Prosecuting Homicide Eighteenth-Century La and Practice

This volume uses four case studies, all with strong London connections, to analyze homicide law and the pardoning process in eighteenth-century England. Each reveals evidence of how attempts were made to negotiate a path through the justice system to avoid conviction and so avoid a sentence of hanging. This approach allows a deep examination of the workings of the justice system using social and cultural history methodologies. The cases explore wider areas of social and cultural history in the period, such as the role of policing agents, attitudes towards sexuality and prostitution, press reporting, and popular conceptions of 'honourable' behaviour. They also allow an engagement with what has been identified as the gradual erosion of individual agency within the law and the concomitant rise of the state. Investigating the nature of the pardoning process shows how important it was to have 'friends in high places' and also uncovers ways in which the legal system was susceptible to accusations of corruption. Readers will find an illuminating view of eighteenth-century London through a legal lens.

Drew D. Gray is the head of Humanities at the University of Northampton.

Routledge Research in Early Modern History

For more information about this series, please visit: www.routledge.com/
Routledge-Research-in-Early-Modern-History/book-series/RREMH

Prosecuting Homicide in Eighteenth-Century Law and Practice

"And Must They All Be Hanged?"

Drew D. Gray

Routledge
Taylor & Francis Group

NEW YORK AND LONDON

First published 2020
by Routledge
605 Third Avenue, New York, NY 10017

and by Routledge
2 Park Square, Milton Park, Abingdon, Oxon, OX14 4RN

First issued in paperback 2022

Routledge is an imprint of the Taylor & Francis Group, an informa business

Library of Congress Cataloging-in-Publication Data
Names: Gray, Drew D., author.
Title: Prosecuting homicide in eighteenth-century law and
    practice : "and must they all be hanged?" / Drew D. Gray.
Description: Abingdon, Oxon ; New York, NY : Routledge
    Taylor and Francis, 2020. | Series: Routledge research in early
    modern history | Includes bibliographical references and index.
Identifiers: LCCN 2019055307 (print) | LCCN 2019055308
    (ebook) | ISBN 9780367460099 (hardback) |
    ISBN 9781003026440 (ebook) | ISBN 9781000047905
    (adobe pdf) | ISBN 9781000047912 (mobi) |
    ISBN 9781000047929 (epub)
Subjects: LCSH: Trials (Murder)—England—History—18th
    century. | Capital punishment—England—History—18th
    century. | Clemency—England—Decision making—
    History—18th century.
Classification: LCC KD371.M8 G73 2020 (print) | LCC
    KD371.M8 (ebook) | DDC 345.42/0252309033—dc23
LC record available at https://lccn.loc.gov/2019055307
LC ebook record available at https://lccn.loc.gov/2019055308

ISBN: 978-1-03-240063-1 (pbk)
ISBN: 978-0-367-46009-9 (hbk)
ISBN: 978-1-003-02644-0 (ebk)

DOI: 10.4324/9781003026440

Typeset in Sabon
by Apex CoVantage, LLC

Contents

Figures

Tables

Acknowledgements

No work of history is completed in isolation: this one has had a very long gestation and owes much to a number of people. I have been working on the case studies that are highlighted here for the best part of a decade. In that time, I've presented my ideas before a number of conferences and seminar series and have discussed them with lots of other researchers. All of these have given advice, useful criticism, and encouragement. So I would like, in no particular order, to offer my heartfelt thanks to the following academic historians, many, but not all of whom, work in my area of criminal history: Bob Shoemaker and Tim Hitchcock (without whom we wouldn't have the Old Bailey Online and its myriad of supporting databases). Thanks too to Mary Clayton, Rosalind Crone, Simon Devereaux, Clive Emsley, Louise Falcini, Elizabeth Hurren, Joanna Innes, Anne-Marie Kilday, Steve King, Randy McGowan, Andrea McKenzie, Ruth Paley, Deirdre Palk, Helen Rogers, Judith Rowbotham, Peter Rushton, Heather Shore, Martin Wiener, Richard Ward, Lucy Williams, and the late Pieter Spierenburg. I must also thank Matthew McCormack and Mark Rothery for their support at Northampton and indeed all of my colleagues there who have made it possible for me to find the time to complete this volume. Most of all, however, I owe a huge debt of thanks to Peter King, who threw most of these cases my way when he finally hung up his history hat and settled into a very well-deserved retirement. Pete has encouraged me more than anyone to tell these stories and I really hope he enjoys the result. Finally, I want to thank my wife for her support which makes it so much easier to get on with writing and my mother for continuing to be that most useful of things, a critical friend.

In July 2017, the field of history lost John Beattie, who made such a seminal contribution to the study of the history of crime. John, along with Pete King and Douglas Hay, have been the biggest influences on my academic career and I will never forget the kindness that John offered me when I was setting out on my postgraduate research. His work forms the bedrock on which the rest of us can build and we all owe him a tremendous debt.

1 Introduction and Themes

'A historical phenomenon can become comprehensible only by reconstructing the activities of *all* the persons who participated in it'.[1]

Images of Execution in Late Eighteenth- and Early Nineteenth-Century London

From 1783 onwards most executions in England's capital took place outside the debtor's door at Newgate Prison. While capitally convicted felons were also hanged at Horsemonger prison (sometimes referred to as the 'New gaol'), Newgate, on Old Bailey, was the preferred site for this ritual of controlled state terror. Prior to 1783, those sentenced to death were transported on a cart from Newgate to Tyburn; when the cart was drawn away, they were left hanging on the 'triple tree' in front of thousands of spectators. In the decades following the removal of the ritual to the more constrained (and arguably more easily controlled) confines of Old Bailey, the crowds, while still huge, were not as extensive as they once were.[2] It is debatable what effect this would have had on the person being executed; they were spared the discomfort and humiliation of a ride in the 'rattling cart' along the furrowed thoroughfare of Oxford Street to modern Marble Arch, but the shock they had when the door of the prison opened onto the gathered throng of witnesses must have been considerable. Just moments earlier the condemned would have been taken from a dark cell to the pressroom to have their shackles removed and their arms pinioned. They would then have processed to the door that opened onto the gallows. It is hard to understand how the condemned felt at this point, but clearly for some this was the moment that they finally realized the enormity of their situation. For one female in 1829 it was all too much:

'A little before 8 o'clock the unfortunate woman was led from the condemned cell to the Press-room; she exhibited a dreadful appearance. The sad procession then set forward, the miserable woman being carried by two men, as she absolutely refused to walk', reported *The Times* on April 14, 1829.[3]

If they managed to steel themselves for the walk to the door, the condemned still had to endure the scene that awaited them, as one eyewitness account recalls:

> The undefined confused murmur of the thousands collected was now heard – an unutterable din, multifarious but not loud, and the movements that the executioner and his attendants made on the scaffold, as soon as the clergyman's voice was heard, was, of course, recognized by the vast assembly, and a cry was heard of – hat's off, stand back, etc.[4]

'Hat's off', of course, should not always (or ever) be read as a sign of the crowd's respect for the gravity of the occasion. As Randall McGowen noted, ' "hats off", far from showing respect for the condemned, only indicated a desire to see better'.[5] In the late eighteenth and early nineteenth centuries those sentenced to hang would have stood on the gallows platform for some minutes while a priest encouraged them to pray and recited the catechism for the dead. As they waited to die they could look down and see and hear the crowd below looking up at them. There might have been familiar and friendly faces there, come to offer support. But equally they would have seen and heard those who came to gloat, sneer, or simply to amuse themselves by watching others die in public. As one historian of American executions has written: 'The stars of the execution ceremony could look forward to pain and death under the close inspection of thousands. Many were understandably frightened'.[6] The fear had been built up over a period of time, of course, with a series of stages leading to the final hanging day. From conviction to sentence at the end of the sessions, the long wait for the Recorder's Report to be actioned and the 'dead warrant' to arrive at Newgate, appeal, petition, possible respites, and frantic attempts to gain a conditional pardon. All this might take days, weeks, or even months, all while the condemned man or woman was held in the dark confines of London's most feared prison. As one observer wrote in 1864, having witnessed the execution of a prisoner outside Newgate, the effect on the individual was hardly less than torture:

> The condemned has been kept a fortnight within hearing of the very footsteps of Death, daily coming nearer and nearer to him. The man is here aware of the intention to kill him. He is brought out alive and well, and conscious, upon the scaffold. Twenty thousand strange eyes glare upon him with hungry, terror-striking warning. He is shown to the excited mob before his face is covered. The spectators see the last spark of hope die out in his soul. No reprieve has come – no shout of pardon is heard – no impossible rescue, which always lingers in the mind of the doomed, occurs. The wretch stands face to

face with inevitable, pitiless, premeditated death. Not the scythe, but the strange, cold, cord of death strikes against his ear, and the crowd know that he knows it. They see the frame quiver and the blood rush to the neck. A thrill passes through the congregated scoundrels whom the Government have thus undertaken to entertain. The noose is adjusted, the click of the drop is heard by the hushed throng, and the wretch descends still in sight; and then the long tramp, the weary hours of standing, the rain, the cold, the damp, the struggling of the hateful night's watching, is all forgotten in the coveted gratification of that horrible minute.[7]

The public nature of executions not only added to the fear of those being hanged; it must have affected those that viewed them. This was not lost on contemporaries either, who, especially from the 1830s onwards, campaigned to remove hangings from public view to behind the confines of prison walls. It was important for justice to be 'seen to be done' but equally the negative effect on the viewer of seeing a ritualized state killing was considered by a growing number of middle-class commentators to be both dangerous and counterproductive.[8] Later observers (particularly those opposed to public execution) were quick to ascribe a lack of humanity to those viewing hanging – even if this was generally assumed to affect the working class audience and not the better educated who also attended. Writing in 1864, having witnessed a number of executions in different parts of the country, George Holyoake wrote: 'He who has feasted his eyes on deliberate strangulation has advanced a step in ferocity. Next time the wife-beater strikes his companion he adds torture to brutality'.[9]

Executions, as Dwight Conquergood has described them, were a form of 'lethal theatre' where spectators were 'encouraged' to 'gaze intently at the body on display and granted extraordinary license for the condemned, especially if they were women, to make spectacles out of their bodies'.[10] Thomas Laqueur was skeptical as to whether public executions really worked, in the way the state must have wanted them to, as palpable demonstrations of power and authority. They were too diverse and unpredictable, he argues, and they drew 'holiday crowds', who were 'boisterous women, men, and children of all ages and classes engaged in festival'.[11] The prevailing emotion at public executions seems to have been curiosity. One observer who recorded his experience of passing near an execution in 1791 was appalled by the crowd, as many middling sort commentators were. As he testified before a parliamentary committee: 'The crowd exhibited a variety of "equally revolting emotions which might be traced in the countenances of all who surrounded me". Some showed an "impatient curiosity", others a "brutal apathy", and still others a "thoughtless levity". He was appalled by the "eager struggles" to get a better view'.[12] Although the crowd reacted in a variety of ways at hangings, as McGowen has written, what the crowd 'did not display was an embarrassment at seeing the event'.[13] This might make modern readers uncomfortable, just as it made reformers in the 1830s uncomfortable. They argued that it was much better to remove the spectacle inside (if it could not be abandoned altogether) because otherwise 'public execution threatened to expose death on the gallows for the ambiguous and compromised solution that it was'.[14]

Accounts of executions in late Georgian and Regency London exist in considerable numbers. Execution broadsides and newspaper accounts are rich in detailed and sensational description of the crimes that the condemned men and women had committed, in the trials that had convicted them, and often of the crowds that came to watch them be 'turned off'.[15] But descriptions of the deaths themselves are minimal and often euphemistic: as well as being 'turned off', convicts were 'launched into eternity' or simply 'fell' as the trap opened beneath them. They usually 'struggled little' and, after being left hanging for the 'the usual time' (an hour in most cases) they were cut down and taken away for burial or (as was the fate of murderers) to be dissected by the surgeons.[16] There were sometimes hints that the death was painful and this was used by abolitionists in their arguments that capital punishment was a barbaric ritual unsuited to a civilized society. 'It was a long time before the body of the poor female seemed to have gone through its last suffering', reported a witness to the execution of Elizabeth Godfrey in 1807.[17] 'Broughton and Francis struggled violently for some moments after all the rest were without motion. The executioner pulled their legs to put an end to their pain more speedily', ran the account of the execution of several persons connected with the alleged would-be royal assassin Colonel Edward Despard outside Horsemonger Gaol in 1803.[18] The pain of hanging was real if not always prolonged but this is generally glossed over in the reports of executions. Despite his suggestion that, amongst people of his class, watching such events was considered 'rather vulgar or prurient', James Boswell attended several hangings in eighteenth-century London and elsewhere. Boswell rarely went into detail on what happened to those dispatched on gallows but, in one case, from August 1785, he stayed around to see the aftermath.

> After hanging an hour, their bodies were cut down; the ceremony of which, though so often mentioned, is unknown to most of our readers. The executioner places himself under the body, which rests on his shoulders, while the hands are brought over his reach. A man on each side also supports the body, and the executioner's man, mounted upon steps, cuts the rope. The body is then tumbled over upon a plank, which is in readiness, and is borne into Newgate to be carried away for internment as soon as may be convenient. These convicts all died very easily. A gentleman,

who is an attentive examiner of shocking scenes [meaning himself]
made Guthrie's cap be pulled up, when the body was stretched
out in Newgate, and there did not appear any distortion in his
countenance.[19]

(*Public Advertiser*, August 18, 1785)

Just occasionally the horror of the hanging process was made abundantly clear, as in this mid-nineteenth-century account:
'The distortions of his countenance, in the agonies of death, could be seen by the crowd: and, as he remained suspended without any covering on his face, the horrid spectacle was most terrific'.[20] Or this, the last execution at Tyburn in 1783: 'The noose of the halter having slipped to the back part of his neck, it was full ten minutes before he was dead'.[21] Mostly, however, after the 'new drop' was introduced outside Newgate, with their heads covered by the cloth of the cap, once the bolt was drawn and the trap opened under them the hanged felon half disappeared from sight and the watching crowd were left to imagine the final moments of their life and death. Before that, bodies would have twitched and squirmed as the hanged men and women at Tyburn and elsewhere strangled slowly or, if they were lucky, died more quickly. In neither scenario did those reporting on executions feel the need to describe the physical act of dying. We can, perhaps, put this down to a natural squeamishness on the part of the writers or a desire not to unduly upset their readership. But the 1700s were not particularly squeamish decades; they are full of death and disease, and executions – in late eighteenth-century London at least – were relatively frequent.[22] Undoubtedly, then, the newspaper reporters, the writers of the ubiquitous execution broadsides, and the 'last dying' speeches of the condemned worked according to a well-worn template and gave their readers what they expected. What they expected was to be told why the felon was standing on the gallows platform in the first place, what crime they had committed, and, if possible, their motives for doing so. The condemned person's fall from grace was important: both to reaffirm their guilt (and thereby justify the judicial killing) but also to warn others that a similar fate awaited them if they strayed from the path of righteousness. Maybe people did not need to be told how the individual had died beyond a fairly standard suggestion that they had died 'well' or, even better, had died 'game' (meaning they had displayed a level of bravado in the moments leading up to their death).[23] Offenders that demonstrated remorse and warned the watching multitude not to follow their errant path would earn praise and some sort of immediate redemption for their sins from the account of their last moments. Executed felons like Richard Turpin, the notorious highwayman hanged at York in 1739, who treated their executions with an air of unconcern, passed into folklore as examples of daring criminals who cared little for the consequences of their actions. Others were defiant, refusing to confess

to their crimes at the last minute, as their executioners – via the priests presiding at the execution – often wanted them to absolve themselves of any accusation that they were killing an innocent man or woman. As Vic Gatrell noted, there was an 'indifference to penal pain which came from too much familiarity with it'. So routine were the reports of hangings that this was 'news merely, recorded as changes in the weather might be'.[24] As Laqueur reminds us in the years before the construction of the 'new drop' outside Newgate Gaol,

> 'the people' were in intimate physical, not semiotic, contact with the scaffold and the body of the condemned. In the days of the 'hanging tree' they . . . literally helped to kill the victim. The body in those days was not so much 'launched into eternity' as left to strangle when the cart upon which it had stood was pulled away.

It was often left to the crowd to pull at the legs of the hanging man or woman, to speed their death.[25]

In reality of course hanging was not (and is not) a painless and clean method of execution. Death, even when modern, scientific, methods of careful measuring of the rope and use of a drop are deployed, is not always quick. As Banner explained:

> Death by hanging could be fast or slow, apparently painless or obviously excruciating, depending on the actual cause of death. If the prisoner was lucky, the force of the drop would fracture vertebrae of his neck and sever his spinal cord, typically between the second and third vertebrae. This is in injury often seen today – and still colloquially known as 'hangman's fracture' – usually after head-on automobile accidents in which the victim's body is thrown forward but his head is snapped back by the windshield. Death by this mechanism was nearly instantaneous and thus caused little or no pain. It was also unusual . . . most people who were hanged died more slowly, as the rope encircling their necks either cut off the supply of blood to their brains or prevented them from breathing, or as the force of the drop wrenched the larynx away from the trachea, again preventing breathing. All these methods of dying took several minutes. The loss of blood to the brain was the least painful, producing unconsciousness within seconds. Asphyxiation, in contrast, left the conscious victim writhing and gasping through the last several minutes of his life. His mouth and nose would turn dark purple, and his eyes would bulge monstrously wide. Convulsions would gradually extend throughout his body, spreading from contortions of the eyes to violent kicking with the legs. He might urinate or defecate. His penis might become erect. Such displays accompanied a significant percentage of hangings.[26]

Rationale and Themes: The Politics of Execution and the Use of Discretion

The effects on the body of the hanged is pertinent to this study, as one of the arguments presented concerns how the visibility of the hanging body may have occasioned debate about the changing nature of executions, from the rudimentary gallows such as that constructed at Tyburn, to the 'new drop' platform outside Newgate Gaol. When the body dropped through the trap following the release of the door by the hangman, it partially disappeared from the sight of the watching crowds. The base of the gallows was shrouded in black cloth, a deliberate move that replaced the carnivalesque ritual at Tyburn with the more austere and sombre backdrop of Newgate prison. The crowd started up to the platform where, eight feet above them, the condemned prisoners waited for the process that was to kill them to unfold. It was more organized, scientific (to a degree), and mechanical than the simple method employed at Tyburn: 'At the middle of the scaffold was a movable platform raised six inches on a system of iron rolling bars. The executioner had simply to pull a lever and felons, standing on this platform with nooses around their necks, would be left dangling over the trapdoor'.[27] This study will suggest that this was a deliberate attempt to sanitize the ritual, in a precursor to its final removal behind closed doors after 1868. Hanging was suspended in England in 1965 and finally abolished in 1998 (although no person was hanged after 1964).[28] About 55 countries still retain the death penalty and several still use hanging as a method of execution.[29] Hanging, then, remains a widely used form of execution in the modern world and not something relegated to a dim and distant past.

This volume is partly a study of hanging and of hanging avoided. In the four case studies presented here, each of the five protagonists faced the possibility, through the actions of which they were accused, of going to the gallows to die in public. Since they were all accused of murder, they faced the additional ignominy of being denied an immediate burial and of having their dead bodies opened up publically so that apprentice surgeons could be taught how to practice medicine.[30] Moreover, as recent work by Elizabeth Hurren has so dramatically established, in a significant proportion of cases the hanged felon on the surgeon's slab was still alive when the post mortem examination began. Hurren demonstrates that in the period men and women were killed 'by degrees'; suspended in the judicial hanging (or 'legal death') before being dispatched at Surgeon's Hall to establish 'medical death'.[31] In one case the accused escaped this awful fate because the case against her collapsed in dramatic fashion before a jury could determine her guilt. In another, two brothers, jointly accused of a very violent and drunken murder, were taken through the process of being brought to be executed only to be spared at virtually the last minute, and on more than one occasion. Ultimately they escaped the rope but certainly they suffered on their roads to freedom. Three other men were not so lucky: one young man died on a public gallows in a provincial town but was spared the associated horror of being anatomized, that small concession was granted to his elderly father as he was a man that had served the Hanoverian state for many years. One of the other two victims of the gallows probably met the worst possible end: executed swiftly close to the place of his alleged crime after a show trial that seemingly ignored the evidence demonstrating not only that he was innocent but that he had actively tried to prevent the very murder he was indicted for.

This then is primarily a book about judicial discretion and the circumstances that surrounded decision-making in the late eighteenth century. The law was supposedly unequivocal when it came to the punishment of murderers. While even serious property offenders might cheat the hangman, condemned murderers were all supposed to die. Those convicted of the less heinous crime of manslaughter would receive a lesser sentence (branding or latterly prison or a fine) but it was very rare for a convicted killer to be treated with the leniency that might be afforded to a felonious thief. So this volume is concerned with understanding why not all of these killers were executed, or, more accurately, *why some were and some were not*. I will suggest that the reasons behind these decisions have a lot less to do with the evidence of guilt or innocence and much more to do with prevailing political circumstances and societal mores. Much historical work has been done to show that some property offenders went to gallows (while others did not) for perfectly understandable and rational reasons. Peter King has demonstrated that the authorities selected examples from amongst the young men convicted of serious, violent, and repeated property crimes to hang and spared the old, women, the very young, and first offenders.[32] Deirdre Palk has likewise revealed that forgers who were prepared to accept a slightly less severe outcome and save the Bank of England the necessity of prosecuting them to a jury trial could avoid the terror of standing on the dread platform outside Newgate Gaol.[33] Yet in all of this very worthwhile effort to demonstrate that reason often featured in judicial decision-making we cannot escape the fact that venality, prejudice, and political expediency all resulted in some men and women being hanged. For, as Simon Devereaux correctly insists, 'Judges did not hang percentages; they hanged people'.[34]

So the purpose of this collection of case studies from the late 1700s is to unpack the rationale behind the decisions that condemned two persons to die and saved three others. There are other stories to be told here; for example, about the nature of execution and how this might reflect contemporary concerns about public decency. The case studies also engage with contemporary politics, notably radical politics, and the use (or rather misuse) of the legal system for political purposes. It considers popular and elite concerns about 'justice' and how these tie into wider societal debates. The role of juries (even post-trial) and the crucial networks surrounding attempts to gain pardons are also exposed by two of these examples. The law itself will be under consideration here, particularly the law surrounding homicide, misadventure (as we understand it), and the little known civil prosecution of unlawful killing, the appeal of murder.

Structure

This book is divided into five chapters and a conclusion. The remainder of this chapter will set the context for the work that follows. It will provide a detailed overview of homicide in London and beyond in the period from 1750–1800, and consider the mechanisms of policing and justice which had developed to deal with it. There was little that changed in terms of policing in the late 1700s but since this study touches directly on the roles of two policing agents (a watchman and a parish constable) both will be outlined briefly. It will look at London's court structure (since London is at the heart of each of these studies, and there will be a justification for this). Having already considered the nature of execution I will say little more about that practice here but will return to it where applicable in subsequent chapters; however, it will be necessary to discuss, albeit briefly, what historians know so far about the mysteries of the pardoning process in the eighteenth and early nineteenth century. There will be a contextual exploration of English politics for the period under consideration and some discussion of London as a growing city but this will be necessarily limited given the availability of considerable other work in this area. While London is central to this study, this is not a study about London but about how power networks and societal issues interconnected to ride roughshod over English notions of 'justice' and 'fair play'.

Chapters 2 to 4 will take the four case studies in chronological order. At the very end of 1769, a murder was committed on Westminster Bridge that led to the arrest and trial of several men for the killing of a duty watchman. Two brothers were condemned to die on the gallows but were later spared and transported to America. Their escape from death may have been down to the difficulty of identifying a culprit for the murder amongst an act of gang violence but, this study will argue, it almost certainly had much more to do with the influence others were able to bring to bear on the government to commute their sentence. Two years later Henry Stroud was not so lucky. He too was involved in a murder in London, this time of a man that had given evidence that led to the execution of others. Again there was considerable doubt over his guilt, but he was hanged and hanged quickly, close to the scene of the murder with a fellow convict hanged beside him for the same killing. In 1788, another man went to the gallows, this time in middle England and not London but also for the killing of a person of authority. He had useful and elite connections, but were they the right connections and at the right time? Finally, the only female killer in this series was charged with murder but her case collapsed as the judge decided to hush up what he believed was an incident that had the potential to offend public morality. This final case poses some interesting questions about contemporary attitudes towards hanging and the execution ritual but was also a product of its specific place in history. Indeed all four cases owe a lot to historical and political circumstance, covering as they do the period from the early reign of 'mad' King George III, through the popular radicalism of John Wilkes, to revolution in the Americas and then France. All of these affected in some ways the fates of the five persons charged with murder and this study will argue that this was, in many ways, more important (to that fate) than the circumstances of the crime they were accused of committing.

The Nature of Micro-History and Case Studies

We have had a glut of micro-histories and case studies in the last decade or so of social history, with notable examples from the history of crime including Anne-Marie Kilday and David Nash's 2017 volume *Law, Crime & Deviance since 1700: Micro-Studies in the History of Crime*. In their introduction, Kilday and Nash argue that the 'micro-study approach is also potentially better able to engage the wider public in the history of crime and the law and is perhaps more readily in tune with how archives and museums frequently present the history of crime'.[35] They acknowledge the risk that such an approach might bring problems but conclude that these are generally outweighed by the benefits that this way of writing history brings. I would agree that this 'holistic method . . . contributes to a wide, deep and nuanced understanding of these areas and the societies in which they occur'.[36] Martin Wiener notes that British historians in particular have generally avoided studies of homicide because it is often 'sensational' and therefore untypical of most crime. But the 'social dramas' that are part and parcel of murder trials are useful to the social historian because, he claims, 'much can be learned about the law as an expression of a society's fundamental values and an instrument of its latent conflicts'.[37] Wiener is referring to the Victorian period but this holds true for the 1700s as well.

Context is crucial to understanding events and decision-making in the past, which I hope will become very evident in this volume. History is contested and the word itself can mean different things to different people at different times but it is worth noting that it is strongly associated with the telling or retelling of stories from the past almost as much as it is with understanding and analyzing the past and the events that shaped it. The Latin word *historia* means a narrative of past events, a story; the Greek ἱστορέω (also *istoria*) similarly means to inquire into, and to narrate the past. Narrative history can sometimes be conflated with 'popular' history (i.e., not 'academic' history) where analysis is eschewed in preference to simple storytelling. But, in Carlo Ginzburg's *Cheese and the Worms* (1966), the author successfully manages to elevate storytelling to meet the requirements of rigorous academic historical analysis. In discussing his approach many years later, Ginzburg writes (in relation to the problematic nature of his sources and the way he had to unpick the details of the life of the miller Menocchio) that:

> The obstacles interfering with the research were integral elements in the documentation and thus had to become part of the account; the same for the hesitations and silences of the protagonist in the face of his persecutors' questions – or mine. Thus the hypothesis, the doubts, the uncertainties became part of the narration; the search for truth became part of the exposition of the necessarily incomplete truth attained. Could the result still be defined as "narrative history"? For a reader with the slightest familiarity with twentieth-century fiction, the answer is obviously yes.[38]

In this volume of case studies, there are all sorts of issues with the sources I have deployed and how I have understood them. There are gaps that can only be filled with informed speculation and, I am sure, alternative conclusions to be drawn from those I will set out. Nevertheless, it is surely both logical and reasonable to ask questions about the ways in which decisions were made behind the closed doors of the Hanoverian justice system and suggest explanations for them. That is what this book sets out to do; it is entirely up to the reader to decide how successful I have been in doing so.

Having set out the structure for this book I will now move on to consider the context: I will start by looking at London, its history in the late 1700s, and at politics and society. There will then follow a detailed analysis of homicide and its prosecution and punishment in the period 1770–1800.

London in the Second Half of the Eighteenth Century

Georgian London, as Dorothy George described it, 'underwent a transformation, indeed a revolutionary one, in the course of the [eighteenth] century'.[39] It expanded, in terms of the space it occupied if not in the proportion of the population that lived there, and it developed as a commercial and cultural centre of the nation. London grew geographically from mid-century to overspill and build upon its fringes. Villages and hamlets north of the City and Marylebone were developed, built up, and occupied as Londoners (generally wealthier ones) moved out of the fetid centre for the calmer and healthier new builds of the north and west. The

1760s and 1770s saw London expand significantly as hundreds of new homes sprang up in Henry Holland and Hans Sloane's development of Chelsea, and Henry Penton's building programme in north London. This was followed in the 1780s by the creation of Somers Town in Bloomsbury and the laying out of Camden Town at the beginning of the 1790s.[40] London was undergoing an important stage of its development as a European centre of culture, of financial and political power, benefitting as it was from the end of war in 1763. While other parts of Britain developed industrially, London prospered financially and politically, and there the growing middling sort rose to prominence as the century unfolded.

Most of the events covered by this volume of case studies (and almost all of the important decisions made) took place in London or by persons living there, and historians have now recognized the peculiarity of the capital in the context of the Hanoverian criminal justice system. As Peter King and Richard Ward have demonstrated, the 'bloody code' was considerably less 'bloody' the further one travelled from London in the 1700s.[41] Despite this, most of the historiography on the 'bloody code' has focused on its practice in the capital and the southeast and for good reasons.[42] Eighteenth-century London was not only by far the largest urban centre in the British Isles it was also the biggest (in terms of the number of people) in Europe as well. The Old Bailey (where three of the four case study trials were heard) was the busiest court in the land and more felons were executed in London than anywhere else in Britain.[43] So while London may not have been typical of the practice of the criminal code in Britain as a whole it informed contemporary opinion about the criminal law and how it operated. As Simon Devereaux has written: 'The experience of execution in London must surely have shaped imaginative perceptions of capital punishment in a more profound and influential way than did that of any other part of the English nation'.[44] So while the newspapers reported stories of crime and punishment from all corners of the country it was events in the capital that most informed contemporaries about the state of the criminal justice system in the nation as a whole. This was reinforced by the reality that while local newspapers could certainly affect the way justice (broadly defined) was practiced most of their news was recycled from the press based in London. There were notable incidents where regional papers clearly influenced the outcomes in local courts. In 1765 a 'crime wave' in Colchester, Essex, was in effect engineered or at least manipulated by competing publications in an attempt to secure circulation (and the subsequent stream of advertising revenue that eighteenth-century newspapers relied upon). A 'moral panic' about footpads and local 'banditti' led to a disproportionate rise in prosecutions and an increase in the severity of punishments.[45] This was a localized occurrence however, and one that did not trouble readers in the capital. However, when in 1788 the attempt by one parent to save the life of his condemned son reached the attention of the London press, the human-interest nature of the story did make it 'national news' and, as Chapter 4 will show, catapulted Northampton (and the tiny village of Pattishall) on to the pages of every London newspaper. This was a rare example of London being interested by the machinations of justice outside of the capital, and there were limits to this interest and to the plight of those concerned, as we shall see.[46] Given that local (regional) papers such as the *Northampton Mercury* or the *Colchester Chronicle* borrowed heavily from the press in the Metropolis, it is likely then that many readers formed their opinions of the justice system and of the extent of crime and criminality more generally, from what they read in the capital's newspapers. Few of them, like few of us thankfully, experienced crime first-hand.[47] Those living in rural England and Wales (and we must remember that in the mid to late eighteenth century this constituted the majority of people) would have encountered crime but rarely, if ever. So while we must be clear about the need to place any study that (once again) focuses its attention on London in context, and appreciate its limitations in terms of what it can say about widespread attitudes towards crime and punishment, the reality was that London and the London press was a prime source of information about crime, particularly serious crime, and its prosecution. Therefore it is reasonable once more to investigate how discretion, contemporary events, and indeed political corruption affected the outcomes of the trials and appeals against execution in the last few decades of the 1700s in England's capital city.

Politics and Society in the Late Eighteenth Century

In the 30 years covered by the case studies this volume deploys, King George III ruled England. However, for some of those years George was king in name only as he was undermined by attacks of the 'madness' that was such a feature of his reign. The first episode seems to have occurred in 1765 as he struggled with what he saw as the attempts of his ministers to manipulate him for their own political ends. This incident – which was dismissed by George Grenville (the sitting Prime Minister) as merely 'a cold' – led to the first discussions about the creation of a regency in the event of the king succumbing to a premature death.[48] The resulting crisis, and Grenville's politically inept judgement in excluding the monarch's mother from the regency bill, saw the end of his ministry.[49] Some 23 years later, when the Prince of Wales was an adult and able to take up the reins of royal power, George III suffered his most serious bout of illness when, in November 1788, he 'fell into a depressed and violent insanity'.[50] What seemed like 'madness' in the 1700s has now been identified as a physical illness, porphyria, but that was not understood at the time and once again the monarch's fitness to rule was questioned. Imprisoned in a straightjacket and treated as a 'madman', the Whig opposition in parliament pressed to have George replaced by his son, the Prince of Wales, whom many felt was entirely unsuited to the role of king due to his excessive love of drinking and gambling. In 1784 William Pitt (the younger) had been made Prime Minster and he stayed loyal to his sovereign (and to his desire to retain political power for the Tories) by resisting attempts to place the future George IV on the throne as Regent. George III recovered from his illness and it was while he enjoyed the therapeutic benefits of his brother's home on the south coast that he was visited by the father of Thomas Gordon, seeking the king's pardon for his son's act of violence. In 1788 George III was incapacitated and while by the summer of 1789 he was well again, he never fully took up the reins of power again. From 1788 onwards it was Pitt that ran the country, as during the 1790s the monarch withdrew almost completely from the day-to-day business of ruling the nation. George fell ill in 1804 and then again in 1810, bringing his errant son to the regency in 1811. In a decade George IV was king in own right, following his father's death in 1820.

George III had succeeded to the throne of England in 1760, the first of the Hanoverian kings to be born in Britain. Educated by his father's favourite, Lord Bute, it is not surprising that King George turned to the Scottish nobleman and politician to become, in effect, the leader of the government following the resignation of his first prime minister, William Pitt (the Elder), in 1761. Bute suffered attacks from the radical opposition (notably John Wilkes) for his failure to negotiate a better postwar treaty with the defeated French at the close of the Seven Years War and he was replaced with Grenville. The elder Pitt re-emerged from that crisis but did not last long, being himself replaced by the Duke of Grafton in 1768. He resigned in 1770 after suffering withering criticism in the press from the anonymous 'Junius'. George now turned to Lord North, and his premiership oversaw a period of rare political calm by comparison to the decade that preceded it. Nevertheless, the 1770s themselves, while relatively tranquil at home, were anything but that overseas. In 1776 the long simmering complaints of the American colonists blew up in the face of the British. By 1781 the American war was effectively lost and in 1783 the Treaty of Versailles recognized the colonists' independence. It cost Lord North his position and propelled the young Pitt to power a year later. In 1789 the French Revolution sent shock waves through the ruling houses of Europe in an even more stark way than the American rebellion against English rule had in 1776. The challenge to the authority of royal power and the subsequent challenge to British dominion on the world stage posed by Revolutionary and then Napoleonic France affected British society profoundly. In the latter case it was not merely the literal removal of the heads of Bourbon France that produced deep disquiet at the palaces of St James and Westminster, it was the ideas that accompanied it. The American Revolution had introduced the ideas of Thomas Paine to many more educated citizens and the French Republic and its soldiers introduced these ideas to new, plebeian audiences. As will be seen in Chapter 5, the notion that the rights of women should be recognized alongside the 'Rights of Man' precipitated a backlash as 'conservative' society attempted to refute the ideas unleashed by these twin revolutions on each side of the Atlantic and put the genie firmly back into its bottle. In Chapter 5 I argue that the case of Susannah Hill must be viewed within the wider context of the so-called sex panic of the 1790s, as analyzed by Katherine Binhammer.[51]

Events in London and England from the early 1770s and throughout the 1780s and early 1790s have to be understood then in the context of what else was happening in domestic and foreign politics, and in all of the case studies chosen for this study external events (by which I mean events not always directly related to the merits of the case itself) were affected by them. It is one of the assertions of this volume that decisions made to prosecute, punish, and to pardon offenders – and in these cases arguably the most serious of offenders – had as much to do with events beyond the control of the alleged perpetrators as anything they were accused of doing themselves. In part, as historians of crime have long recognized, this is due to the very nature of the criminal justice system of the eighteenth century which was rooted much more deeply in the exercise of discretion to mitigate the worst excesses of the sanguinary system of public execution.[52] Before moving on to look at the nature and extent of homicide and its prosecution and punishment in the last three decades of the 1700s, it is necessary to briefly consider that system of justice and the other factors that influenced the prosecution and punishment of offenders.

Crime and Policing in Late Hanoverian England

In 1723 the Waltham 'Black' Act created, at stroke, an additional 50 offences that could be punished capitally (in other words, by some form of execution – most usually hanging in public). Edward Thompson noted that the 'Black Act' represented the 'onset of the flood-tide of eighteenth-century retributive justice'.[53] In fact the 'long' eighteenth-century saw the passing into law of more than 200 separate acts that prescribed the death penalty, many of them localized, specific, and probably hardly ever applied.[54] In reality most of those hanged in Hanoverian England and Wales were executed for crimes that had been capital well before the Glorious Revolution of 1688–1689. Those hanged were convicted of murder (capital since medieval times), petty treason (made capital without benefit of clergy under Henry VIII), various forms of robbery (made capital without clergy in the Tudor and Elizabethan period), burglary (again, Elizabeth I), the theft of horses (capital under the Tudors), and infanticide (James I). The late 1600s and early 1700s saw offences such as shoplifting (1689), counterfeiting and uttering (1727), and rioting (1714) made capital, reflecting the changing nature of society and the growth of the property-owning elites.

Overwhelmingly, the criminal law operated to protect private property and while contemporaries were quick to suggest that since the theft of even the smallest amount of property was punishable by death this meant that everyone was treated equally under the law, the reality was somewhat different. The vast majority of those sent to the gallows in the 1700s were from the labouring poor and most had committed a crime that involved some form of theft from a person of a higher social status.[55] Age and gender were also reflected in the statistics of those executed in London and elsewhere. Men, and more specifically young men (aged 18–25), were disproportionately more likely to be convicted of property crimes than women. Historians of the eighteenth century are not as well served as those studying the Victorian period when it comes to age, since this was but rarely recorded. However, King's survey of the age and gender of offenders on the Home Circuit in the 1780s reveals that 'more than two-thirds of those indicted for property offences . . . were under 30'.[56] Women only represented 13 per cent of property criminals prosecuted in Essex between 1740 and 1804 and a mere 'handful' of these were for the most serious property crimes (the ones that most usually resulted in executions).[57] In Surrey from 1660–1800 the pattern described by John Beattie is similar: men were responsible for three-quarters (76 per cent) of all property offending prosecuted in the jury courts. However, this proportion rises to 91.5 per cent for robbery (theft with violence) and 85.9 per cent for burglary.[58] In London, where the majority of the case studies of crime offered up in this study were prosecuted, women were held accountable for crime more often than elsewhere in the country. Here, more women were prosecuted for property crimes such as picking pockets, shoplifting, and coining or uttering and more were convicted and sentenced to death.[59] However, women were still much less likely to have their sentences carried out than men were, and some (notably married women) were able to benefit not only from the discretionary nature of Hanoverian justice but also the peculiarities of a legal system rooted in patriarchy.[60]

While hanging remained the primary form of punishment for much of the eighteenth century, many of those sentenced to hang were ultimately spared a public death at the end of a hangman's rope. The image of the Hanoverian justice system is probably best illustrated by William Hogarth's engraving of the 'idle apprentice' being taken to London's Tyburn execution site on a cart accompanied by a parson and a coffin (see Figure 1.1).

Large crowds turned out to watch executions, which demonstrated the power of the state and served as a deterrent to those watching. At least that was the intended purpose of such a draconian form of public display; the reality was – as Hogarth's satire reveals – that criminals infested

Figure 1.1 William Hogarth, "The Idle Prentice Executed at Tyburn": *Industry and Idleness*, plate 11. September 30, 1747. Harris Brisbane Dick Fund, 1932

Source: www.metmuseum.org/art/collection/search/399844

the crowds at executions suggesting that their ability to deter others from emulating the crimes of those dangling from the 'triple tree' was limited at best. This was a reality not lost on contemporary commentators who bemoaned the inefficiency of execution and the justice system as a whole.[61] As the century unfolded, voices calling for reform became more clarion and the loss of access to the American colonies (after 1776) as a place to dump those offenders who were granted a reprieve from death saw an increased debate about the merits of alternative forms of punishment.[62] Transportation as a 'soft' alternative to execution had been practiced throughout the late Stuart and early Hanoverian period but had only been enshrined in law (and supported by government funding) in 1718.[63] Merchant ships transported felons from England to the American colonies of Maryland and Virginia where they would be sold as indentured labour to work in the fields cultivating the cash crop of tobacco. While such a punishment was considered severe it was not as feared as execution and, given that escapes were not uncommon and the Americas not too distant to preclude return, some felt that it offered a chance at redemption and reform rather than simple banishment.[64] Following defeat in the American War of Independence, the government and legal authorities looked for new alternatives as the execution rate (in London at least) began to rise again.[65] The utilitarian ideal of the panopticon was proposed by Jeremy Bentham while other, less ideological, systems of imprisonment were suggested by reformers such as John Howard, George Onesiphorous Paul, and, later, Elizabeth Fry. In 1787 the First Fleet sailed to the recently occupied colony at Botany Bay, in modern New South Wales, to begin a new chapter in the transportation of felons out of Great Britain as an alternative to killing them at home.

Contemporaries were arguably well aware that most of those sentenced to hang (and some of those sent for transportation) would be spared from either of the most serious (at least in terms of being commonly deployed) punishment available to the Hanoverian state. Offenders could escape the gallows in a number of ways, which bears testimony to the highly discretionary nature of the penal system. In the first instance it was the victim of crime who determined what happened to an offender (with the obvious exception of the victims of homicide). Given that eighteenth-century England had no professional system of organized policing, the onus to prosecute rested with the individual who had been (for example) robbed, burgled, or defrauded. While it is certainly incorrect to describe England under the reign of George III as 'unpoliced', most historians would accept that its ability to effectively deter crime and punish criminal acts was limited at best. In urban areas – and in London's central parishes in particular – the night watch patrolled the streets from dusk to dawn. A medieval innovation, the watch was largely made up of low paid, poorly organized, and badly equipped men who had possibly previously served their country and/or were no longer able to find better employment. The watch was widely criticized by those advocating a more professional form of policing but contemporary accusations of laziness, corruption, and ineptitude should be treated with caution as the voices of those with vested interest in change. Throughout the second half of the 1700s the watch in London underwent considerable reform at parish level and was very far from being the broken system that men like Patrick Colquhoun and Henry Fielding derided.[66] In the City of London as well as in Westminster the watch improved considerably across the last quarter of the eighteenth century and the first decades of the nineteenth.[67] In Chapter 2, the victim in the homicide case described was himself a member of the night watch that attempted to keep the peace on Westminster Bridge. His actions that night in confronting a group of violent and drunken men who had already perpetrated a number of violent and destructive acts is consistent with bravery and a sense of civic duty, not the careless and cowardly passivity that was so often used by critics of the night watch in the pages of the newspapers.

Nevertheless while the watch did catch criminals in the act or soon after and deterred others by their presence or by alerting householders to unlocked portals into their homes, shops, or warehouses, they were a responsive unit, not a proactive one. For that element of policing

Londoners had to look to the thief-takers. These were entrepreneurial 'police' who could be hired to find stolen property and secure, if possible, the culprits. Thief-takers benefitted from the reward system that was started in the reign of Queen Anne and which continued into the early 1800s. Ordinary subjects could earn a financial reward, payable upon conviction at the discretion of the presiding judge, as well as gaining exemptions from onerous forms of public service.[68] Thief-taking was open to corruption as a result of the money that could be made from it and there were more than one high profile examples of 'blood-money' scandals in the 1700s.[69] The most infamous of all thief-takers was Jonathan Wild the self-proclaimed 'thief-taker general' of 1720s London. Wild was, in effect, a crime 'boss' running criminal networks in the capital, a 'gangster' to modern eyes and a 'celebrity criminal' like the escapologist burglar Jack Sheppard that he helped bring to 'justice'.[70] Heather Shore recently described Wild as 'thief-taker and thief-maker, a man who artfully navigated the entrepreneurial justice system of the early eighteenth century'.[71] Wild was hanged in May 1725 and large crowds turned out to see him travel on his humiliating procession from Newgate Gaol to Tyburn, apparently jeering him as they had previously cheered Sheppard. In the middle of the century, the newly appointed magistrates at Bow Street, Henry and his half-brother John Fielding, set about recruiting and developing their own version of the thief-taker model. 'Mr Fielding's people' or the 'Runners' as they were referred to were a small group of paid thief-takers who profited (as Wild had) from finders' fees for stolen items and by earning rewards (government and private) for catching and prosecuting thieves. Theoretically the Bow Street Runners (as history has come to know them) were less corrupt and more efficient than many of the thief-takers that had existed previously and they soon established themselves as recognized experts when appearing at the Old Bailey to prosecute or to give evidence in cases against serious property defendants.[72] As the century went on, the 'runners' developed a sophisticated system of information gathering and John Fielding was instrumental in lobbying the government of the day to obtain funds to create day and night 'patroles', expanding the role of his officers beyond that of mere thief-taking. The Bow Street office now began to send its men out of the capital to investigate crime in the home counties and even further afield.[73]

Finally, Londoners could also turn to the parish constables that were hired on a nominally annual basis to serve their communities. Unlike the watch or thief-takers, parish constables were a national institution. Men – initially propertied men of reasonably high social standing – were elected to act as constables for a year (sometimes two) and would be unpaid save for any expenses incurred. It was often deemed to be a thankless task – escorting vagrants out of the parish, shooting unwanted birds that damaged crops, attending at courts and executions, or responding to members of the public when a crime had been committed. Since constables were drawn from amongst the ranks of the middling sorts or propertied tradesmen, their living was often affected by the call of duty.[74] Not surprisingly then it was increasingly common for men to hire substitutes to serve in their place as the century unfolded. In the City of London, which had a relatively efficient system of police in the second half of the eighteenth century, many constables had been substituting continuously for several years.[75] Outside of the capital the system of electing constables may have survived longer, due in part to far less dangerous levels of crime and disorder. Notwithstanding this, the newly elected constable of Pattishall in Northamptonshire was shot dead as he tried to exercise a warrant as his first real action in the role. So, while contemporaries may have not always felt that their society was policed enough we can see that it was not unpoliced either. However, the personal nature of the justice system – and thus the role of the victims of crime – was still very much its defining characteristic. Discretion therefore rested, as noted earlier, in the hands of the prosecutor who could decide whether or not he (or she, but more usually it was a 'he') wanted to pursue the arrest, investigation, and prosecution of a suspect. All of the aforementioned policing agents could help, some would cost, others were free, but it still could take considerable time and effort on the part of a victim to act against someone that had stolen or in other ways wronged them. Rewards were offered with this in mind, to encourage prosecutions by ordinary people so that criminals would be caught and fellow citizens protected. Once a prosecution had resulted in the arrest, further layers of discretion now affected the outcome.

Courts, Juries, and the Administration of Justice

If an accused was indicted for a crime, he or she would undertake a journey that had a variety of outcomes. If the crime was minor (a petty theft, misdemeanor, or not fatal assault for example), it might be dealt with locally by a justice of the peace (a magistrate). In all of the case studies covered by this volume a magistrate played a role in the decision-making but because each of the examples involved homicide that role was limited. Nevertheless, whether it was the Northamptonshire JP Mr Eccles or Mr Wilmot in Spitalfields, the pretrial hearing offered an important opportunity for the facts of the case (such as they were) and the narrative of the subsequent trial to be established. Once a formal indictment had been secured, this was passed up to the jury courts. Outside of London this involved either the courts of quarter sessions or the assizes. The former met four times a year and dealt with, generally at least, non-capital crimes and a huge range of local administrative business. The assizes were normally held twice yearly (quarterly in Surrey but only once a year in Cumberland, Durham, Northumberland, and Westmoreland)

and were accompanied by great pomp and ceremony.[76] Judges from the Westminster courts were dispatched on circuits to 'deliver' to the gaols of provincial England and Wales and travelled from county town to county town, hearing trials, passing sentence, and recommending mercy where it was appropriate. In London the Old Bailey was in effect the capital's assize court and it sat eight times, served by local judges. There were two sets of jurisdiction: London and Middlesex, which recognized the City of London's separate status. As a result two sets of jurors were impaneled and the Recorder of London (the City's chief legal officer) often sat in judgement there on London cases (although he was frequently present, but not presiding, at all cases at the Old Bailey). Judges had considerable discretion in both the way they conducted trials and in the sentences they awarded but discretion also rested with the two sets of jurors that determined whether an accused would be found guilty of a crime and therefore subjected to the judge's sentencing power. At assizes, and therefore at the Old Bailey, indictments were first considered by the grand jury, a larger and generally more affluent group of higher status individuals than the petty jury (which determined the guilt or innocence of defendants). The grand jury decided whether an indictment was 'true' (and thus could proceed to trial) or not, in effect determining whether the accused had a case to answer.[77] The published accounts of trials at Old Bailey (the 'Old Bailey Sessions Papers' or 'Proceedings') only list those cases that made it to trial while the bound sessions files held by the London Metropolitan Archives (hereafter LMA) reveal those that did not. Not all trials were written up by the authors of the Proceedings; those that ended in 'not guilty' verdicts were sometimes omitted on the grounds that it might have encouraged offenders to believe they could get away with crime or reveal defences that were successful in persuading a jury of the innocence of the person standing in the dock.[78] Some offenders were adept at deploying effective defences to sow doubt in the minds of jurors or to undermine prosecution witnesses. The serial thief Charlotte Walker managed to evade conviction on numerous occasions at the Old Bailey by recognizing that jurors could be swayed by her control of the narrative of events surrounding the crimes she was accused of committing. Her luck did eventually run out but only after she had enjoyed a fairly long criminal 'career'.[79] In the 1790s the Proceedings had a moratorium on the publishing of trials that contained subversive or immoral content, stipulating that 'No trials of remarkable indecency or for any unnatural should be published'. This was not necessarily that new however, as Devereaux notes: 'Evidence on such sorts of trials – especially sodomy and rape cases – was often omitted or at least limited in the Sessions Paper throughout the eighteenth century'.[80] This may have affected the reporting of one of the cases within this study, that of Susannah Hill who was tried for the murder of the Czech musician Francis Kotzwara in 1789 (see Chapter 5). However, this study will argue that there were other reasons for the suppression of the reports of Hill's case, which touched on wider social concerns at the time.

Juries mattered of course; the English judicial system was adversarial, although until the later years of the 1700s barristers were relatively rare in criminal trials.[81] Prosecutors (either the victim of crime or his or her legal representative) had to persuade the jury that their version of the 'truth' was more believable than that offered up by the defence. For the defendant in the dock the task was simple if desperately difficult. They had to demonstrate their innocence to the satisfaction of the court, often without any legal counsel at all, and do this when they were ill-prepared having often been dragged from a prison cell with little or no warning that their trial was 'coming on'. Evidence was extremely limited in the Hanoverian justice system and consisted almost entirely of verbal testimony. Hearsay was largely permitted and forensic evidence rarely available. The evidence given was credited with more authority if the person testifying was seen to be respectable and of a good social standing. Thus, in many cases the only reported defence evidence is that of character witnesses who, if called in time, appeared to say what a good employee, peaceful neighbour, or otherwise unsullied individual the accused was. In the first half of the century perjured testimony was fairly common and the reward system certainly encouraged this. It was alleged that 'straw men' could be bought for a few shillings to say anything in the Old Bailey, and those accused of conspiracy with others could be expected to turn 'King's evidence' to save their own necks. Jurors had considerable discretion in whom they believed and whose evidence they rejected. Trials were notably short, and for many years Old Bailey jurors conducted their deliberations in court, not retiring to a jury room as they do today. The life of a defendant could be decided in a matter of moments and the judge could influence the jury's decision-making.

Juries could and did, however, act to corral judges' power. In very many cases juries delivered partial verdicts in capital cases that effectively took away the opportunity for a judge to hand down a death sentence. This practice, dubbed 'pious perjury', often involved downgrading the value of stolen goods to ensure that the capital element of charge was not met. For example, in some cases where a person was accused of stealing property from a dwelling house, the jury would find the accused guilty of stealing goods valued at 39s when the capital statute only applied to the theft of goods worth more than 40s. Similarly a pickpocket could be hanged for 'stealing privately' from the person – remove the 'privately' charge and the case was no longer deemed to be capital. Discretion then extended from the victim/prosecutor, through the juries (petty and grand), to the judge himself, but it did not end with sentencing. While there was no legal appeal against conviction in the 1700s it was possible to beg for clemency by petitioning the monarch. The pardoning process is of vital importance to understanding the operation of the criminal justice system in Hanoverian England, so this chapter will now spend some time outlining what historians know about it.

The Pardoning Process

Historians have been interested in the importance of pardoning in the criminal justice system since Douglas Hay published his seminal essay in 1975. This is not the place for a root and branch reappraisal of Hay's thesis but we might usefully look at the key tenets. Hay outlined the three key principles underpinning the Hanoverian criminal justice system, which he termed 'Majesty', 'Justice', and 'Mercy'. The first referred to the way the law was seen and, importantly, was intended to be seen as a visible representation of the power of the monarch and state.[82] This idea is articulated in dramatic style by Michel Foucault at the beginning of his own powerful study of punishment and power in 1975.[83] Foucault described in detail the execution of Robert-François Damiens for the attempted murder of Louis XV in Paris in 1757. Hay equates the criminal assizes trial (from the arrival of the judges to the final denouement of execution), with its emphasis on ceremony and ritual, to religion. By 'justice' Hay meant that the law had to be seen to be fair and the oft-cited execution of an aristocrat, Lord Ferrers, for the murder of his servant, was intended to demonstrate that no one was above the law.[84] The argument has been made by Hay's fiercest critic, John Langbein, that a better a way to demonstrate the equality of the law was the fact that even the property of the poorest subject of the nation was protected under legislation that made the theft of goods valued at a mere shilling or more punishable by death.[85] What mitigated this 'terror' was the 'mercy' shown to the vast majority of individuals condemned to die slowly on the gallows in the period. The process was supposedly 'mysterious' and certainly unknown to the bulk of the watching public. Decisions were made behind closed doors, or at least away from prying eyes. This helped preserve the fiction that the decision-making process was in some way fair and rational, when in reality is it was anything but (as this study will go some way to demonstrate). Hay's wider point was that the criminal law operated to sustain 'the hegemony of English ruling class' in the absence of a standing army or national police force.[86]

Since Hay published his thesis, historians of crime have attempted to test, demolish, and support it and again this is not the place to unpack that debate. We are still struggling to understand exactly how the process of obtaining a pardon operated. Gatrell was famously distracted enough by a chance encounter with the records of pardoning held by the National Archives to focus his entire attention on it for several years. Gatrell explains that in the period to 1837 (when Victoria ascended the throne) a parallel system of reviewing pardons operated in London and the provinces. Immediately following an Old Bailey session, the monarch and his or her council would 'determine the fates of those whom the judges or recorder had condemned there, ticking off those who would live or die' with what Gatrell terms 'sleazy insouciance'.[87] London had a unique status in England in Wales in regards to pardons because here, as Devereaux reminds us, 'the final decision for life or death amongst its capital convicts lay directly in the hands of government rather than the assize circuit judges'.[88] Conditional pardons (the commuting of death to transportation) were fairly common before the late 1770s or 1780s and around 50–60 per cent of London's condemned escaped execution.[89] Outside of London, decisions were delegated to 'directly to the judges [on circuits] or the secretary of state'. In principle they had still to be signed off by the king but in reality this was 'impractical'.[90] The judges were central in Gatrell's analysis, making decisions about whom to make an example of in a system which chose selected victims rather than opting for the wholesale slaughter of all those sentenced to death. This helped keep the public on side, as Hay had argued cogently in his earlier article.[91] The most tangible record of the pardoning process is the existence of thousands of petitions for mercy that are held at Kew providing testimony, particularly in the 1800s, to the desperation of individuals to avoid death on the gallows or transportation to Australia. These arrived most often on the desk of the home secretary from the 1820s onwards when the system seems to have become more streamlined. These were from offenders (or their supporters) convicted outside of London; the capital cases from the metropolis still went before the king and his council. Appeals became more sophisticated as well as more common in the nineteenth century though not necessarily more successful.[92] Felons waiting in London's Newgate Gaol for the outcome of the king's decision suffered the agonies of not knowing whether they would gain a reprieve or not.[93] Their families waited outside the walls in the nineteenth century, possibly inside in the eighteenth, hoping the messenger would arrive in time to save their loved ones from the noose.[94] One of the consequences (indeed the intentions) of the 1752 Murder Act (25 Geo. II, c. 37) had been to make the obtaining of pardons more difficult. Offenders were supposed to be executed and their bodies handed over to the surgeons within two days of conviction (Sundays excluded).[95] In two of the cases under scrutiny in this volume this did not happen, but in one it did. Again, we might reasonably ask why the letter of the law was applied for Henry Stroud (see Chapter 3) but not in the case of Matthew and Patrick Kennedy (Chapter 2) or Thomas Gordon (in Chapter 4)?

Before continuing with this discussion it is necessary to pause briefly and look at the process that led in London to the determination of the fates of those sentenced to death at the Old Bailey. This was led by the City chief legal authority, the Recorder of London, a position that was held between 1770 and 1800 by Sir James Eyre (1763–78), John

Glynn (1778–79), James Adair (1779–89), and Sir John William Rose (1789–1803).

The Role of the Recorder

At the end of each Old Bailey session the Recorder of London would present the names of those prisoners condemned to death before a council of the king and his ministers. It is likely that the Recorder, as the person who 'pronounced all the sentences at the conclusion of the session' was present on the bench in 'most trials'. As a result he was ideally suited to advising the king and his ministers on the merits for and against mercy in any given capital case.[96] Along with the Recorder and the king the council would have included the Lord Chancellor and the Lord Chief justice as well as other senior ministers. It was these men that determined who was to hang in London in the eighteenth century while outside the capital initial decisions were made by the judge at assizes before subsequent pardons were directed to the king via the Home Office. There is little evidence to suggest that the council tarried overlong in making their decisions. Beattie could see nothing in the early records (from the period before 1720) that supported an idea that they looked at any additional documentation beyond the Old Bailey Sessions Papers[97] and the Recorder's written report. The latter was short and to the point and, even after the 1720s, when the report ran to 'four or more manuscript pages', decisions were most likely to follow the Recorder's recommendation.[98] If the Recorder had not been present at a trial he would request the shorthand writer's notes either directly or, after 1785, from the publisher of the Sessions Paper.[99] Of course, as Beattie recognized, without detailed minutes of the meetings we cannot be sure how much (or how little) discussion preceded these judgements on the lives of the men and women waiting in the condemned cells at Newgate. Nor can we be sure what criteria the council members applied. However, Beattie was surely correct when he suggested that the

> council and lords justices drew distinctions among the convicted men and women in accordance with certain guidelines, if not principles. To judge by the decisions they made, the decisive issues were the gravity of the offence and the character of the offender, though what was thought to be the current level of crime was always likely to be an important consideration, as indeed were personal and political influences: the cabinet council and the lords justices were after all highly partisan bodies.[100]

It is clear to Devereaux that short as most trial reports were in the OBSP, they were deemed sufficient on their own to determine whether someone lived or died or was transported or granted a full pardon. It may be that this was augmented by individual statements on the prisoner's character and the judge's report, but the crucial evidence regarding the crime itself was contained within the trial report alone.[101]

Once the council had made their deliberations the fate of those waiting at Newgate was delivered to the gaol in the form of the 'dead warrant'. At this point petitions for mercy could still be written and applied for (and so the Recorder would be required to report once more)[102] but prisoners would have to hope for respites and last minute reprieves, something the Kennedy brothers experienced on more than once occasion. For this an inmate of Newgate would need friends or family and some access to money and a scribe (if they could not write themselves). None of that was easy and time was certainly not on their side. The passing of the Murder Act narrowed this window considerably meaning that, after 1752, convicted murderers had very little chance to avoid the noose. Indeed those left to hang by the Old Bailey judge under the terms of the Murder Act did not have their cases considered by the Recorder at all.[103] In the winter of 1788–9, when George III was taken ill with his first episode of 'madness', this system was effectively stalled, meaning that 'no less than four accumulated sessions [had] to be dealt with by the time he had recovered his health'.[104] This was to have severe implications for one of the individuals showcased in this volume, as will become evident in Chapter 4.

So, despite the amount of attention that has been focused on those condemned to die for a range of offences across the long eighteenth century and beyond and much debate on the campaign to abolish the Tyburn and later Newgate execution ritual, we still are not much closer to a good understanding of how decisions were made or what influenced them. Notably we have Peter King's immense contribution to the debate around Hay's thesis which identified that, for property offenders at least, quite understandable factors influenced whether they were sentenced to death or not, and whether those judgements were carried out in full.[105] Other sources are surprisingly quiet or even silent on the detail of the pardoning process, with Gatrell's being a clear exception for the nineteenth century at least.[106] This study will try, therefore, to add a little to our knowledge in this area.

Homicide: The Nature and Punishment of Murder and Manslaughter in the Late Eighteenth Century

Having looked at the operation of the eighteenth-century criminal justice system, from the identification of a crime, through arrest, trial, sentence and possible punishment, and then pardoning, it is now necessary to focus on the extent to which the cases presented in the subsequent chapters of this book are, or were, typical of crimes prosecuted at the time. Fundamentally, of course, they were not at all typical because most prosecuted crime in the 1700s was property crime, not homicide. Even within the broad category of indicted property crime (that which went before a judge and jury) violence played a very small part. Highway robbers and footpads (the criminals most likely to deploy violence to achieve their aims) were always in a minority compared to burglars, pickpockets, shoplifters, and 'common' larcenies. Interpersonal non-fatal violence also relatively rarely made the Old Bailey or assizes, being more usually dealt with a quarter sessions or by the magistracy in their Petty Sessions.[107] So these cases are, by definition, exceptions to the rule that the Hanoverian justice system was obsessed with the protection of private property. Nevertheless, as Martin Wiener argued, we can still learn a lot about a society by the study of the way it dealt with homicide.[108] It is important then to establish the level of homicide in London and more widely in the period these four case studies were prosecuted. To what extent were they typical of homicide *per se*, were the contexts in which they happened typical, and were the outcomes those we might expect, having studied the nature of homicide and judgements made more generally? We might usefully start by attempting to measure homicide in the second half of the eighteenth century, particularly in London where most of the cases used in this book played out.

Measuring Homicide in London in the Last Quarter of the Eighteenth Century

Arguably it is easier to measure actual homicide rates than those of virtually any other recorded crime in the eighteenth century. This is because, as Lawrence Stone argued in 1982, homicide engenders such a strong emotional reaction that we (meaning society) are impelled to report it and so it is much more likely to be investigated and prosecuted. In the 1700s very many offences went unreported or unprosecuted—such was the nature of a victim-led society—but murder and manslaughter were less likely to be ignored, Stone insisted, given the involvement of the coroner who was tasked with investigating all 'suspicious' deaths.[109] Historians of crime and criminologists are well aware of the so-called dark figure of unreported crime but, while there are certainly problems with accepting the records of English coroners as accurate at face value, Pieter Spierenburg argued that this 'dark figure' is 'negligible'.[110] That said we should be cautious of attempting to reach any definite figure for homicides before the modern age (and some might even urge caution today, regardless of the forensic armory available to twenty-first-century police forces). However, for the purposes of this study it is only necessary to provide a contextual framework for understanding first, how common murder or manslaughter was in the eighteenth century (in London and outside of the capital), and second, what forms this lethal violence took. The nature of homicide will be considered later but for the time being the levels of unlawful killing will be explored so far as the data is available.

The homicide rate in urban and rural Surrey in the period 1780–1802 was just 0.9/100,000 people.[111] Homicide is usually measured as a ratio of population since this allows comparison across time periods (something which is crucial to the now well-travelled historical debate in to the long term decline of homicide in Europe from the medieval to the modern period). The figure for urban Surrey (the area of London south of the river Thames) had been significantly higher the 20 years before 1780; at 1.7/100,000 it was almost double but this was still a fall from previous decades according to John Beattie's long chronological study of crime in the county. His study of indictments presented at the Surrey assizes reveal that in the immediate Restoration period (from 1660–1679) rates were as high as 8.1/100,000 remaining high into the reign of Queen Anne (where they stood at 3.9/100,000) and the first of the Hanoverians, George I. Thereafter they tumbled to 1.7/100,000 by the beginning of George III's rule in 1760.[112] Homicide rates were always lower in rural Surrey, away from the taverns and streets of the capital where, it was assumed, violence was more common. Rates were falling in both urban and rural Surrey, however, and the same pattern is evident in James Cockburn's long study of homicide in Kent from the sixteenth to the twentieth century.[113] Given that most of this book is concerned with homicide in London, that is where it will concentrate its attention, but it is necessary to look briefly at the available statistics for Northamptonshire in the late 1700s because this is where the killing of Constable Linnell took place in 1788. Unfortunately the complete assize records for Northamptonshire in the 1780s no longer exist and the register of trials held by the National Archives at Kew (hereafter NA) begins its series in 1791, just four years too late for our purposes.

Nevertheless it is possible, using the records of those executed in the county, to establish that, in the period 1770–1799, 32 people went to the gallows in Northamptonshire, the vast majority of which (29) were men.[114] Of the women, one (Elizabeth Nokes) was convicted of infanticide, while Catherine Parker went to her death for the killing of Thomas Cottingham and Jane Cross for her part in a highway robbery. Highway (and mail) robbery was the most common reason for executions with 14 men and Cross being hanged (including John Roberts whose body was afterwards gibbetted at Boughton to deter others).[115] Four of those hanged for robbery were members of the notorious Culworth Gang and their mass execution in August 1787 drew record crowds to watch them be 'turned off'. There were only four murders in that 30-year period, one of which was the killing of George Linnell by Thomas Gordon, the subject of Chapter 4. Thomas Pool and William Howell were the other men hanged for murder in the county (in 1780 and 1786, respectively). So homicide (or rather successful prosecutions for homicide) was rare in Northamptonshire in the last quarter of the eighteenth century and executions were running at about three a year. However, in 14 out of the 29 years between 1770 and 1799 there were no executions for any offence, seeing someone in Northamptonshire was, relatively speaking compared to London, an unusual event. This supports the analysis undertaken by King and Ward in their study of the operation of the 'bloody code' outside of the metropolis.[116]

London was quite different as executions there were much more frequent, especially in the late 1770s and early 1780s when war with the American colonists effectively removed the state's only concrete alternative to hanging, exile by transportation. Indeed Devereaux's research reveals that the actual number (if not the proportional rate) of executions at the Old Bailey increased to a century high in the mid-1780s, reaching its 'awful peak' in February 1785.[117] For example, in 1779, London saw 60 death sentences with 23 executions, considerable by comparison to provincial towns like Northampton but nothing compared to the 97 'turned off' in 1785. Moreover, a higher proportion of those condemned were actually being executed, as Tim Hitchcock and Robert Shoemaker have pointed out. In 1785 64.2 per cent of those receiving a death sentence were killed; in 1787 this had risen to a staggering 81.4 per cent; in 1779 that figure had been around 38 per cent.[118] This means that in the period within which most of the cases considered in this study (and all of those that resulted in a public execution) hangings were a frequently occurring event in the lives of ordinary people in London. The question that we might ask, however, is how many of those state sanctioned killings were inflicted on those that had taken the lives of others?

For London we are able to deploy the records of the Old Bailey – the printed proceedings – to explore the extent of homicide prosecutions in the last three decades of the eighteenth century. The Old Bailey Proceedings (or Sessions Papers) are not an exhaustive or perfect record of prosecutions and trial content for the period but, at least as far as homicide cases go, they are probably the best guide we have to indicted homicide in the capital. The Old Bailey Proceedings do not always represent a verbatim transcript of trials, nor are all trials recorded there, but in our period there is evidence to suggest that the Sessions Papers were considered to be an accurate representation of what happened in court and were being used to inform decisions on which convicts hanged and which were spared.[119]

From January 1770 (when the case against Matthew and Patrick Kennedy was heard) to the end of December 1799, the Old Bailey Proceedings records 271 offences involving some form of unlawful killing, with some 243 victims and 366 defendants. Given that this section is concerned most with the numbers of incidents of homicide in the period (and to avoid infanticide which represents a very different subset of killing), I have decided to restrict my analysis to the 243 records that reveal a victim. Of these, set out in Table 1.1, the vast majority (221) were prosecuted as murder.

Table 1.1 Trials for Killing at the Old Bailey, January 1770 to December 1799, Counting by Victim

	Manslaughter	Murder	Petty Treason	Other	Total
1770s	2 (2.13%)	90 (95.74%)	1 (1.06%)	1 (1.06%)	94 (38.68%)
1780s	10 (12.35%)	68 (83.95%)	1 (1.23%)	2 (2.47%)	81 (33.33%)
1790s	5 (7.35%)	62 (92.65%)	0 (0%)	0 (0%)	68 (27.98%)
Total	17 (7%)	221 (90.95%)	2 (0.82%)	3 (1.23%)	243 (100%)

Source: Old Bailey Proceedings Online (www.oldbaileyonline.org, version 8.0, 26 February 2019)

The three cases that were defined as 'other' by the modern digitization of the Old Bailey Proceedings were Bennet Storer in January 1777 who was acquitted of the manslaughter of George Keith; Thomas Apostle whose cart was involved in a fatal road traffic accident; and William Clipson for neglecting a prisoner in his care. Storer shot Keith when he forced his way into his lodgings at a public house near Westminster Bridge. It seems as if the jury, for lack anything to clearly pin the murder on Storer, viewed it as a case of self-defence.[120] In 1782 Thomas Apostle was convicted of the manslaughter of James Edwards, a carman. The cart Edwards was driving collided with the coach of Lord Verney, throwing him under the spokes of the oncoming coach and four. Edwards was crushed under the wheels, dying before the apothecary that Lord Verney summoned could treat him. It was prosecuted as a deliberate act but the peer's testimony on behalf of his coachman probably helped reduce the charge in the minds of the jury to the lesser one of manslaughter and Apostle was sentenced to be branded and released.[121] Finally, in December 1789, William Clipson, a turnkey (or gaoler) at the Fleet prison, was accused of causing the death, by neglect, of a prisoner in his care. William Garrow, arguably the foremost barrister of his generation, successfully defended Clipson and the London jury acquitted him.[122]

The other minor category (in terms of numbers of defendants if not seriousness) was that of 'petty treason' which was the killing of husbands by their wives. Until June 1790, when the punishment was abolished, women found guilty of husband murder could be executed by burning at the stake, as were those convicted of coining.[123] Petty treason was considered to be 'an aggravated degree of murder' as defined by the Treason Act of (1351), involving as it did the killing of a master by their servant or a husband by his wife.[124] In 1772 Elizabeth Herring was burnt at Tyburn for stabbing her husband Richard in the neck with a knife.[125] Henrietta Radbourne was spared such an awful punishment when she was convicted of her mistress' murder but it was ruled not to be 'petty treason'.[126] While Radbourne avoided a slow painful death by fire she was still publically hanged on December 14, 1787 outside the debtor's door at Newgate Gaol.

Of the 221 trials for murder, just over half (50.23 per cent) resulted in a guilty verdict. In 88 cases (39.8 per cent) the defendant/s was acquitted, and there were 21 'multiple verdicts' and one 'special' verdict. This last case involved Mary Adey who was convicted of killing a man named William Barnet. Barnet worked at the Bow Street Police office (as one of John Fielding's 'runners') and had gone to execute a warrant to arrest Adey's lover, known only by the name 'Farmello'. Adey stabbed Barnet as he tried to take her partner away but the jury was unsure whether it was deliberate or not.[127] The multiple verdicts include those that included several defendants, not all of whom were convicted of murder. So, for example, in the case of Thomas Dempsey, Thomas Welch, James Delaney, Philip Corbet, Dennis Sherry, and Andrew Nihil – all of whom were indicted in 1776 for the murder of Thomas Grimsley – Delaney, Corbett, and Nihill walked free from court, acquitted of any offence. The other three men were found guilty of manslaughter only, not murder. The case – which involved a group of men and plenty of alcohol – has some similarities with that of the Kennedy brothers, but because it was not deemed to be murder the worst punishment the culprits could expect was to be imprisoned for a relatively short period. No punishment is recorded by the Proceedings however.[128]

So that leaves the 111 cases where a conviction for murder was found. Table 1.2 reveals the nature of the punishments handed out to those convicted, by the gender of the defendant.

This shows that no women were set for execution by an Old Bailey judge for simple murder in their own right in the period of this study. However, Antis Horsford (in 1771), Elizabeth Pigott (in 1778),[129] and Jane Taylor (in January 1792)[130] were all found guilty of some degree of homicide. Taylor was imprisoned; for Pigott the outcome is unclear; and Horsford's case is considered in Chapter 3 alongside that of Henry Stroud and Robert Campbell.

Even in this much smaller sample there are cases where the accused was convicted of the lesser offence of manslaughter and punished accordingly.

Table 1.2 Outcomes for Trials for Murder at the Old Bailey, January 1770 to December 1799, Counting by Victim

	Death	Branding	Multiple	Prison	Fine	Respited	Unknown	Total
Male	25	15	31	2	10	2	14	99
Female	0	3	3	0	1	0	2	9
Mixed	1	1	1	0	0	0	0	3
Total	26	19	35	2	11	2	16	111

Source: Old Bailey Proceedings Online (www.oldbaileyonline.org, version 8.0, 26 February 2019)

Twenty-four of the men tried for murder at the Old Bailey in the 1770s had their crimes downgraded to manslaughter; each of them were branded in the hand and given a short term of imprisonment. Two others, Oliver Davis in September 1774 and Edward Britain in May 1775, were also branded, having been accused of 'feloniously killing' rather than with 'willful murder'.[131] In the 1780s, men eight men found guilty of manslaughter instead of murder were branded, while 14 others were merely fined and imprisoned. Branding was abandoned in 1789 and so it is unsurprising that the nine men convicted of manslaughter in the following decade (having been charged with murder) were simply fined and locked away for six months to a year.[132] Eighteen other men were fined, having been convicted of manslaughter.

Of those sentenced to death, two men, Peter Conoway and Michael Richardson, were executed and their bodies hanged in chains as an additional disgrace for the crime they had committed (the shooting of William Venables at point blank range).[133] Twenty-two men received sentence of death in the 1770s: Matthew and Patrick Kennedy, Charles Stevens, John Pursel, Richard Hewett, Henry Stroud, Frederick Wilkie, William Edwards White, Alexander Tate, Robert Williams, Joseph Bull, Benjamin Harley, Thomas Henman, Robert Harley, Peter Tolosa, Francis Mercier, and John Howse and all but two of them went to gallows, with several of them being anatomized and dissected afterwards in accordance with the 1752 Murder Act. The Kennedy brothers were the only two capitally convicted murderers not to be executed in London in the 1770s, and the reasons for this will be unpacked in Chapter 2. Henry Stroud, convicted in July 1771, was executed quickly after conviction, near the scene of his alleged crime, and his story is told in Chapter 3.

In the 1780s seven men were executed: Francis Gray, John Clarke, Henry Morgan, William Higson, John Hogan, William Woodcock, and Cornelius Carty. Carty's execution, for killing Michael Williams as he and his family travelled on the roads through Hendon to the north of London, was followed by the display of his body in an iron cage as a warning to other highwaymen.[134] Carty and Woodcock had the dubious distinction of making the pages of the Newgate Calendar, where they were described as 'atrocious villains'.[135] Daniel Macginnis, a 60-year-old labourer who was convicted of stabbing John Hardy to death with a bayonet, had his sentence commuted to transportation for life. There was clearly some doubt in the case as to whether this was a murder or a manslaughter but the jury convicted him as charged and did not recommend him to mercy. His age, and the underlying doubt over his guilt, may well have influenced the decision to reduce his sentence.[136] Kenith Mackenzie also escaped death after he was freed in February 1785.[137] Mackenzie was held responsible for the death of (confusingly) Kenith Murray Mackenzie in an unauthorized execution. The victim was tied to the mouth of a cannon and, on Mackenzie's orders, blown to bits.

Mackenzie was convicted by the Old Bailey jury and the judge sentenced him to be hanged and then anatomized, but he was later pardoned.[138] Finally, William Power, who was convicted of murder and sentenced to death, had this commuted during the Old Bailey session and was burned in the hand instead.[139]

In the 1790s Jacintho Phararo, Anthoni Murrini, and Stephen Apologie were all executed for the murder of a fellow Italian sailor named Josephi. They were each dissected and anatomized within days of the trial (in this case just as the Murder Act prescribed).[140] Seven other men went to their deaths following convictions for murder at the Old Bailey in the 1790s: Thomas Masters, Edward Welch, Charles Taylor, Francis Hubbard, Robert Anderson, John Bond, and George Dingler. James Eyres had his sentence of death and dissection for killing Gabriel Franks in a riot against the Bumboat Act, in which Eyres was considered to be a leading player. However, there was clearly no actual proof that Eyres fired the pistol that killed Franks (who was in some way connected to the Thames Police office at Wapping) and this may have helped him get his sentence commuted to transportation to Australia for 21 years.[141] Eyres sailed on the *Royal Admiral* in March 1800 and is listed as surviving the journey to New South Wales.[142]

There is some duplication in the statistics set out in Table 1.3 because of the way the Old Bailey Online database records outcomes. So, of the 37 men sentenced to hang for murder at the Old Bailey in the three decades covered by this collection of case studies, only six men escaped that awful punishment. Of these, one, Kenith Mackenzie, was an officer in the armed forces. Another, Daniel Macginnis, was an old man in his sixties. In the case of James Eyres there was considerable doubt as to who had fired the gun that had ended the victim's life. Similar doubts may have allowed William Power's capital sentence to be commuted. What this brief analysis of convictions for murder at the Old Bailey in the period from January 1770 to December 1799 reveals is that most of the sentences of death handed down to those convicted of homicide were carried out. As this

Table 1.3 Sentencing in Trials for Murder at the Old Bailey, December 1769 to December 1799, Counting by Punishment, Where the Defendant Is Male

	Death[*]	Branding	Prison	Fine	Respited	Unknown	Total
1770s	22	26	1	2	1	15	67
1780s	13	8	11	14	1	7	54
1790s	12	0	9	18	0	16	55
Total	57	34	21	34	2	38	176

Source: Old Bailey Proceedings Online (www.oldbaileyonline.org, version 8.0, 26 February 2019)

[*] Includes 'death and dissection', 'hanging in chains', and 'executed'

study will hopefully show, the case of Kennedy brothers was exceptional while that of Henry Stroud and Robert Campbell perhaps better fitted the 'normal' pattern. Just why this was the case will be the main subject of the book, which aims to illustrate, through a series of cases studies, that discretion (and sometimes discretion exercised as a result of political corruption) can explain why certain individuals escaped the noose even when they had been convicted of the most heinous crime.

The importance of discretion both to the outcomes of trials and the ultimate execution of capital sentences has long been established by historians and this study will both add to that research and extend it to consider where specific instances of societal attitudes, political convenience, corruption in high places, and individual circumstances might also have affected the outcomes of trials, sentencing, and appeals for clemency. In any consideration of homicide it is necessary to look at the contexts in which it occurred, and so this study will now look in some detail at the nature of murder and manslaughter, as prosecuted at the Old Bailey in the last three decades of the eighteenth century.

The Nature of Homicide in the Eighteenth Century

Once again the Old Bailey Online's database is invaluable in providing the raw data from which to construct a typology of homicide in the late 1700s. However, a useful starting point for this is professor of criminology Fiona Brookman's working typology from 2005.[143] Brookman sets out ten contexts for homicide, as shown in Table 1.4 that follows:

Understandably, given Brookman's background as a criminologist, this is aimed at explaining modern occurrences of homicide and so needs some adjustment to be relevant to the eighteenth century. It is possible to create two relatable typologies of homicide for the period covered by this volume: one that adapts Brookman's and the other that considers the gendered relationship between killer and victim (see Table 1.5).

Table 1.4 Brookman's Homicide Contexts

Domestic Homicide
Homicide in the Course of Other Crime
Gang Homicide
Confrontational Homicide
Jealousy/Revenge (Unrelated Individuals)
Reckless Acts (Unrelated Individuals)
Racial Violence
'Other' Unspecified Circumstances
Context/Motive Unknown
Unusual Cases (i.e., Serial Murder, Terrorism, Mass Homicide, Homicide
    Among Children

Table 1.5 Killer/Victim Relations in Homicide Cases

Male on Male	165 (66.80%)
Male on Female	53 (21.45%)
Female on Male	13 (5.26%)
Female on Female	9 (3.32%)
Mixed on Male	6 (3.64%)
Unknown	1 (0.40%)
Totals	247

Source: (Tabulating defendant gender against victim gender where offence category is killing, between December 1769 and December 1799. Counting by offence)[144]

That men allegedly perpetrated 88 per cent of homicides will come as no surprise to historians of crime and criminologists. Violence is most commonly associated with male actors although this is somewhat altered when the victims is an infant or newborn child. Given that infanticide was considered to be a specific offence, committed by unmarried women, and subject to a quite different interpretation of law in the 1700s, I propose to exclude it from this study. Infanticidal mothers, therefore, are excluded from the statistics in Table 1.4. This removed 24 'unknown' relationships from the results of the survey. The others were determined by studying the trial transcripts, only one of which actually stated that the victim was 'unknown' to the jurors, that of James Warren in February 1798.[145] The small number of women who were accused of killing men included just four cases (that of Elizabeth Herring, 1773; Mary Owen, 1776; Henrietta Radbourne in July 1787; and Mary-Ann Winter in 1798) of spousal murder. Not all of these were prosecuted as, or convicted of, 'petty treason', which carried (until 1790) the dread punishment of being burned at the stake.[146]

Wife killing was much more prevalent than husband murder, even allowing for suggestions that the latter was more common than records show.[147] In 24 of the cases where women were the victims of men we can be clear that husbands murdered (or were accused of murdering) their wives or lovers. While 19 of the women killed were described as the wife of the accused, in five cases the victims were women who lived with the defendant and were considered to be their wives by witnesses testifying at the Old Bailey. In three other cases, it is evident that there had been a connection between the deceased and their killer, quite possibly a romantic one. This was the case for Charles Griffiths who was cleared of murdering Charity Lee, a woman that had left him to care for himself and their sick children on his own.[148] Three of the homicide victims were otherwise associated with the accused, two shared a house, and another was a nurse in a workhouse who was killed by the actions of an inmate. Four of the victims were infants or children but not clearly ones related to the prisoner at the bar, and in 16 cases there was no obvious relationship between the woman that died and the man accused of killing her. Thus 53 per cent of murder or manslaughter trials at the Old Bailey in this period, where the victim was a female and the accused male, we can reasonably place in the category of domestic homicide alongside the previous four women accused of murdering their husbands.

It is much more complicated to establish the connections and motives in the 165 cases where men were accused of killing other men, although some of these are apparent in the context in which they occurred and in the evidence given by witnesses in the transcripts of trials. Eighteen of the victims would appear to have been killed in the course of the committal of a property crime, most often a form of robbery. For example, in May 1797, Martin Clinch and James Mackly were tried for the murder of Sidney Fryer earlier that month. Fryer and his young female cousin were walking towards Islington from central London when they were set upon by robbers. Sidney Fryer was shot and killed by a man wearing a handkerchief over the lower part of his face. His cousin Ann testified that the same man then approached her:

> he then came up to me with a pistol, and desired me to deliver my money; my hand trembled, and I could not get to my pocket, he said, make haste, give me your money; and I gave him my purse, with some money in it.

The man then ran away.[149] It would appear to be a fairly classic highway robbery by footpads, in the open country to the north of the city. Clinch and Mackley (both young men in their early twenties) were convicted and executed at the beginning of June.[150] In May 1782 four companions were travelling across the north of London when they encountered four men near an Islington tavern. The robbers demanded their money with menaces and in the ensuing scuffle John Herd received a mortal wound in his eye and died almost instantly. Francis Gray was the only man tried for the crime since the others escaped custody. There were doubts as to whether he had dealt the killing blow but the judge, Justice Nares, thought that was 'immaterial'; Gray was convicted and ordered to be hanged and his body anatomized.[151]

There were seven cases where there is evidence that the killings were a consequence of a duel or a prearranged fist fight. Bennet Allen fought a duel with Lloyd Dulany in June 1782 after a quarrel that had its origin in the divided loyalties of the American Revolution.[152] The pair stood eight yards apart and Allen shot his rival in the chest. Duelling amongst gentlemen was coming under increased if not sustained criticism in the last quarter of the eighteenth century. This has been explained as part of wider move away from violence by the urban gentry class and towards 'politeness' and this in turn gradually led to more prosecutions when duels ended in fatalities.[153] It took Lloyd Dulany three days to die from the wound he sustained at Gloucester Gate. In the trial the prosecuting counsel, John Silvester – one of the Old Bailey's 'most active' barristers[154] – emphasized the point that Allen had practised shooting his pistol at a target prior to the encounter and that his second and fellow defendant, Robert Morris, had insisted that the duellists stand just eight yards apart rather than the more conventional (and less lethal) ten or twelve.[155] The duel took place in the evening, around nine, and although it was close to midsummer the light was failing and it had been wet. At the raising of the hats of the two seconds both men fired and Dulany fell down. He was taken away in a hackney coach but never recovered. In his defence Allen, a clergyman, claimed he never wished to fight, that it had been forced on him and that he was ill prepared for it. Moreover he was blind in one eye, saw 'very imperfectly', and had never fired a pistol before, while Dulany was proficient with weapons, having fought more than one duel previously. The jury, who only considered their verdict for 15 minutes, found Morris not guilty and Allen guilty, but of manslaughter rather than murder.

James Adair, who held the position of Recorder of London between 1779 and 1789, noted that 'duelling has been justly reprobated by the laws of every well-regulated state' and condemned it as 'subversive of every tie of morality and religion'. However, he satisfied himself with sentencing the convicted man to six months in Newgate and a one-shilling fine.[156] Two years later Cosmo Gordon was indicted for the murder of Frederick Thomas, a fellow officer in the army. They had fought together in America and an acrimonious dispute had arisen between them concerning an engagement where Thomas, as the junior officer, had led his men to occupy high ground only to find that Gordon did not come to his support. The quarrel ended in a court martial case and rumbled on after the pair had returned to England. According to a nineteenth-century account the pair met at Hyde Park and agreed to 'fire when they pleased'. The two men measured eight paces, turned, and presented their pistols. They each fired on three occasions and the final exchange resulted in Thomas sustaining a mortal wound.[157] The judge, Baron Eyre, while pointedly criticizing the practice of duelling as being 'in direct opposition to the feelings of mankind, and the prevailing manners of the present time', pretty clearly directed the jury to acquit Colonel Gordon, which they did.[158] At this time duels involving officers in the armed forces accounted for around a quarter of such violent encounters, making the Gordon case fairly typical.[159] The duel was a formalized method of settling disputes, albeit if the rules that were followed were ones devised informally given the illegal nature of the activity. The fist fight was also recognized as a means of dispute resolution amongst men but here the lines are much more blurred between what constituted a prearranged contest (as duelling was) and an argument that got out of hand and ended in raised fists and even the recourse to any weapons that might be close to hand.[160] Edward Britain and James Lewis were drinking together at a pub called the *London Apprentice* in April 1777. An argument began and the two men rose and exited the pub, agreeing to fight each other outside. They traded blows for about eight minutes before one landed by Britain knocked the other to ground. He hit his head as he fell and was knocked unconscious. The injured man was taken inside and then to a nearby hospital where he died. At the trial the few witnesses that appeared testified that it was a fair fight with no 'foul blows' but that Britain had also behaved badly 'cursing and swearing' and the jury convicted him of manslaughter. The judge ordered him to be branded on the hand.[161]

In about 20 cases the cause of death was a clear accident. Most of these were driving (road traffic) accidents that would not usually be prosecuted as murder or manslaughter in a modern court but were in the 1700s.[162] A jury acquitted John Knutt after he was accused of causing the death of James Moody, who died under the wheels of one of the coal carts he was guiding along Fleet Street in the summer of 1777. Moody was on horseback and had got himself between two heavily laden carts and lost control of his horse. The horse reared and threw its rider, who was unable to prevent himself falling between the heavy wheels of the coal carts. He died less than an hour later.[163] Matthew Wright was crossing Bishopsgate Street in October 1770 carrying a tray of vegetables when he was run over by a hackney coach. Witnesses deposed that James Tompion's coach was driving 'furiously' and was unable to stop. In his defence Tompion claimed that his reigns were broken and he had lost control. Several character witnesses appeared to speak up for the coachman and the jury downgraded the murder charge to one of manslaughter. Tompion was branded and sent to Newgate.[164] Thomas Plata (or Plato) and Francis Parker were tried for the murder of James Messenger in an incident that may have resulted from an illegal act of bullock hunting near Smithfield market. Bullock hunting (not unlike the popular pastime of bull running as practised in Stamford, Lincolnshire, and other English towns in the eighteenth and early nineteenth centuries) was a perennial problem for the authorities in London. Cases of bullock hunting, where single beasts were separated from a herd and chased through the streets of the City by 'yahooing' gangs of youths, were not infrequently brought before the magistrates at Guildhall and Mansion House to be dealt with summarily.[165] Plata and Parker (both drovers) had apparently identified the animal as being 'wild' and offered to help its owner take it to a secure pound. However, it seems that the two men separated the animal, goaded it, and ran it through the streets, whether for the sport or in an attempt to keep it away from the larger herds they were tasked with driving. In the event the bullock run amok and gored Messenger who died of his injuries in hospital. Plata was acquitted by his co-defendant was convicted of manslaughter and burnt in the hand.[166]

In a couple of cases the accidental nature of the death was made clear at the state of the trial – where a pistol had gone off accidently, or someone had fallen under a carriage after being jostled on the street – but the word 'accident' was also regularly used in many of the cases which ended up being deemed to be manslaughters rather than murders. Indeed in many of the cases that clearly arose from an unscheduled fight (as opposed to a duel or 'fair' fist fight) – which constituted the vast majority (45 per cent) of all male on male killings – the tone of the trial suggested that there was no intention to kill on the part of those involved. As a result many of these ended up being downgraded from murder to manslaughter. Unsurprisingly quite a large proportion of these quarrels that ended in homicide charges requiring a jury trial began (and often ended) at a tavern or public house. Alcohol was clearly a factor in very many of these deaths, and that conforms to what we know about the proliferation of casual violence in the eighteenth century.[167] While contemporaries like Bernard Mandeville recognized that drink made men 'quarrelsome, renders 'em brutes and savages, sets 'em on to fight for nothing, and has often been a cause for murder',[168] drunkenness was frequently used in mitigation of actions considered otherwise out of character for 'sober' men. Dana Rabin has highlighted evidence of localized toleration of drunkenness as a mitigating factor in deaths and injuries caused by tavern brawls, when the victim and perpetrators knew each other: 'Testimony of deep friendship with no history of conflict between the killer and his victim recurs with predictable regularity in the depositions', she notes, and '[d]escriptions of camaraderie accompany the defendant's expression of deep regret and sorrow'.[169] However, while juries might have taken the fact that a person was drunk in some mitigation of their actions the law was less tolerant. Sir James Stephen, a sitting judge at Queen's Bench, writing in 1883 noted that while a man who was 'wildly excited by drink can hardly be said to know at the moment of that excitement that any particular act which he may do is either right or wrong', he could not excuse his actions on account of his drunkenness since he 'did wrong in getting drunk' in the first place.[170]

In the case of Matthew and Patrick Kennedy and their co-defendants (the subject of Chapter 2) the excessive consumption of alcohol on Christmas Eve 1769 led to a drunken brawl and eventually to the murder of a watchman on Westminster Bridge. At least two other incidents that started in pubs also resulted in deaths in the period covered by this study are worth considering to see these trials were prosecuted and what they tell us about this sort of interpersonal homicide in the late 1700s. In 1771 three men left an establishment in Shoreditch and walked arm in arm in high spirits on their way home. They soon encountered a group of family and friends coming in the opposite direction and, as they passed, John Foy accidentally collided with the wife of Joseph West. West flew into a rage and a fight broke out. The watch was called as a large affray was underway near the *Black Dog* public house and many arrests were made. In the process Foy was knocked to the floor by West and kicked and stamped on by one of his companions, Stephen Paris. Foy died soon afterwards and West, Paris, and another man, Samuel Randall, were indicted for murder and for aiding and abetting West in the killing.[171] The trial was a long one by eighteenth-century standards, lasting from ten in the morning until four in the afternoon, partly because the defence insisted that all of the witnesses be examined separately. Randall was acquitted while West and Paris were found guilty only of manslaughter, not wilful murder. Each of the convicted men were branded and released.[172]

In April 1776 six men were put on trial for the murder of a watchman following a brawl in the *Coach & Horses* public house in Cockspur Street. John Shakespeare had jostled a group of men who were standing around the fire and had ended up being knocked to the ground for his pains. A brawl ensued and the watch were called. The reports of witnesses vary but it seems as if some of the defendants had armed themselves with everyday tools to use as weapons and the watch had come in brandishing their hangers and cutlasses. As Thomas Grimsley and other members of the watch tried to corner the men on the stairs he was hit on the head with an axe and collapsed. In all of the confusion and the conflicting witness testimony it was hard to work out who had hit whom and with what but despite the efforts of a surgeon at St George's hospital – who attempted to trepan the deceased – Grimsley died. Thomas Dempsey, Thomas Welch, James Delaney, Phillip Corbet, Dennis Sherry, and Andrew Nihil were all acquitted of his homicide.[173]

In 1792 Francis Hubbard joined a group of at least seven of his friends at the *Crown & Anchor* in Chick Lane. The men were described in court in derogatory terms by William Garrow, prosecuting, as a 'riotous mob' who were the associates of common prostitutes. Everyone had been drinking and arguments broke out before this spilled out on to the street where a number of passers-by were abused and assaulted seemingly for no reason. They chased a man through the streets, beating him and cutting at him with knives, before he took refuge in a grocer's shop on Saffron Hill. The grocer's wife saw Francis Hubbard and others beating the man, Jordan Hosty, and remonstrated with the gang while the injured man was dragged inside to safety. Unfortunately for Hosty it was too late to save his life and he expired soon afterwards. The surgeon that examined him attributed his death to a stab wound in his buttocks from which he would have lost a lot of blood. Hubbard had only recently been released from prison and that probably counted against him in court. He and John Noble were found guilty of the murder of Jordan Hosty and were sentenced to death; the other men involved were acquitted.[174] Hubbard was executed on April 2, 1792 and his body sent to Surgeons' Hall to be anatomized.[175]

This handful of cases reveals that an excess of alcohol could clearly be a factor in aggravating disputes and escalating fairly trivial altercations to the point at which pushing and shoving descended into fist fights which ended in the use of lethal weapons. If these ended in injury, assault prosecutions might follow, or charges of riotous or disorderly behaviour could be brought by watchmen or constables, but unless the riot act had been read these would usually only trouble a jury at a quarter sessions or a magistrate sitting summarily. Thus the cases that reached the Old Bailey were in themselves unusual or atypical of the normal run of pub and tavern brawls that must have been a very regular part of daily life in the eighteenth-century capital.[176] In many respects the Kennedy case was of itself fairly typical of this small subgroup, but, while Francis Hubbard was executed for murder outside Newgate Gaol, the two brothers, Patrick and Matthew, were able to escape a similar fate. The reasons behind this are complicated and have much more to do with their personal circumstances than the circumstances of the crime they were convicted of committing. We can move on to consider another selection of homicides in the same data sample that arose from fights or quarrels to see what lay at the heart of them.

There were around 70 deaths that can be attributed to violence that arose out of everyday squabbles and petty jealousies visible in the prosecutions for homicide at the Old Bailey between January 1770 and the end of December 1799. While all of these were the result of the death of one of those 70 men, relatively few of the 94 men tried for homicide were convicted for murder and hanged. It seems to have been generally believed that death was an inevitable (and possibly acceptable) consequence of men squaring up to each other in public which, given the prevailing state of contemporary medicine, is perhaps understandable. As the work of James Cockburn has indicated, our modern society might appear considerably more dangerous were it not for important developments in medical science, not least the discovery and application of antibiotics after the First World War.[177] This was exacerbated by the easy availability of weapons (blunt and sharp edged) in the 1700s and the lack of any restrictions on carrying them. While sword carrying among the elite had declined considerably by the second half of the eighteenth century, leading to fewer fatalities, it is far from clear that working class men abandoned their knives and tools that were often essential for their daily existence.[178] Moreover men did not need to be in possession of a lethal weapon to deploy one in a fight; almost any situation in which quarrels erupted presented opportunities to seize something that could end a person's life. This was what occurred at the end of October 1770 on board a ship that had recently docked at the London quays. An argument broke out between George Newton and George Atkinson and insults were exchanged on deck. The men squared up to each other while several other members of the crew tried to intervene, without success. Newton had picked up a capstan bar (a long wooden pole used to turn the capstan that helped haul up ropes and cable) that had been stowed in a longboat. In effect he had armed himself with a stave and he 'swore he would knock down the first man that near him'. Atkinson moved forward and was about to take a handspike from the same long boat. This was probably also made from wood but may have had a metal tip; at least one witnesses suggested that the handspike was a 'dangerous weapon'. Before he could get control of it however, Newton hit him twice about the head and body with the capstan bar and knocked him to the deck. Atkinson never recovered and died of a fractured skull three days later in the London infirmary. Newton was tried for murder but acquitted.[179]

William Saddler also died of a fractured skull when John Cotton hit him with a hammer. Cotton was a bricklayer and on June 22, 1774 he and some co-workers had completed a job in London and were returning north in the direction of Muswell Hill. Saddler ran a public house there with his wife Ann and he claimed that Cotton owed him money. The pair met in Crouch End where Cotton's employer was treating his workers to a well-earned drink and after words were exchanged a fight started. Saddler was the bigger man and he managed to push the other man into a ditch. The pair grappled before Cotton hit him a couple of times on the head with his work hammer. Saddler died on July 9 and Cotton was indicted for his murder. In September 1774 an Old Bailey jury acquitted him of murder but found him guilty of manslaughter. He was branded in the hand and imprisoned for six months.[180] Weapons were not always necessary to cause fatal injuries; a man's fists coupled with falls and bad landings could be just as lethal. When Francis Jenkins and William Anderson clashed outside a pub where the latter had just unloaded his dustcart, neither was armed. Jenkins had come out of a nearby public house and demanded the repayment of a debt. The dustman said he had no money to pay it and the other man lost his temper and attacked him. The first blow hit Anderson on the head and he laughed it off as nothing serious, which may have enraged Jenkins still further. According to several witnesses Jenkins then kicked his victim in the groin, pulled him unceremoniously off his cart, and hit him again several more times in the head. Bystanders watched all of this but did nothing to intervene; Jenkins was in such a belligerent mood that at least one witnesses stated that he was too scared to get between him and Anderson. The stricken man was eventually helped to the Marylebone Infirmary where he died from the wounds he received to his head. Jenkins was tried for murder, but the jury downgraded it to manslaughter after considering their verdict for some time. Nevertheless, the judge made it clear to Jenkins that he was responsible for another man's death as a result of his 'brutality'. By 1786 branding was in decline and so the convicted man was sentenced to a year's imprisonment in Newgate Gaol.[181] In many of the cases indicted as murder but downgraded to manslaughter very similar circumstances occurred. The jury appears to have taken into consideration whether the killing took place as the result of a 'fair fight' between relative equals. If it could be shown (by witnesses) that two men had quarrelled and agreed to fight then it was unlikely that any charge of murder would stick. If both men had used force, with or without weapons, they were similarly reticent to find one man more complicit than the other and those cases were most likely to result in a not guilty verdict. Where the accused had demonstrated that he was assaulting someone smaller, older, or weaker than himself, or where the other had not attempted to fight back, a charge of manslaughter (if not deliberate murder) was more likely to be upheld. Historians have discussed the concept of the 'fair fight' (particularly amongst working class men in nineteenth-century Britain) and however problematic the term is it does seem that Old Bailey juries in the eighteenth century understood it as a mitigating factor in homicide cases.[182]

Alongside all the fights, duels, and group brawls (drunken of otherwise), some small number of the encounters that ended in indictments for murder were clearly the result of jealousies concerning relationships between men and women. This is one of Brookman's ten contexts for homicide and one of the more popular themes for drama representations of murder. Jealousy was one factor but revenge was another that led to homicides in the 1700s. There were eight trials at the Old Bailey in the period under study that appear to have resulted either from jealousy amongst rival males or as a result of some deep seated quarrel that required avenging. Joseph Rickards appears to have killed his former master Walter Horseman, after he was discharged from his service one or two months earlier. The fact that Rickards broke into the house and that the murder, with an iron bar, was seemingly premeditated counted against him both with the jury and the judge. Rickards, who was only 18 years of age, was convicted and executed close to the scene of his crime in Kentish Town.[183]

There were other factors which led to homicide cases being heard at the Old Bailey, not all of which easily fit into an obvious typology. One, the alleged murder of William Poole, a child of 12, by his schoolmaster, is particularly distressing. Poole had been reading in class but was not acquitting himself very well according to other pupils present. The schoolmaster John Barney aimed a strike at the lad's head with an open hand that made his head collide with the chimneybreast. The blow concussed William who was taken downstairs where he vomited before being dragged back up to continue his lessons. He was made to sit at his bench unable to complete a simple maths test before it was time to go home at five o'clock. His parents' servant reported that he came home sick so was sent straight to bed where he was discovered dead the next morning. It was a tragedy but because there was no clear intent in Barney's action and several people, including his pupils, spoke up for him in court; he was acquitted of murder and manslaughter.[184] This casual cruelty towards a school child was nothing compared to the calculated abuse meted out to William Ringrose by his master Stephen Self. Ringrose was one of three apprentices under the tuition and care of Self, a hairdresser in Marylebone. Ringrose had not settled well into Self's service and ran away from it. Captured, he was brought before Sir John Fielding by his master and punished with a spell in Bridewell, a not uncommon outcome for disobedient apprentices.[185] In what reads like an early version of *Oliver Twist* Self continued to punish his charge thereafter by starving him of food and making him sleep on the kitchen floor. One of the other apprentices claimed that the boy was forced to fight for food with the hairdresser's dog and on January 22, 1776 he finally died of malnutrition. Despite managing to produce several witnesses to his character Self was convicted, not of murder but of the lesser charge of manslaughter, and was burned in the hand and sent to Newgate.[186]

It should have now become fairly self-evident that in the eighteenth century, in London and most likely elsewhere in the country, homicide was part and parcel of everyday life. However, even though deaths from brawls or street accidents were commonplace and largely accepted, more serious planned murders were considerably less common. The laws concerned with unlawful killing were, arguably at least, designed either to provide some sort of compensation for those bereaved when a breadwinner was killed or to prevent careless or wanton murders. Murder was the ultimate crime, proscribed by statute law and by religious text, but it came in many guises and, while the eighteenth-century criminal justice did not recognize the division between first degree and second-degree murders, juries appear to have applied some commonly held perceptions of what these might have been. The case studies chosen for this volume all involve accusations of murder that might have been considered as manslaughter, but were not. Before we leave the topic of homicide then I think it necessary to be very clear about how the law defined murder and manslaughter and what constituted a legal defence for either, or both, in the 1700s.

The Law of Homicide in the Eighteenth Century

As John Beattie stated 'there is no question that murder retained its hold over the public imagination' in the 1700s.[187] Murder, according to the great eighteenth-century jurist William Blackstone, was when 'a person of sound memory and discretion unlawfully killeth any reasonable creature . . . with malice aforethought'.[188] The key factor here was 'malice' and the emphasis was on proving intent. Justice Stephen recognized that it was the 'malice' that mattered more than the 'aforethought' in legal terms, at least when it came to murder. For him, malice meant one of four 'states of mind', the most important of which was: 'An intention to cause the death of, or grievous bodily harm to any person, whether such person is the person actually killed or not'.[189] The legal difference between murder (intentional homicide) and manslaughter (unintentional or accidental killing) emerged from legal disputes in the 1500s and continued to be debated into the eighteenth century as the latter was not normally punishable by death.[190] Malice could be implied – for example, if the attack was on a serving peace officer (a constable or watchman, for example, as it was in two of the case studies in this book), malice was implied and the crime seen as murder. Poisoning was also viewed as a malicious attack, because it could be deemed both to be premeditated and unprovoked.[191] Both could be contrasted with a 'fair fight' or even a tavern brawl where two or more men exchanged relatively equal blows, each retaliating to the aggression of the other. Crucially the law expected someone accused of murder to be able to demonstrate that they had not acted maliciously and were, for example, provoked. Even revenge, if left too long, could be deemed malicious and therefore murder rather than manslaughter. Simply, in order to escape a charge of murder you had to be able to show that you were forced to act in the heat of the moment unless, that is, you could demonstrate you were acting in self-defence or were in some other way justified.

Under eighteenth-century law a prosecution for murder could be brought if a person died of wounds received within a year and a day of the attack that caused them. Additionally that prosecution had to be pressed within a year and day of the victim dying. The law also allowed the wife or family of the person killed to bring a private appeal if a conviction could not be gained though the criminal system. This was a complicated and rarely used legal device but it was deployed in the case of the Kennedy brothers and so I will confine my discussion of it to Chapter 2.

Hopefully, the preceding discussion of homicide, and its contexts and typologies, has established the background for the case studies or microhistories that follow. In each there will need to be further contextual discussion: of Georgian society and politics, policing and courts, punishments, law, and media representations of crime. An introductory chapter can only achieve so much before it is necessary to delve more closely into the detail of the sources under investigation. Chapter 2 will start, therefore, with the casual murder of a policing agent on Christmas Eve 1769.

Notes

1. Carlo Ginzburg, 'Microhistory: Two or Three Things I Know About It', in Carlo Ginzburg (ed.), *Threads and Traces: True False Fictive* (Berkeley, CA, University of California Press, 2012), pp. 204–5.
2. Steve Poole, ' "For the Benefit of Example" ': Crime Scene Executions in England, 1720–1830', in Richard Ward (ed.), *A Global History of Execution and the Criminal Corpse* (Basingstoke, Palgrave Macmillan, 2015), p. 73. As Poole notes, there is a debate about the reasons for moving executions from

the open space of Tyburn to Newgate. For this debate, see Simon Devereaux, 'Recasting the Theatre of Execution: The Abolition of the Tyburn Ritual', *Past and Present*, Vol. 202 (2009); Greg T. Smith, 'Civilized People Don't Want to See That Kind of Thing: The Decline of Public Punishment in London, 1760–1840', in Carolyn Strange (ed.), *Qualities of Mercy: Justice, Punishment and Discretion* (Vancouver, 1996); Stephen Wilf, 'Imagining Justice: Aesthetics and Public Executions in Late Eighteenth-Century England', *Yale Journal of the Humanities*, Vol. 5, No. 1 (1993), pp. 51–78.

3. Alan Newman, *Criminal Executions in England with Remarks on the Penal Code, Prison Discipline and Abuses, and Other Subjects Connected with the Punishment and Prevention of Crime* (Paternoster Row, London, B. Steill, 1830), p. 219.

4. *The Spiritual Times*, 24 July 1829, quoted in Newman, *Criminal Executions in England*, pp. 217–18.

5. Randall McGowen, 'Civilizing Punishment: The End of the Public Execution in England', *Journal of British Studies*, Vol. 33, No. 3 (July 1994), p. 268.

6. Stuart Banner, *The Death Penalty: An American History* (Cambridge, MA, Harvard University Press, 2003), p. 39.

7. George J. Holyoake, *Public Lessons of the Hangman* (London, 1864), p. 6.

8. Randall McGowen, 'A Powerful Sympathy: Terror, the Prison, and Humanitarian Reform in Early Nineteenth-Century England', *Journal of British Studies*, Vol. 25, No. 3 (July 1989), pp. 312–34.

9. Holyoake, *Public Lessons of the Hangman*, p. 4.

10. Dwight Conquergood, 'Lethal Theatre: Performance, Punishment, and the Death Penalty', *Theatre Journal*, Vol. 54, No. 3 (October, 2002), p. 349.

11. Thomas W. Laqueur, 'Crowds, Carnival, and the State in English Executions, 1604–1868', in A. L. Beier et al. (eds.), *The First Modern Society* (Cambridge, Cambridge University Press, 1989), p. 332.

12. Evidence of George Sinclair quoted by McGowen, 'A Powerful Sympathy', pp. 319–20.

13. McGowen, 'Civilizing Punishment', p. 271.

14. Ibid., p. 282.

15. McGowen, 'A Powerful Sympathy', p. 319.

16. Elizabeth T. Hurren, *Dissecting the Criminal Corpse: Staging Post-Execution Punishment in Early Modern England* (Basingstoke, Palgrave Macmillan, 2016); Peter King, *Punishing the Criminal Corpse, 1770–1840: Aggravated Forms of the Death Penalty in England* (Basingstoke, Palgrave Macmillan, 2017).

17. Leigh Yetter (ed.), *Public Execution in England, 1573–1868. Volume 5: Public Execution in England, 1777–1868* (London, Pickering & Chatto, 2010), p. 241.

18. Ibid., p. 182.

19. *Public Advertiser*, 18 August 1785.

20. Yetter (ed.), *Public Execution in England*, p. 176.

21. On the execution of John Austin on November 7, 1783 for highway robbery: he was the last person hanged at Tyburn before the execution ritual moved to a new site outside Newgate Gaol. Devereaux, 'Recasting the Theatre of Execution', p. 129.

22. Ibid., pp. 153–54.

23. Andrea McKenzie, *Tyburn's Martyrs: Execution in England, 1675–1775* (London, Hambledon Continuum, 2007), pp. 114–15.

24. V. A. C. Gatrell, *The Hanging Tree: Execution and the English People, 1770–1868* (Oxford, Oxford University Press, 1994), p. 282.

25. Laqueur, 'Crowds, Carnival, and the State', p. 352.
26. Banner, *The Death Penalty*, pp. 46–47.
27. Wilf, 'Imagining Justice', p. 70.
28. The last executions in England took place on the same day. Peter Anthony Allen was hanged at Walton Prison, Liverpool and Gwynne Owen Evans at Strangeways, Manchester. They were co-convicted for the murder of John Alan West. The Murder (Abolition of Death Penalty) Act of 1969 renewed the five-year temporary suspension ordered in 1965 and the Crime and Disorder Act (1998) and Human Rights Act (1998) finally removed hanging as a punishment in England and Wales.
29. At the time of writing, this includes India, Japan, Pakistan, and Singapore.
30. This was the new stipulation of the Murder Act passed in 1752 to add 'some further terror and peculiar mark of infamy to the punishment of death', Tim Hitchcock and Robert Shoemaker, *London Lives: Poverty, Crime and the Making of a Modern City, 1690–1800* (Cambridge, Cambridge University Press, 2015), p. 221.
31. Hurren, *Dissecting the Criminal Corpse*, pp. 47–62.
32. Peter King, *Crime, Justice and Discretion in England, 1740–1820* (Oxford, Oxford University Press, 2000).
33. Deirdre Palk (ed.), *Prisoners' Letters to the Bank of England, 1781–1827* (London Record Society, 2007).
34. Simon Devereaux, 'England's "Bloody Code" in Crisis and Transition: Executions at the Old Bailey, 1760–1837', *Journal of the Canadian Historical Association*, Vol. 24, No. 2 (2013), p. 82.
35. Anne-Marie Kilday and David Nash (eds.), *Law, Crime & Deviance Since 1700: Micro-Studies in the History of Crime* (London, Bloomsbury, 2017), p. 9.
36. Ibid., p. 9.
37. Martin Wiener, 'Murder and the British Historian', Presidential Address of the North American Conference on British Studies, 2003, *Albion: A Quarterly Journal Concerned with British Studies*, Vol. 36, No. 1 (Spring 2004), p. 2.
38. Ginzburg, 'Microhistory', p. 204.
39. M. Dorothy George, *London Life in the Eighteenth Century* (Harmondsworth, Penguin, 1925, 1966), p. 15.
40. Jerry White, *London in the Eighteenth Century: A Great and Monstrous Thing* (London, The Bodley Head, 2012), pp. 68–81.
41. Peter King and Richard Ward, 'Rethinking the Bloody Code in Eighteenth-Century Britain: Capital Punishment at the Centre and on the Periphery', *Past and Present*, Vol. 228 (2015).
42. Jon Walliss, *The Bloody Code in England and Wales, 1760–1830* (Basingstoke, Palgrave Macmillan, 2018), p. 4.
43. Devereaux, 'England's "Bloody Code" in Crisis and Transition'.
44. Ibid., p. 76.
45. Peter King, 'Newspaper Reporting, Prosecution Practice and Perceptions of Urban Crime: The Colchester Crime Wave of 1765', *Continuity and Change*, Vol. 2, No. 3 (1987), pp. 423–54.
46. Drew D. Gray and Peter King, 'The Killing of Constable Linnell: The Impact of Xenophobia and of Elite Connections on Eighteenth-Century Justice', *Family & Community History*, Vol. 16, No. 1 (2013).
47. Peter King, 'Newspaper Reporting and Attitudes to Crime and Justice in Late-Eighteenth and Early-Nineteenth-Century London', *Continuity and Change*, Vol. 22, No. 1 (2007), pp. 73–112.

48. J. Steven Watson, *The Reign of George III, 1760–1815* (Oxford, Clarendon Press, 1960), p. 109.
49. Stephen Brumwell and W. A. Speck, *Cassell's Companion to Eighteenth Century Britain* (London, Orion, 2001), p. 170.
50. Watson, *The Reign of George III*, p. 304.
51. Katherine Binhammer, 'The Sex Panic of the 1790s', *Journal of the History of Sexuality*, Vol. 6, No. 3 (1996), pp. 409–34.
52. King, *Crime, Justice, and Discretion*; Deirdre Palk, *Gender, Crime and Judicial Discretion, 1780–1830* (Woodbridge, Boydell & Brewer, 2006); Wallis, *The Bloody Code*.
53. E. P. Thompson, *Whigs and Hunters: The Origin of the Black Act* (Harmondsworth, Penguin, 1975, 1990), p. 23.
54. John H. Langbein, 'Albion's Fatal Flaws', *Past and Present*, Vol. 98 (February 1983).
55. Peter Linebaugh, *The London Hanged: Crime and Civil Society in the Eighteenth Century* (Harmondsworth, Penguin, 1991).
56. King, *Crime, Justice, and Discretion*, p. 170.
57. Ibid., p. 196.
58. John Beattie, *Crime and the Courts in England, 1660–1800* (Princeton, NJ, Princeton University Press, 1986), p. 239.
59. Palk, *Gender, Crime and Judicial Discretion*.
60. King, *Crime, Justice, and Discretion*, pp. 200–1; Palk, *Gender, Crime and Judicial Discretion*, pp. 22–23.
61. Wilf, 'Imagining Justice'.
62. Gatrell, *The Hanging Tree*; McGowen, 'A Powerful Sympathy'; Randall McGowen, 'The Body and Punishment in Eighteenth-Century England', *Journal of Modern History*, Vol. 59 (1987); McGowen, 'Civilizing Punishment', pp. 257–82; Harry Potter, *Hanging in Judgment: Religion and the Death Penalty in England from the Bloody Code to Abolition* (Norwich, SCM Press, 1993).
63. Drew D. Gray, *Crime, Policing and Punishment in England, 1660–1914* (London, Bloomsbury, 2016), pp. 290–92.
64. A. Roger Ekirch, *Bound for America: The Transportation of British Convicts to the Colonies, 1718–1775* (Oxford, Clarendon Press, 1987); Gwenda Morgan and Peter Rushton, *Eighteenth-Century Transportation: The Formation of the Criminal* Atlantic (Basingstoke, Palgrave Macmillan, 2004); Anthony Vaver, *Bound with an Iron Chain: The Untold Story of How the British Transported 50,000 Convicts to Colonial America* (Westborough, MA, Pickpocket Publishing, 2011).
65. Devereaux, 'England's "Bloody Code" in Crisis and Transition'.
66. Francis Dodsworth, *Masculinity as Governance: Police, Public Service and the Embodiment of Authority, c. 1700–1850* (Basingstoke, Palgrave Macmillan, 2007); Elaine Reynolds, *Before the Bobbies: The Night Watch and Police Reform in Metropolitan London, 1720–1830* (Redwood City, Stanford University Press, 1998).
67. Drew D. Gray, *Crime, Prosecution and Social Relations: The Summary Courts of the City If London in the Late Eighteenth Century* (Basingstoke, Palgrave Macmillan, 2009).
68. John Beattie, *The First English Detectives: The Bow Street Runners and the Policing of London, 1750–1840* (Oxford, Oxford University Press, 2014), pp. 18–22.
69. Ruth Paley, 'Thief-Takers in London in the Age of the McDaniel Gang, c.1745–1754', in D. Hay and F. Synder (eds.), *Policing and Prosecution in Britain, 1750–1850* (Oxford, Oxford University Press, 1989).

70. Gerald Howson, *Thief-Taker General: The Rise and Fall of Jonathan Wild* (London, Hutchinson, 1970).
71. Heather Shore, *London's Criminal Underworlds, c.1720–c.1930: A Social and Cultural History* (Basingstoke, Palgrave Macmillan, 2015), p. 25.
72. Beattie, *The First English Detectives*.
73. David J. Cox, *A Certain Share of Low Cunning: A History of the Bow Street Runners, 1792–1839* (London, Routledge, 2012).
74. Joan R. Kent, *The English Village Constable 1580–1642: A Social and Administrative Study* (Oxford, Oxford University Press, 1986).
75. Gray, *Crime, Prosecution and Social Relations*.
76. Douglas Hay, 'Property, Authority and the Criminal Law', in D. Hay (ed.), *Albion's Fatal Tree: Crime and Society in Eighteenth-Century England* (Harmondsworth, Penguin, 1975).
77. Palk, *Gender, Crime and Judicial Discretion*, p. 17.
78. Robert B. Shoemaker, 'The Old Bailey Proceedings and the Representation of Crime and Criminal Justice in Eighteenth-Century London', *Journal of British Studies*, Vol. 47, No. 3 (2008), p. 567.
79. Mary Clayton, 'The Life and Crimes of Charlotte Walker, Prostitute and Pickpocket', *The London Journal*, Vol. 33, No. 1 (2008), pp. 3–19.
80. Simon Devereaux, 'The City and the Sessions Paper: "Public Justice" in London, 1770–1800', *Journal of British Studies*, Vol. 35, No. 4 (October 1996), p. 491.
81. John H. Langbein, *The Origins of the Adversary Criminal Trial* (Oxford, Oxford University Press, 2003).
82. Hay, 'Property, Authority and the Criminal Law'.
83. Michel Foucault, *Discipline and Punish: The Birth of the Prison* (Harmondsworth, Penguin Books, 1977).
84. Hay, 'Property, Authority and the Criminal Law'.
85. Langbein, 'Albion's Fatal Flaws'.
86. Hay, 'Property, Authority and the Criminal Law', p. 48.
87. Gatrell, *The Hanging Tree*, p. 201.
88. Devereaux, 'England's "Bloody Code" in Crisis and Transition', p. 80.
89. Tim Hitchcock and Robert Shoemaker, *Tales from the Hanging Court* (London, Hodder Arnold, 2006), p. 200.
90. Ibid.
91. Hay, 'Property, Authority and the Criminal Law'.
92. Gatrell, *The Hanging Tree*, pp. 206–7.
93. Ibid., p. 42.
94. For a description of life inside eighteenth-century Newgate, see Michael Ignatieff, *A Just Measure of Pain: The Penitentiary in the Industrial Revolution, 1750–1850* (Basingstoke, Macmillan Press, 1978), pp. 39–42.
95. Hitchcock and Shoemaker, *London Lives*, p. 221.
96. John M. Beattie, *Policing and Punishment in London, 1660–1750: Urban Crime and the Limits of Terror* (Oxford, Oxford University Press, 2001), p. 349.
97. The OBSP was bring used to 'facilitate decision-making in council' according to Devereaux, and this may explain why the length of trial reports increased in the late 1770s. Devereaux, 'The City and the Sessions Paper', p. 467.
98. Beattie, *Policing and Punishment in London*, pp. 451–52.
99. Devereaux, 'The City and the Sessions Paper', p. 475.
100. Beattie, *Policing and Punishment in London*, p. 456.
101. Devereaux, 'The City and the Sessions Paper', pp. 479–80.
102. This time to the Secretary of State rather than the council. Beattie, *Policing and Punishment in London*, p. 449.

103. Devereaux, 'Recasting the Theatre of Execution'.
104. Simon Devereaux, 'The Bloodiest Code: Counting Executions and Pardons at the Old Bailey, 1730–1837', *Law, Crime and History*, No. 1 (2016), p. 24.
105. Peter King, 'Decision-Makers and Decision-Making in the English Criminal Law, 1750–1800', *Historical Journal*, Vol. 27, No. 1 (1984), pp. 25–58.
106. Gatrell, *The Hanging Tree*; Andrea McKenzie's 100 year study of execution has nothing to say about the pardoning process for example. McKenzie, *Tyburn's Martyrs*.
107. Gray, *Crime, Prosecution and Social Relations*; Drew D. Gray, 'Making Law in Mid-Eighteenth-Century England: Legal Statutes and Their Application in the Justicing Notebook of Phillip Ward of Stoke Doyle', *The Journal of Legal History*, Vol. 34, No. 2 (2013); David Lemmings, *Law and Government in England During the Long Eighteenth Century: From Consent to Command* (Basingstoke, Palgrave Macmillan, 2011).
108. Wiener, 'Murder and the British Historian', p. 2.
109. Lawrence Stone, 'Interpersonal Violence in English Society, 1300–1980', *Past and Present*, Vol. 101 (1983); Pieter Spierenburg, *A History of Murder: Personal Violence in Europe from the Middles Ages to the Present* (Cambridge, Cambridge University Press, 2008).
110. Spierenburg, *A History of Murder*, p. 4. For the wider debate see: John E. Archer, 'Mysterious and Suspicious Deaths: Missing Homicides in North-West England (185–1900)', *Crime, History & Societies*, Vol. 12, No. 1 (2008), pp. 45–63; M. Beth Emmerichs, 'Getting Away with Murder: Homicide and the Coroners in Nineteenth-Century London', *Social Science History*, Vol. 25 (2001); Peter King, 'The Impact of Urbanization on Murder Rates and on the Geography of Homicide in England and Wales, 1780–1850', *The Historical Journal*, Vol. 53, No. 3 (2010); J. A. Sharpe, 'Debate: The History of Violence in England; Some Observations', *Past and Present*, Vol. 108 (1985); Howard Taylor, 'Rationing Crime: The Political Economy of Criminal Statistics Since the 1850s', *Economic History Review*, Vol. 51 (1998).
111. See Table 3.4. 'Homicide Indictments in Urban and Rural Parishes of Surrey and in Sussex, 1660–1800', Beattie, *Crime and the Courts*, p. 108.
112. Ibid.
113. J. S. Cockburn, 'Patterns of Violence in English Society: Homicide in Kent 1560–1985', *Past and Present*, Vol. 103 (1991).
114. www.capitalpunishmentuk.org/northant.html [accessed 5 July 2019].
115. For the peculiar punishment of gibbeting, see Zoe Dyndor, 'The Gibbet in the Landscape: Locating the Criminal Corpse in Mid-Eighteenth-Century England', in Ward (ed.), *A Global History of Execution*, pp. 102–25.
116. King and Ward, 'Rethinking the Bloody Code'.
117. Devereaux, 'England's "Bloody Code" in Crisis and Transition', p. 86.
118. This was in part because the home secretary, Lord Shelburne, had decided in 1782 that all pardons would be refused to anyone convicted of robbery or burglary if those crimes were considered to have been 'attended with acts of great cruelty'. Hitchcock and Shoemaker, *London Lives*, p. 363.
119. Shoemaker, 'The Old Bailey Proceedings and the Representation of Crime'; Devereaux, 'The City and the Sessions Paper'.
120. Old Bailey Proceedings Online (www.oldbaileyonline.org, version 8.0, 26 February 2019), January 1777, trial of BENNET STORER (t17770115-37).
121. Old Bailey Proceedings Online (www.oldbaileyonline.org, version 8.0, 26 February 2019), April 1782, trial of THOMAS APOSTLE (t17820410-51).

122. Old Bailey Proceedings Online (www.oldbaileyonline.org, version 8.0, 26 February 2019), December 1789, trial of WILLIAM CLIPSON (t17891209-114).

123. Simon Devereaux, 'The Abolition of the Burning of Women in England Reconsidered', *Crime, History & Societies*, Vol. 9, No. 2 (2005), pp. 73–98.

124. Beattie, *Crime and the Courts*, p. 100.

125. Old Bailey Proceedings Online (www.oldbaileyonline.org, version 8.0, 26 February 2019), September 1773, trial of ELIZABETH HERRING (t17730908-6).

126. Old Bailey Proceedings Online (www.oldbaileyonline.org, version 8.0, 26 February 2019), July 1787, trial of HENRIETTA RADBOURNE, otherwise GIBBONS (t17870711-1).

127. Old Bailey Proceedings Online (www.oldbaileyonline.org, version 8.0, 26 February 2019), September 1779, trial of MARY ADEY (t17790915-74).

128. Old Bailey Proceedings Online (www.oldbaileyonline.org, version 8.0, 26 February 2019), April 1776, trial of THOMAS DEMPSEY THOMAS WELCH JAMES DELANEY PHILIP CORBET DENNIS SHERRY ANDREW NIHIL (t17760417-59).

129. Old Bailey Proceedings Online (www.oldbaileyonline.org, version 8.0, 26 February 2019), June 1778, trial of RICHARD LINDALL Elizabeth Pigott (t17780603-69).

130. Old Bailey Proceedings Online (www.oldbaileyonline.org, version 8.0, 26 February 2019), January 1792, trial of SAMUEL TAYLOR JANE TAYLOR, otherwise MORGAN (t17920113-53).

131. Old Bailey Proceedings Online (www.oldbaileyonline.org, version 8.0, 11 March 2019), September 1774, trial of OLIVER DAVIS (t17740907-64); Old Bailey Proceedings Online (www.oldbaileyonline.org, version 8.0, 11 March 2019), May 1777, trial of EDWARD BRITAIN (t17770514-28).

132. Branding had been abolished as a separate punishment in 1779 but clearly the Old Bailey retained it as an alternative to more extreme penalties. Hitchcock and Shoemaker, *London Lives*, p. 362; Beattie, *Crime and the Courts*, pp. 88–89.

133. Old Bailey Proceedings Online (www.oldbaileyonline.org, version 8.0, 26 February 2019), July 1770, trial of PETER CONOWAY MICHAEL RICHARDSON (t17700711-35).

134. Old Bailey Proceedings Online (www.oldbaileyonline.org, version 8.0, 11 March 2019), January 1789, trial of CORNELIUS CARTY (t17890114-6).

135. Andrew Knapp, *The New Newgate Calendar . . . To Which Is Added a Correct Account of the Various Modes of Punishment of Criminals in Different Parts of the World*, Vol. 3 (London, 1826).

136. Old Bailey Proceedings Online (www.oldbaileyonline.org, version 8.0, 11 March 2019), January 1783, trial of DANIEL MACGINNISS, otherwise MACGENISE (t17830117-1).

137. www.digitalpanopticon.org/life?id=obpt17841210-1-defend8.

138. Old Bailey Proceedings Online (www.oldbaileyonline.org, version 8.0, 11 March 2019), December 1784, trial of KENITH MACKENZIE (t17841210-1).

139. Old Bailey Proceedings Online (www.oldbaileyonline.org, version 8.0, 11 March 2019), September 1789, trial of WILLIAM POWER (t17890909-109).

140. Old Bailey Proceedings Online (www.oldbaileyonline.org, version 8.0, 11 March 2019), April 1790, trial of JACINTHO PHARARO ANTHONI MURRINI STEPHEN APOLOGIE (t17900416-1).

141. Old Bailey Proceedings Online (www.oldbaileyonline.org, version 8.0, 11 March 2019), January 1799, trial of JAMES EYRES (t17990109-5).

142. Great Britain. Home Office, & State Library of Queensland (1948). James Eyres, One of 301 Convicts Transported on the Royal Admiral, March 1800, Criminal: Convict transportation registers [HO 11].

143. See Table 2.14. Fiona Brookman, *Understanding Homicide* (London, Sage, 2005), p. 50.

144. Old Bailey Proceedings Online (www.oldbaileyonline.org, version 8.0, 26 February 2019).

145. Old Bailey Proceedings Online (www.oldbaileyonline.org, version 8.0, 11 March 2019), February 1798, trial of JAMES WARREN (t17980214-63).

146. Devereaux, 'The Abolition of the Burning of Women'; see also Ruth Campbell, 'Sentence of Death by Burning for Women', *Journal of Legal History*, Vol. 5 (1984), pp. 45–59.

147. Spierenburg, *A History of Murder*, p. 136.

148. Old Bailey Proceedings Online (www.oldbaileyonline.org, version 8.0, 11 March 2019), December 1786, trial of CHARLES GRIFFITHS (t17861213-104).

149. Old Bailey Proceedings Online (www.oldbaileyonline.org, version 8.0, 12 March 2019), May 1797, trial of MARTIN CLINCH JAMES MACKLY (t17970531-1).

150. The Digital Panopticon Martin Clinch b. 1775, Life Archive ID obpt17970531-1-defend44 (www.digitalpanopticon.org/life?id=obpt17970531-1-defend44). Version 1.1, consulted 12th March 2019.

151. Old Bailey Proceedings Online (www.oldbaileyonline.org, version 8.0, 12 March 2019), October 1782, trial of FRANCIS GRAY (t17821016-11).

152. Robert B. Shoemaker, *The London Mob: Violence and Disorder in Eighteenth-Century England* (London, Hambledon Continuum, 2004), p. 261.

153. Ibid.; Robert B. Shoemaker, 'The Taming of the Duel: Masculinity, Honour and Ritual Violence in London, 1660–1800', *Historical Journal*, Vol. 45, No. 3 (2002), pp. 525–45.

154. Hitchcock and Shoemaker, *London Lives*, p. 362.

155. Old Bailey Proceedings Online (www.oldbaileyonline.org, version 8.0, 19 March 2019), June 1782, trial of BENNET ALLEN ROBERT MORRIS (t17820605-1).

156. Ibid.

157. John Gideon Millingen, *The History of Duelling: Including, Narratives of the Most Remarkable Personal Encounters That Have Taken Place from the Earliest Period to the Present Time*, Vol. 2 (London, 1841), p. 119.

158. Old Bailey Proceedings Online (www.oldbaileyonline.org, version 8.0, 19 March 2019), September 1784, trial of COSMO GORDON (t17840917-1).

159. Antony Simpson, 'Dandelions on the Field of Honour: Dueling, the Middle Classes, and the Law in Nineteenth-Century England', *Criminal Justice History*, Vol. 9 (1998), p. 106; see also, Donna Andrew, 'The Code of Honour and Its Critics: The Opposition to Duelling in England, 1700–1850', *Social History*, Vol. 5 (1980), pp. 409–34.

160. See Clive Emsley, *Hard Men: The English and Violence Since 1750* (London, Hambledon Continuum, 2005); John Carter Wood, *Violence and Crime in Nineteenth-Century England: The Shadow of Our Refinement* (London, Routledge, 2004); Martin Wiener, *Men of Blood: Violence, Manliness, and Criminal Justice in Victorian England* (Cambridge, Cambridge University Press, 2004).

161. Old Bailey Proceedings Online (www.oldbaileyonline.org, version 8.0, 19 March 2019), May 1777, trial of EDWARD BRITAIN (t17770514-28).

162. Cockburn, 'Patterns of Violence in English Society'.

163. Old Bailey Proceedings Online (www.oldbaileyonline.org, version 8.0, 19 March 2019), September 1777, trial of JOHN KNUTT, otherwise COUNT (t17770910-75).

164. Old Bailey Proceedings Online (www.oldbaileyonline.org, version 8.0, 19 March 2019), October 1770, trial of JAMES TOMPION (t17701024-52).

165. Gray, *Crime, Prosecution and Social Relations*, pp. 136–47.

166. Old Bailey Proceedings Online (www.oldbaileyonline.org, version 8.0, 19 March 2019), October 1786, trial of THOMAS PLATA, otherwise PLATO FRANCIS PARKER (t17861025-37).

167. Gray, *Crime, Prosecution and Social Relations*, p. 97; Peter King, *Crime and Law in England, 1750–1840: Remaking Justice from the Margins* (Cambridge, Cambridge University Press), p. 251.

168. Bernard Mandeville, *Fable of the Bees: Or, Private Vices, Public Benefits* (London, 1714), 'Remark (G)', p. 86.

169. Dana Rabin, 'Drunkenness and Responsibility for Crime in the Eighteenth Century', 2005, *Journal of British Studies*, Vol. 44, No. 3 (July 2005), pp. 471–72.

170. Sir James Fitzjames Stephen, *A History of the Criminal Law of England*, Vol. II (London, Macmillan & Co., 1883), p. 165.

171. Old Bailey Proceedings Online (www.oldbaileyonline.org, version 8.0, 19 March 2019), February 1771, trial of JOSEPH WEST STEPHEN PARIS SAMUEL RANDALL (t17710220-27).

172. *Middlesex Journal or Chronicle of Liberty* (London, England), 21–23 February 1771.

173. Old Bailey Proceedings Online (www.oldbaileyonline.org, version 8.0, 19 March 2019), April 1776, trial of THOMAS DEMPSEY THOMAS WELCH JAMES DELANEY PHILIP CORBET DENNIS SHERRY ANDREW NIHIL (t17760417-59).

174. Old Bailey Proceedings Online (www.oldbaileyonline.org, version 8.0, 19 March 2019), March 1792, trial of FRANCIS HUBBARD alias NOBLE JAMES JONES alias PASTE alias DEACON JAMES ARMSTRONG alias OGDEN JOHN BAILEY alias TAYLOR alias DISDALL JAMES SAVAGE PETER DOUGLAS JAMES FRERE JOHN CARRYL (t17920329-26).

175. The Digital Panopticon Francis Hubbard b. 1772, Life Archive ID obpt17920329-26-defend243 (www.digitalpanopticon.org/life?id=obpt 17920329-26-defend243). Version 1.1, consulted 19 March 2019.

176. Peter King, 'Punishing Assault: The Transformation of Attitudes in the English Courts', *Journal of Interdisciplinary History*, Vol. 27, No. 1 (Summer 1996), pp. 43–74.

177. Cockburn, 'Patterns of Violence in English Society'.

178. Shoemaker, 'The Taming of the Duel'.

179. Old Bailey Proceedings Online (www.oldbaileyonline.org, version 8.0, 26 March 2019), December 1770, trial of GEORGE NEWTON (t17701205-43).

180. Old Bailey Proceedings Online (www.oldbaileyonline.org, version 8.0, 26 March 2019), September 1774, trial of JOHN COTTON (t17740907-84).

181. Old Bailey Proceedings Online (www.oldbaileyonline.org, version 8.0, 26 March 2019), July 1786, trial of FRANCIS JENKINS, otherwise GIPPEY (t17860719-86).

182. John E. Archer, ' "Men Behaving Badly"? Masculinity and the Uses of Violence, 1850–1900', in Shani D'Cruze (ed.), *Everyday Violence in Britain, 1850–1950* (Harlow, Longman, 2000); Emsley, *Hard Men*; Wiener, *Men of Blood*.

183. Old Bailey Proceedings Online (www.oldbaileyonline.org, version 8.0, 26 March 2019), February 1786, trial of JOSEPH RICKARDS (t17860222-1);

The Digital Panopticon Joseph Rickards b. 1768, Life Archive ID obpt17860222-1-defend49 (www.digitalpanopticon.org/life?id=obpt17860222-1-defend49). Version 1.1, consulted 26th March 2019.

184. Old Bailey Proceedings Online (www.oldbaileyonline.org, version 8.0, 26 March 2019), October 1770, trial of JOHN BARNEY (t17701024-55).

185. Gray, *Crime, Prosecution and Social Relations*.

186. Old Bailey Proceedings Online (www.oldbaileyonline.org, version 8.0, 26 March 2019), February 1776, trial of STEPHEN SELF (t17760221-38).

187. Beattie, *Crime and the Courts*, p. 79.

188. William Blackstone, *Commentaries on the Laws of England*, Vol. 4 (Oxford, 1765), p. 195.

189. The others were:

   (a) Knowledge that the act which causes death will probably cause the death of, or grievous bodily harm to any person, whether such person is the person actually killed or not, although such knowledge is accompanied by indifference whether death or grievous bodily harm is caused or not, or by a wish that it may not be caused.

   (b) An intent to commit any felony whatever.

   (c) An intent to oppose by force any officer of justice on his way to, in, or returning from the execution of the duty of arresting, keeping in custody, or imprisoning any person whom he is lawfully entitled to arrest etc. Stephen, *A History of the English Criminal Law*, pp. 119–20.

190. Since manslaughter was subject to benefit of clergy, a system which had begun as a method for members of the clergy to avoid a death sentence and had evolved to allow almost anyone to escape the noose if they could read a set religious text – Psalm 51, to so-called 'neck verse'. By the early 1700s almost anyone who successfully applied for clergy was transported to the colonies in America. Beattie, *Crime and the Courts*, p. 81.

191. Richard Burn, *Justice of the Peace and Parish Officer*, Vol. 2 (London, 1785), p. 508.

2 'Mercy Without Justice'? Press Criticism of the Pardoning Process in Late Eighteenth-Century London
The Kennedy Case of 1770

Introduction

In April 1770, a newspaper article explicitly criticized the incumbent Lord Chief Justice, William Murray, the 1st Earl of Mansfield, and King George III for their misuse of judicial discretion. The letter writer ended by stating:

> His Majesty is bound by his oath 'to execute JUSTICE WITH MERCY'. Mercy without justice would not only be contrary to oath, but a most alarming cruelty for all his innocent subjects.[1]

This letter was part of a campaign of attack orchestrated against Mansfield by those radicals that resented his skilled use of the libel laws against them. However, it reveals that the supposedly private process of obtaining pardons for condemned felons was actually far from opaque.

This was because the brutal murder of a watchman on Westminster Bridge on Christmas Eve 1769 set in motion a chain of events that revealed the supposedly hidden machinations of the pardoning process. In turn, this highlighted an ongoing and very public exchange of views between the supporters of the king and his government and their opponents. At the heart of this debate was the role of judicial discretion and the extent to which those in high office manipulated it. Those convicted of the murder were soon the beneficiaries of the elite connections that they were able to bring into play, but this victory was only temporary. Within weeks of being conditionally pardoned they were back in court facing a private prosecution from their victim's widow. Once again, however, their well-placed supporters managed to extricate them from a fatal outcome and they were allowed to escape to relative freedom in America. Throughout this process, the London press kept up a steady commentary on the case and its outcomes—a commentary that reflected the political allegiances of the newspapers concerned.

Douglas Hay argued that the Hanoverian elite were able to manipulate the criminal law and control the mechanism of appeal.[2] He stated that petitions for pardon 'were most effective from great men' . . . pleas were 'passed up through increasingly higher levels of the social scale, between men bound together by the links of patronage and obligation'.[3] These links were revealed as this case developed. The greatest 'great men' of the day were involved but their motivations for doing so had little to do with the criteria that Peter King identified in his study of judicial decision-making.[4] Here, while previous 'good character' might reasonably be put forward as an excuse not to hang two 'respectable' young men, the violence associated with their actions and the drunken excess that accompanied it militated against them. Moreover, the target they chose, a part-time watchman employed to protect a crossing over the Thames, was a clear and direct attack on authority. Hay argued that the criminal law supported the hegemony of the ruling elite and that the pardoning process was crucial to this. Decisions turned on seemingly arbitrary judgements about 'character' and so it was vital for defendants in court to be able to show they had the support of 'respectable' character witnesses. Moreover, their lives depended on their ability to have a person of note speak up for them and help their petition for a pardon. By contrast, King argued that in the eighteenth century discretion was not based on elite connections but instead on more measurable factors such as age, gender, previous conviction, 'good' character, and the nature of the offence. Instead of privilege and power, circumstance and context were the driving factors in determining who hanged in the 1700s.[5] The case of Matthew and Patrick Kennedy suggests that, while both of these eminent historians may be correct to some degree, it is important not to overlook the reality that special circumstances could, and did, impact the way the justice operated. As a result both of their theses require some qualification. In response to criticism of his work, Hay robustly defended his position. He acknowledged that judges may have 'felt obliged to offer a selection of acceptable excuses for a pardon – youth, good character, an offence not aggravated by violence', ('factors' that both King and Beattie claimed were crucial). However, these were merely 'excuses', allowing the impression that discretion was based not on the influence of the 'respectable' patronage' but on rational and persuasive mitigating factors.[6] This study supports Hay's defence by offering an examination of how the pardoning process ignored the culpability of those involved in favour of extending mercy to individuals that were closely connected to 'persons of quality'.

Hay's work concentrated on the appeal process outside of the capital, and, as I acknowledged in Chapter 1, this was technically different from the one that operated within. Appeals outside of London were lodged in the first instance with the presiding judge at assizes, who sent his report to the Home Office for final consideration. The monarch was supposedly involved in signing off any final pardon but in reality decisions were made at Westminster and the judges' reports were crucial. In London, requests for pardon followed the Recorder's report on those left to hang by the Old Bailey judges. This report, as has been outlined in the previous chapter, was heard by the king and his ministers in council, whose decisions were then relayed to the condemned and the prison authorities by the Recorder of the City of London.[7] All of this, along with any subsequent petitions for mercy, was supposed to take place in private and behind closed doors. Of course Hay and King were both concerned with the operation of the law as it pertained to property crime, not violence and homicide. It is possible that decision-making was different when it came to questions around conditional pardons for murder as opposed to, say highway robbery or horse stealing, but to what extent? One of the questions this volume needs to consider then is just how atypical its chosen case studies are, and, taking this into account, what might we usefully glean from the study of them?

In this case study, the links between the two young men involved, their family, and the men (and women) of influence they were able to marshal the support of are slowly revealed as this case develops in the aftermath of an Old Bailey trial and the sentencing of the two young men to death. The 'great men' of the day were involved but their motivations for doing so had little to do with the criteria that King identified in his study of judicial decision-making.[8] Here, while previous 'good character' might reasonably be put forward as an excuse not to hang two 'respectable' young men, the violence associated with their actions and the drunken excess that accompanied it would surely have militated against them being deemed 'worthy subjects' of the king's mercy. Moreover, the target they chose, a watchman employed to protect a major crossing point over the Thames, represented a clear and direct attack on authority. In 1788, in rural Northamptonshire, the killing of a parish constable resulted in the execution of another young man with an impeccable character despite his father's excellent elite connections, as Chapter 4 will demonstrate.[9] Hay's suggestion that pardons were 'most effective' when the petitioners were well connected needs some amendment, therefore. This chapter will argue that such connections have to be the *right* connections, made at the *right* time and within the *right* context if they were to withstand competing pressures to 'let justice take its course'. This case had a very public face; every twist and turn of it was reported in the pages of the London press and the process and those involved in it were subject to close scrutiny. This drew considerable criticism and became interwoven with debates about politics and the role of government and the judiciary. Thus, this also allows some engagement with David Lemmings' suggestion that there was a 'growth of discursive public comment or criticism [of] the administration of justice' in the period.[10] That criticism was loud in this case, even if – arguably at least – it ultimately failed to affect those in power or the outcome of events.

This case study will therefore bring the process of pardoning into much deeper scrutiny than has so far been the case. This was a system that was supposed to be private and to happen behind closed doors so the machinations of elite discretion were hidden from view and made all the more 'mystical' and effective as a result.[11] However, in this example there was an attempt to subvert the discretionary power of the elite by the use of an ancient right to private redress, which exposed the appeal process to public debate. As a result, every twist and turn was reported in the pages of the London press and those involved were subjected to criticism and scrutiny. This became interwoven with debates about politics, the role of government, and the judiciary as it played out in newspapers.

This case also allows us to investigate the rarely used private Appeal of Death (or Murder). This archaic legal device allowed the victim's wife and family to pursue 'justice' against their loved one's killers in spite of the concentrated attempts of some significant members of the ruling elite to influence the outcome. In effect, they found a legal mechanism that circumvented the power of the elite to control proceedings. Ultimately, they failed in their endeavours and two young men escaped the awful consequences of their violence, but this was only achieved by paying off the bereaved with a considerable sum of money. During the process there was even an attempt to quash this action in parliament as a bill was introduced to remove this ancient right. This legal device has had little examination by historians despite the fact that it seemingly undermined the monarch's ability to intervene to pardon those subjects he (or his government) believed to be worthy of saving from the gallows.[12] At least one contemporary correspondent challenged the right of the king to interfere at all in the judgements of the jury courts and this also offers us an interesting insight into the contemporary views of the law and the criminal justice system. In addition, this case offers a rare (if fleeting) opportunity to look at functions of the King's Bench court. The private appeal against the defendants was brought just as they were about to start their voyage to America having, they must have believed, secured their escape from the gallows in return for accepting exile. It brought this journey to an abrupt halt and forced the convicted killers to present themselves before the judges at King's Bench. In this case that meant that it was heard before the Lord Chief Justice of the day, Lord Mansfield. Mansfield was attended by William Blackstone, the noted jurist, who wrote up the case for posterity. Mansfield's judgements in a number of libel cases were being widely discussed as a result of an ongoing campaign by the anonymous legal writer 'Junius' who alluded to Mansfield's handling of this case and others as examples of what he saw as the corrupt manipulation of judicial discretion.[13] The case was complicated and allowed Mansfield considerable licence to delay matters—a situation that benefitted the accused at the expense of the prosecutrix. Ultimately, the case was arguably decided not on its merits, nor on any evidence, or even on the class or status of those involved but instead by the technicalities of the legal process and the ability of a determined and elite cadre to exert their influence and financial muscle.

Finally, this case study reveals the way in which a politically motivated press was able to use this episode as a weapon to attack the government of the day. Various anti-government authors and papers cited the case and those involved as evidence of corruption in the *ancien regime* and refought battles over the publication of parliamentary debates and the treatment of the radical 'hero' John Wilkes. On the other side, less radical organs used the situation of the condemned men as a 'human interest' story and as evidence of state cruelty. In effect, then, the papers allowed the murder of a watchman and the fate of his killers to become a political football to be kicked around the coffee houses of the capital. In the end, the establishment won this particular bout because the opposition was divided and weak. Again, this demonstrates the importance of timing and context in the success of pardoning petitions in the 1700s. As we shall see later in this volume, in 1789 the killer of Constable Linnell failed to secure the royal mercy at a time of domestic and international instability, when any attempts to resist authority were viewed with particular concern, thus demonstrating that elite connections in and of themselves are not enough.[14]

The chapter is divided into five parts: First, the events that precipitated the pardoning process – the killing of a Westminster watchman – are set out in a narrative of the murder followed by an analysis of the Old Bailey trial. Section three will explore the campaign to save those involved from execution. The fourth part examines the Appeal of Death and the legal context in which this was applied. The press campaign is analyzed in the fifth section of the article, which also looks at the aftermath of the failed appeal and at what happened to the protagonists. Finally, I will conclude this chapter with a summary of the findings of this research and the implications it has for understanding the pardoning process in the 1700s and Hay and King's respective theses concerning the role of the criminal justice system in the Hanoverian period.

The Murder of John Bigby

The events that led to the conviction of two young men for murder were widely reported in the newspapers and later detailed in the records of the proceedings at the Old Bailey. It is possible to reconstruct what happened, with the caveat that this information is entirely derived from witness statements given in court (and only those recorded and published by the Old Bailey Proceedings) and so must be treated with the caution that always applies to such source material. On Christmas Eve 1769, a group of five young men, four of whom were sons of wealthy London tradesmen and one of their servants, were enjoying a night out. Their revelries included food, entertainment, and a considerable amount of alcohol.

What started as festive celebrations ended up, however, in tragedy as several innocent bystanders were injured, one killed, and another so badly shaken by the experience that he too would die some months afterwards.

The party gathered at a pub in Wood Street, Westminster, run by George Mallard. Mallard later told the Old Bailey court that five men came into his hostelry between five and six o'clock in the afternoon.[15] The five were Stephen Grant, Michael McMahon, Matthew and Patrick Kennedy, and John Evans (who was servant to the brothers' father). They were good friends and members of London's long-established Irish community. Mallard and his staff served them with alcohol in a back room until around nine in the evening when they came into the taproom. They ordered 'two half pints of brandy, a pot of beer, . . . and four half-crown bowls of punch' between them, so we might reasonable expect them to have been quite affected by the time they decided to join the main community of the pub in the front bar.[16] Up until that point the group had behaved 'very honorable' and had given no cause for alarm but the amount of drink they had consumed now began to take hold of them. Once they reached the public bar what seemed at first to be a friendly squabble broke out, with the men pushing and shoving each other, but this quickly escalated into what the landlord later described as 'a riot'.[17] In the fracas Patrick Kennedy wrestled Grant to the ground. It was probably little more than youthful high spirits occasioned by the consumption of too much alcohol but the fight caused Mallard to intervene. Grant was one of his regular customers while the other men were unknown to him. If the desire to protect his 'regulars' was not sufficient cause to try and stop the violence getting any more serious then self-preservation surely was. After all, he would have had a care to his licence (and his property) and so needed to maintain order on his premises.[18]

However, if the landlord hoped to quiet things down by stepping in he was sadly mistaken. The group of friends now turned their anger on the landlord and attacked Mallard and then a number of other customers who attempted to intervene. What had started as a wrestling match had swiftly turned into a barroom brawl involving a dozen or more individuals. The trigger for the altercation may well have been the landlord's refusal to sell them any more drink. This was not to do with their ability to pay however; Mallard later testified that the men had given him money up front, emphasizing that these were relatively wealthy young men.[19] In the course of the fight one man was badly beaten and Mallard sustained a broken nose. Eventually, about 15 minutes after the altercation had started, the men grabbed their belongings and exited the pub with a cry of 'take up your hats and run!'[20] Patrick Kennedy, whose stick had been broken in the fight, armed himself with a poker he had removed from the pub, adding theft to his already growing list of offences. John Atkinson was able to testify to the chaos they caused and then left behind. He was walking along Wood Street that evening when he saw a man dressed as a brewer's servant stagger out of the pub. At first he thought he was drunk then he released he had been beaten up and was bleeding from the nose and head. He had no time to react before a man wearing a smart green coat, trimmed with gold thread, and a bright red waistcoat, appeared at the door. The man shouted at Atkinson, demanded to know where his hat was, and then attacked him with the poker he was carrying. As Atkinson fell against the doorway under the force of the blow he narrowly avoided being hit again, the poker thudding into the doorframe instead. Fortunately, his assailant abandoned the fight and hurried away with his companions, leaving the injured men behind him.

The Kennedy brothers and their companions left the pub at about a quarter past nine in the evening and now ran along Millbank towards Old Palace Yard where the next person they met was Samuel Vincent, a young lad. In his testimony, given in the subsequent trial at the Old Bailey, Vincent described them as a 'mob' and said that Patrick Kennedy squared up to him, accused him of being a robber, and threatened him with an iron poker, most evidently the one he had stolen from the Wood Street hostelry. As Vincent sidestepped the blow, he was pulled backwards into a nearby alley, rescued by a stranger who had seen what was unfolding from the door of the pub opposite. A group of onlookers outside the *Ship* inn now intervened more forcefully and were attacked. Two men were knocked to the ground, one (George Lucas, a coachman) requiring treatment in the pub (his head being washed with gin as a crude form of antiseptic) before the group took off towards Westminster Bridge. At this stage, this was an unpleasant but not unusual example of boorish behaviour and drunkenness, in which several people had been beaten, bloodied, and knocked to the ground, but it was to get much worse.

George Bracegirdle (a Thames lighterman) and John Bigby were chatting on Westminster Bridge. The latter was a bricklayer's labourer who also worked as a watchman. On that night he served as a private security guard for a man named Goodchild but was dressed in his watchman's greatcoat and red waistcoat. So even setting aside the fact that he was not carrying a lantern and staff (the usual accompaniments of a parish watchman) there could be no misunderstanding his position.[21] Despite the work of Elaine Reynolds and a handful of other scholars we still know relatively little about watchmen.[22] By 1736, most parishes 'had night watch systems modeled on those in Piccadilly and Hanover Square' but private systems still continued.[23] As a parish watchman Bigby might have earned around £15 a year to patrol his beat. That was a hardly a huge amount of money and probably explains why he had two occupations and acted privately for Mr Goodchild. We also know he had a wife and a brother because they were both important players in the story that was about to unfold. That night, as was apparently normal practice for Westminster Bridge, there were five watchmen on duty, two at each end and another in the middle with a the duty constable of the night, who on this occasion was William Shillitoe.

As Bigby and Bracegirdle walked across the bridge, Patrick and Matthew Kennedy came running up behind them, somewhat out of breath as they had been trying to escape from the alteration they had caused outside the *Ship*. According to several witnesses that night – several of whom were later able to formally identify the brothers and others in their party – once they had left the *Ship* they were pursued by several people all angry at the violence they had meted out there and at Mr Mallard's house in Wood Street. Additionally, they must have known the watch and local constables would have been called out after the chaos and violence they had served on anyone and everyone they had encountered that evening. The brothers now ran past the two friends watching on the bridge and then turned and attacked them, for no apparent reason.[24] Patrick hit Bracegirdle over the head with a cane while Matthew set about Bigby with his fists. Matthew seized his brother's weapon – the iron poker stolen from the pub – and started to hit Bigby with it. The senior watchman was quite clear that it was Matthew that struck Bigby, identifying him in court before pointing at Patrick as the person that had hit him (Bracegirdle). Bracegirdle then reported that two others arrived, presumably these were the Kennedys' companions but in the dark and confusion he could not swear to them in court. Bracegirdle was badly hurt, needing assistance from a passer-by to get to his feet. John Bigby, however, was much more seriously hurt: when the other watchmen of the bridge arrived they propped him up and he said 'O George! I am very bad' and there was a lot of blood on the back of his head where he had been struck.[25] Bigby was taken to the Westminster infirmary where he died of his wounds within a few hours.

Patrick Kennedy was apprehended after a struggle. While the constable of the bridge, Shillitoe, and his men tried to take him to the watch house he attempted an escape near the *Bear* public house, aided by his friends. In the melee the constable was hit on the head (by Patrick) and sustained a head wound that was cited as a causal factor in his death some years later.[26] Matthew was picked up soon afterwards in Channel Row (which ran parallel to Parliament Street close by) while the others (excepting Grant) were rounded up in the following week and committed to trial by Sir John Fielding at Bow Street. The brothers' father deposited the murder weapon at a grocer's shop in the Strand but if this was an attempt to conceal evidence it failed, as Bigby's brother Joseph managed to trace it and it was brought before the magistrate and was produced in court for various witnesses to swear to. Bigby's family were closely involved in the hunt for John Bigby's killers; while Joseph traced the weapon Robert Bigby 'endeavored to find out all [he] could', capturing Evans himself.[27] This was just the start of a long struggle to gain justice for the murder of their relative and helps reveal just how personal the criminal justice system was in this period before professional policing. In fact, the determination of Joseph Bigby and his sister-in-law (Anne Bigby) to bring the first prosecution and then return later when the Kennedy family conspired to save the brothers from the judicially prescribed consequences of their actions is evidence of how much effort was required by prosecutors and victims in a system that relied on the activity of those involved.

The Trial of Matthew and Patrick Kennedy

The court trial was fairly straightforward. While there was some confusion as to the exact details of who hit whom and with what, there were ample witnesses that could identify the Kennedy brothers and their associates as being actively aggressive on the night and who could place Patrick and Matthew on Westminster Bridge at the time Bigby was attacked. Witnesses like George Lucas, William Shillitoe, George Bracegirdle, and John Quick (who kept the *Ship* inn) all swore to the Kennedys participation in the violence that evening. Several people clearly saw a poker and a cane or stick in one or other of the brothers' possession at various points, but it was less clear to what extent Evans, Grant, or McMahon were culpable in the killing of the watchman and that certainly contributed to all three of them being acquitted. It was dark that night and not all of those who gave evidence would swear to all of the companions in the dock being involved. There was at least one misidentification when John Quick touched Evans on the shoulder when asked to pick out Matthew Kennedy.[28] This doubt, while it did not affect the jury's decision-making on the day, may have given some comfort to those seeking a conditional pardon for the two men later.

One report of the trial claimed the brothers were intoxicated in court, suggesting a level of disrespect or perhaps simply fear.[29] Matthew offered nothing more than a denial; 'I know nothing of it' he told the court in his defence.[30] Patrick was more careful to construct an alternative narrative of events. He confirmed the reports of the drinking bout and melee at the pub but framed it so that Mallard and the other drinkers were the instigators. He said nothing of the fight outside the *Ship* and suggested he and his brother had crossed the bridge to the Surrey side before returning and being chased by the watchmen. He claimed he was knocked down and robbed (perhaps alluding to the altercation with the young man outside the *Ship* inn who he accused of attempting to rob him before hitting with his stick). When they were held at Tothill Fields Bridewell, Matthew Kennedy alleged that some of the witnesses who appeared were demanding money not to testify against them.[31] This introduced another small amount of doubt to the proceedings but it was not enough to shake the jury's conviction that the brothers were guilty. There was one witness for the brothers who offered a different version of events that night. James Justice Culvertson claimed to have seen another man, much larger (taller and 'more corpulent') than any of those on trial, strike the watchman that night.[32] His facts were very different to the accounts given by the watchmen and the other witnesses. He said he saw 50 or 60 people surrounding the watchmen on the bridge. There may be an explanation for this discrepancy. When pushed he said he had come forward in response to a plea from the brothers' father for information regarding the death of Bigby and the robbery of his sons (which was the story told by Patrick). 'Old Mr Kennedy' was already attempting to use his money and influence to save his offspring from what was potentially a fatal encounter with the criminal justice system. He must have known that if they were convicted they would hang and hang quickly under the terms of the Murder Act (1752). Moreover, it seems evident that the Kennedys were well known and this was not lost on those potentially coming forward as witnesses. A mixture of opportunism and fear informed the actions of men like Bracegirdle who probably recognized that their information was valuable. The eighteenth-century court system was undoubtedly open to corrupt practice with witnesses being paid for their silence or to offer false testimony (as Culverhouse clearly had).

This was followed by another curious exchange in court with a character witness named as Mr St John presented himself. St John deposed that Bracegirdle (in the company two other 'ill looking' men) had visited him asking for money not to testify against the brothers in court. St John was at pains to say that he refused their demand for £10 to keep quiet and in doing so it is pretty clear his purpose was to undermine the watchman's evidence. Had Bracegirdle tried to profit from the death of his colleague and friend John Bigby? It is entirely possible since £10 was a great deal of money in 1770 but I think we should be cautious of taking St John's word at face value. St John was closely connected to the brothers, as later events will show and I think his actions and appearance at the end of the Old Bailey trial can be better interpreted as an early attempt to set up the grounds for a petition for a conditional pardon for Patrick and Matthew.[33] At the end of the trial, the Kennedys and the other defendants were able to produce a series of character witnesses that demonstrated their connections to the business world and wider community in London; an auctioneer (as the brothers were), haberdasher, gilder, shoemaker, and the Attorney General of the Island of St John's all testified to the good character of those on trial. It failed to save Matthew and Patrick and on conviction the brothers were sentenced to death with the additional penalty of being anatomized and dissected in accordance with the terms of the Murder Act. So, while there might have been some slight grounds for suggesting that conditions made it hard (on 'a very dark night') to identify either of the brothers as the person that had dealt a killing blow to John Bigby, it was pretty clear that they were responsible for his death. Significantly, given the discussion of contemporary homicide trials at the Old Bailey in the opening chapter the jury did not believe there was any case to downgrade the actions that night to manslaughter. In this case, the fact that all of the protagonists involved in John Bigby's death had been drunk and were, by all accounts, quite intoxicated, seemed to count for nothing. Here there was no mitigation as Rabin has described elsewhere,[34] and the pair were convicted of murder, with all that entailed for their punishment thereafter.

The Campaign to Save the Brothers

Almost as soon as the sentence was passed, the campaign to save the brothers' lives began in earnest. The London newspapers reported that the death sentence had been met with 'tears of pity and compassion' in court, especially from the 'softer sex'.[35] This might have been expected since the brothers were 'respectable' sons of an elderly and 'reputable tradesman' and not the usual occupants of the Old Bailey dock.[36] Their supporters were almost certainly in court with them that day, and this may have included their sisters who were well connected in their own right. The brothers were set to be executed on the Monday morning following their trial but a stay of execution arrived for Patrick just in time. According to one press report, one of those acquitted of the murder (McMahon) had subsequently sworn an affidavit admitting to having struck Bigby. Having already been cleared of murder he presumably believed himself immune from prosecution and was taking the blame to save his friends.[37] Matthew's respite arrived on the following day, both brothers could breathe a little more easily but the campaign to overturn their death sentences had only just begun; they were far from safe yet.[38]

The pardoning and petitioning process remains somewhat shrouded in mystery and that supposedly suited those presiding over it. Yet this does not mean that the public was entirely in the dark about how it operated, a reality that goes some way to undermine Hay's argument that it was this very secrecy that allowed the justice system as a whole to act as an effective arm of state control.[39] As far as most English men and women understood it, conditional pardons and reprieves were authorized by the king himself, after his attention had been brought to the plight of those 'left to hang' by the judges at Old Bailey or on the circuit. The reality was probably quite a bit different, with George III being counselled by his ministers and the judiciary (and mostly by the Recorder if Beattie is correct in his assessment).[40] One contemporary (writing at length to the editor of the *London Evening Post*) presumed to challenge the right of the monarch to intervene at all in the execution of convicted murderers. The judge, he said, was entitled to order a respite if he felt there were grounds for doing so (such as a doubt over conviction), but the king did not.[41] Regardless, on this occasion a respite bought valuable time for the Kennedys and it is indicative of the power of their connections because under the terms of the Murder Act appeals for clemency had been made that much more difficult. Execution of sentence was supposed to take place within three days and this severely limited the opportunities to draw support from well connected parties. However, for the Kennedy brothers this was not a problem; they were very well connected and had the ear of those in positions of power. No lesser figures than the Duke of Manchester and Sir George Savile took an interest in the Kennedy case.[42] George Montagu, 4th Duke of Manchester, served as lord of the bedchamber until the year of the Kennedys' trial, giving him virtually unrestricted access to George III.[43] Savile was a 'trimmer' who shared the beliefs of the Whigs but maintained a position as an independent MP.[44] Both shared similar political views and were well placed to intervene on behalf of the Kennedys.

A further respite followed for Matthew at the end of February and now the press revealed yet more information about the pardoning process and those engaged behind the scenes.[45] According to reports, no less than 13 noblemen had signed a petition to spare Matthew and Patrick, which had been presented to the king by a triumvirate of the 'great and good' made up of the Earl of Carlisle, Lord Robert Spencer, and Sir George Selwyn. Selwyn was an incumbent politician who used his position to cover his gambling debts. A one-time friend of Robert Walpole, Selwyn clearly knew his way around the establishment and so was a useful ally and 'fixer'.[46] Frederick Howard, 5th Earl of Carlisle, was a man on the up and was to go on to have a glittering career in politics.[47] He and Selwyn were close friends. Spencer was also an MP and a part of Charles Fox's circle of Whigs who enjoyed the advantages for pleasure that a life in politics brought with it. Spencer was a gambler and someone described by Fox as 'a great arranger' for his personal negotiation skills.[48] It would seem likely that these three men had much in common and would have met frequently in parliament, at court or in their clubs. It is clear that the Kennedy brothers had some important connections to persons in government and at court. What is far less clear is how the sons of a 'respectable tradesman' had acquired these connections and to what extent they could be brought to bear on the king and his ministers.

The respite, welcome as it would have been for the brothers, could not remove their anxiety completely. Reportedly, Matthew was suffering in gaol; the 'fears and terrors of his expected destiny, and the glimmerings of hope' had made him 'extremely ill'.[49] Meanwhile, as the press reported the week-to-week unfolding of the saga, small snippets of the case emerged. The petitioners had not only failed to keep their own names out of the public domain, but now the legal niceties of the case were open to scrutiny. In early March, there was another reference to George Bracegirdle's supposed willingness to accept a bribe.[50] The same report expressed concern for the Kennedys' experience of being continually respited at the last minute, stating that the process of being made ready for execution only to be spared as the respite arrived (on one occasion by a messenger who tripped and fell, so fast was he running) was taking its toll on the brothers' nerves.[51] What emerges is the existence of a polarized debate on the merits of pardoning in the late 1700s, something that was to become much more sharply focused in the early 1800s as the move to restrict capital punishment gathered momentum. The Kennedy case reminds us that this debate was already under way and was here applied to a murder case, while most of the historical discussion has centred on pardons for property offenders.[52]

The press was undoubtedly keen to exploit the human-interest story that surrounded the brothers. The *Independent Chronicle* reprinted the depositions from the trial (in several parts) so that its readership had some context.[53] But the reportage also unveiled something much more interesting; namely, the intervention of some members of the original Old Bailey jury who took to the press to refute allegations made against them and to criticize the petitioning process. In mid-March, an advertisement appeared placed by members of the petty jury that convicted the Kennedys. It was signed by five men and reiterated their belief that they had made the correct decision, despite the emergence of the affidavit signed by McMahon that he had delivered the blow that had killed John Bigby. The letter referred to the pardoning petition; evidently some pressure was being brought to bear (by 'some Noblemen') on the jurors to append their signatures to that petition and there was a suggestion that a huge bribe had been offered.[54] Seven jury members had already signed the petition and the letter writers noted that this 'method of exculpating criminals, by getting the Jury to sign a Petition, has lately been practiced with great success'.[55] It seems the decision on whether or not to hang Matthew and Patrick was now subject to intense public discussion and was not the mysterious and private process that supposedly allowed elite hegemony to be maintained.[56] Moreover, the otherwise fairly routine decision over whether to hang two convicted felons was now being used for political purposes, with commentators on both sides weighing in and linking the Kennedy case to wider issues of the day.

The fate of the brothers remained in the balance throughout the spring with a series of stays of execution. As late as April 13 it was reported that Matthew became very ill at the news that he was set to be executed.[57] On April 16 or 17, two noblemen entered the press yard at Newgate and demanded Matthew's irons be 'knocked off'. They paid 6s for his '[r]oom, gave him money for other purposes, and promised he should want for nothing'.[58] Soon afterwards the brothers were formally spared when the press reported that 'his Majesty had extended his Royal mercy to them on the following condition; Matthew to be transported for life, and Patrick for 14 years'.[59] It would seem that the efforts of those 'of the first rank' had been successful and the two young men were now set for a new life in the American colonies where they might expect to receive favourable conditions given the connections they had. Transportation across the Atlantic did not hold the same terrors that the later introduction of exile to Botany Bay did and presented ample opportunities for escape.[60] The brothers would have hoped to have immediately regained their freedom on arrival in the Colonies. As Ekirch has written:

> Wealthier transports also gained their liberty once ships docked at colonial ports . . . Normally payment of a sum equivalent to what the transport could have fetched as a servant was required to satisfy ship masters, whose legal responsibility lay only in conveying transports to the colonies.[61]

The average cost of a male servant bound for transportation was £13, as opposed to the cost of a slave (at £35–44) so this was relatively inexpensive for someone as seemingly well connected as the brothers.

Matthew Kennedy was sent on board a merchant ship. Here he was visited by another nobleman, this time James Duff, the 2nd Earl of Fife, who found him in a parlous state: 'chained to a board, in a hole not above sixteen feet long; more than fifty with him; a collar and padlock about his neck, and chained to five of the most dreadful creatures I ever looked on'. The earl gave Patrick 15 guineas and paid to have his irons struck off before speaking to the ship's captain, a fellow Scot, to ensure that he would be well looked after on the voyage (and possibly on arrival in the Americas).[62] Fife then wrote to Selwyn to express his concerns about the treatment both brothers had received, noting that Matthew had been 'at least four times hanged'. Importantly in his letter he urged Selwyn to act in private, stating that: 'If you make any contribution, I humbly think it should be v private', suggesting that he believed that these machinations were best kept secret and away from the glare of public scrutiny. It would appear, however, that in this at least he failed.[63]

So clearly the Kennedys had powerful allies. Not only had their lives been spared but their futures in the colonies had been secured.[64] We might ask how the Kennedys' supporters managed to persuade the king to grant a conditional pardon and this was certainly something that was the subject of debate at the time, notably by the radical politician John Horne Tooke. Amongst all the reaction to the decision, however, one individual was not amused. John Bigby's widow, Anne, now chose to pursue a seldom-used path to find justice for her husband.

Anne Bigby's Appeal for Murder

There existed under English law a right of redress for those who felt the criminal justice system had failed them in such circumstances.[65] The legislation allowed a private prosecution to be brought; in effect a civil suit that was lodged by the 'wife, heir, or closest kin of the deceased person, within a year and a day of the latter's death'.[66] Even by the sixteenth century it was rarely used but examples can be found right up until the early 1800s.[67] The Kennedy case was rare and set a legal precedent and so we are fortunate that Sir James Burrow wrote it up at length.[68]

So what was the Appeal of Death (alternatively and perhaps more properly titled an 'Appeal of Murder'[69]) and how did it work? The law allowed an exception to the principle of English law that a person could not be tried twice for the same offence (so-called double jeopardy). The appellant was entitled to bring a writ of appeal against the accused person.[70] It was an ancient law that survived from a time before the state had taken such a prominent role in regulating the behaviour of its subjects. As one critic of the Appeal noted in 1818 (following the high profile case of Ashford vs. Thornton), the device was outdated in a modern age where criminal trials were conducted with lawyers and evidence, and the notion of the feud was a medieval one.[71] The appeal was literally 'a call' (appeler), a summons of the person deemed responsible for the act of homicide. Blackstone described it as a 'private process for the punishment of public crimes' although in reality what it was used for was as a mechanism to prosecute those private offences that the public courts failed to prosecute.[72] The appeal had to be brought by the wife of the deceased or by a male heir and in person; only a wife had the right to be represented by an attorney and only after a change to the law in 1486, because the principle was that the appeal would result in a trial by combat. If the wife had remarried, she lost her right of appeal. So it would seem (something that was later pointed out in the Kennedy case) that the appeal of murder was seen as a device to get compensation rather than 'justice' in the purest sense of that word. Crucially the appeal removed the monarch (and the mercy allowed by him) from the equation. While the king could pardon a subject that had been convicted of a public crime, he or she had no power to overturn a sentence delivered following a private appeal for murder. Indeed in the medieval period the appellant and their family chose where and when to bring the condemned to execution using 'a long rope'.[73] This then was a very personal system of justice.

This was something that the contemporary legal expert Edward Kendall found intolerable because, as he put it, the appellant stepped 'between the King (or the nation) and the accused'.[74] The appeal was also problematic because of course it allowed a defendant to be tried twice. As one of the few researchers to look at this topic observed: 'the maxim of law, *nemo debet bis vexari pro una et eadem causa*, was violated'.[75] Moreover, the appeal bypassed the grand jury because the right was an older legal instrument. Thus the appeal, unlike the indictment under which most accused were brought to trial, did not have to go through the same level of legal scrutiny.

It also had one gaping loophole. The accused could, if they were aware of the process or had an astute enough lawyer to advise them, claim their right to 'trial by battle' (in other words, by combat). So long as the appellee quoted the right set of words and threw down a glove in court at the appropriate time he could avoid a trial by jury and instead elect to have his accuser confront him in a duel. Naturally, as was seen in the case of Abraham Thornton, the appellant was hardly likely to wish to take up such a challenge and so the accused could escape scot-free. This did not apply to Anne because, since 1486, a wife had the right to be represented by an attorney, as 'a woman could not fight'.[76] In 1774 a parliamentary debate on whether the Appeal of Murder applied to the American colonies encompassed a debate about the process itself. MPs spoke at length on either side of the argument with Charles Fox intervening forcefully to say that the appeal should be abolished because it undermined the role of the monarch to pardon convicted felons and this took away a very useful mechanism of reversing miscarriages of justice (there was no appeal against conviction in England in the eighteenth century, only the recourse to clemency).[77] In the aftermath of the Thornton case Parliament again discussed the abolition of the Appeal.[78] The bill was hotly debated with opponents of abolition arguing that it provided an important check on the misuse of discretion and influence by government and the monarch. Sir Francis Burdett made explicit reference to the Kennedy case and stated that the Appeal acted to 'check the illegal exercise of the power of the Crown in pardoning criminals'.[79] Regardless, the bill finally received the Royal Assent in July 1819.[80]

Given that this legal device was so little used in the 1700s (it was deployed on just two occasions before 1770),[81] how did Anne discover this method to prosecute her husband's killers and, moreover, how did she finance the legal team required to bring it to the King's Bench? It would seem that she too had useful friends in high places, or at least interested parties who had some vested interest in making sure the state's interference in the execution of a justice did not go unchallenged or unexposed. Just who these 'interested parties' were will be addressed shortly, but in the meantime we must return to the narrative of events in the spring of 1770.

In late April 1770, Anne lodged her appeal at the Old Bailey but only one of the Kennedy brothers was brought into court to hear it. This situation ultimately undermined Anne's attempt to ensure that the full force of the law was brought to bear on her husband's killers. Patrick was called to the bar at Old Bailey but Matthew was already onboard a merchant ship. Indeed some sections of the London press reported false information that his vessel had sailed.[82] It had not, and a few days afterwards the second brother appeared in court to face the appeal. Once again there is evidence of intervention on both sides: as reportedly the Lord Mayor of London had overridden an attempt to prevent Matthew from being returned to the capital. The City's chief magistrate had personally signed the warrant for Matthew's return and wrote to the keeper of Newgate to ensure he 'detained Patrick Kenny [sic]', adding that 'no murderer should ever escape justice while he lived'.[83] The press described Matthew as looking 'greatly dejected' at this turn of events, as well he might; from believing he had at last escaped the danger of being hanged, he was now back in prison.[84] If convicted under the Appeal, both men faced the death penalty, but this time with no prospect of a pardon. The king had the power to issue respites to delay execution but he had no power to make the respite permanent; the lives of the brothers now rested in the hands of the King's Bench and, crucially, Bigby's widow.[85] However, the legal process and those that administered it would also determine their fate, and here it was Anne Bigby who was severely disadvantaged. The private appeal process was costly and time-consuming and someone in Anne's situation – a widow of a poor bricklayer's labourer and watchman – could not expect to compete with those supporting the brothers. The key for the Kennedy camp was to attempt to delay the case until Anne ran out of funds or succumbed to pressure to accept a payoff.

The first obstacle Anne and John Bigby's brother Robert faced was indeed a legal one: the Kennedys' counsel argued that the bill was 'exhibited against Matthew, before Patrick was in custody: Therefore it can't [sic] affect Patrick'. He called for another bill of prosecution.[86] This was because while Patrick was in Newgate, his brother had been in Maidstone Gaol at the time the original bill was presented. After a delay the bill was brought and read again, but the defence now objected on the grounds that it contained a 'false fact', namely that the brothers had been brought to court at the same time, when clearly they had not. The defence moved to adjourn on the grounds that his clients were being asked to plead on a bill they had had no prior notice of and that they had not known they would be in court on that day.[87] Since Anne did not object the case was adjourned until the next term. For later critics this legal wrangling had the hidden hand of Lord Mansfield all over it.[88]

The defendants were sent to the Marshalsea Prison to wait for the next session of King's Bench. When they reappeared the defence again objected to them having to plead to a writ they had not seen. The court ordered that the original writ be produced and the men remanded again in the meantime. All of this process is as confusing to the uninitiated as it must have been to Anne. Even Blackstone, observing the case in court, was unclear of exactly what legal procedure should be followed.[89] The Bigbys were severely disadvantaged, both by the complexities of the law and the imbalance in funding between themselves and the Kennedys.

By contrast the brothers were served by a well-organized judicial team and had Lord Mansfield's tacit support. Mansfield (as the presiding judge at King's Bench) had found ways to prosecute libel that had made him an implacable opponent of the radicals inside and out of parliament. Mansfield was, as Arthur Cross has described him, 'like many judges before him, a creature of government and the court'.[90] One of the radicals that attacked the Lord Chief Justice and George III's other minsters was

John Horne, a one-time ally of Wilkes who later found himself drawn into a war of words with his former radical friend. In January 1771, he wrote to Wilkes to refute accusations of personal corruption. Within a long missive was a forceful denial that he had directed the appeal against the Kennedys on Anne Bigby's behalf and had raised (and pocketed) the subscription to pay for it. He condemned Mansfield as a judge who 'so dexterous in finding out or creating obstacles to a trial in the antient [sic] mode of appeal for murder'. He supported (in principle at least) the widow's case and revealed that the subscription had raised £110 16s and that he had paid Anne's attorney £150 (and so was some £39 out of pocket).[91] Horne's letter also referred to an attempt to abolish Appeal of Death in the House of Commons by bringing in a private member's bill. This attempt failed but it is another reminder of just how widespread the conspiracy to save the brothers' lives was.

Meanwhile the papers ran a series of reports suggesting that Anne had accepted money to stop her prosecution. There had been rumours as early as June 1770 that she had settled with the family and friends of her husband's killers. One suggested that she had been offered 'a large sum of money' by 'a certain lord'.[92] In October the *Middlesex Journal* stated that: 'it is confidently said that Mrs Bigby . . . some time since compromised the said affair, on condition of receiving the sum of 500L'.[93] This was quickly denied in a rival broadsheet who 'assure[d] the public' that this report was 'without foundation'.[94] However, it would seem that the papers were mostly correct. One suggested that a baker in Westminster had paid a sum of £350 to Anne and that she had left London to 'settle in the country'.[95] Another claimed that the Kennedy's counsel had advised those supporting the brothers' cause to 'count out the gold before her, throw it in to her lap and see if she will refuse it'.[96]

On November 6, 1770 both men appeared in the King's Bench court. Anne was called three times but did not appear. The defence moved that a nonsuit be recorded and Mansfield obliged. The defendants were remanded into the custody of the Marshal and effectively cleared of the appeal. In his write up of the case, Blackstone noted that Anne 'accepted a Sum of Money from the Friends of the Appellees'; in other words the Kennedys and their supporters had finally bought her off.[97] This must have been a difficult decision for Anne as one report alludes:

> An evening paper says that when she went to receive the money (350L) she wept bitterly, and at first refused to touch the money that was to be the price of her husband's blood; but being told that nobody else could receive it for her, she held up her apron, and bid the attorney, who was to pay it sweep it into her lap.[98]

£350 was a life-changing sum of money in 1770 and represents a huge incentive not to pursue her complaint against the brothers. It was suggested that Anne's motives in taking the money were not out of context with the spirit of the appeal in law anyway. According to one correspondent, the 'law of appeal was invented by the founders of our constitution for no other purpose than of giving a compensation to the nearest relation for the death of the person slain'.[99] It was blood money or 'wergild', as the Anglo-Saxons would have understood it.

Press Reaction and Aftermath

Following the collapse of the appeal, the Kennedy brothers remained in custody while the authorities worked out what to do with them. In April 1771, Matthew and Patrick were set before the bar at Old Bailey, this time to be told once more that the king had granted them a pardon on condition they accepted transportation to the colonies, Matthew for life and his brother for 14 years.[100] In the aftermath, newspapers that opposed the brothers' release published a series of reports which alleged that they were either being treated far too well or had escaped from custody altogether.

Matthew and Patrick were held in the King's Bench Gaol. The prison housed debtors and criminals alike and one commentator was critical of the ways in which it operated. It came under the stewardship of Lord Mansfield and Francis Browne accused the Lord Chief Justice of misappropriating the fees paid by inmates for his own uses. Along with an accusation that Mansfield and the City Marshall were 'plundering the wretched' within the gaol, he made a direct reference to the conditions under which the Kennedys were being held. Under the rules, debtors and criminal inmates were supposed to be kept apart, the latter in leg irons. However, it seemed that the two brothers were being allowed considerable privileges, including mixing with the debtors and being 'suited with a pair of irons, so prodigiously easy, as to render them able to pull them off every night, [as] they would a stocking'.[101]

Not only were the brothers able to live comfortably within the gaol, they were also terrorizing its inmates. 'Complaints were frequently made', Brown alleged, that the Kennedys had 'discovered a savageness of disposition' and that 'they actually beat, bruised, and bit, an unhappy debtor, in a manner, so unmerciful, that he kept his bed for two days, and is not to this hour recovered'.[102] In February, it was reported that the Kennedys' irons had been removed altogether so they could enjoy the same privileges as other, non-criminal inmates of the prison.[103] As the year unfolded the violence associated with the brothers continued. A fight broke out between them:

> The two Kennedies, who have long been a terror to all the prisoners in the King's Bench, and having wounded and ill-treated all who fell in their way, have at length fallen upon one another; one of them having last week bit a piece out of the other's breast.[104]

Later it was suggested that the brothers would have commissions in the army when they reached America: 'one a captain's, worth 1000L, the other a lieutenant's, worth 600L'.[105] These rumours of special treatment, violence, and future financial security were unsubstantiated but reported as fact in the opposition press.

The brothers were set to sail to Virginia[106] in July 1771 and the press reported that their sisters went aboard to make their farewells. This made explicit in print what must have been well known at the time, that Matthew and Patrick's sisters were intimately involved in their reprieves. The *Middlesex Journal* noted that: on 'Friday the two Miss Kennedies went on board the transport ship lying below Deptford, to take their leave of their brothers, and while they were on board one of them had her pocket picked of a 10l. bank note, which was intended to be given to their brothers at parting. Some of the Convicts who stood nearest to them were searched'.[107] Conveniently, nothing was found and the allegation of special treatment could continue to linger in the minds of the capital's reading public.

The transport ship *Scarsedale* sailed for America with the brothers on board but what happened to them afterwards is impossible to ascertain.[108] They almost certainly went equipped with letters of introduction and probably the funds to ease their passage and secure their freedom at the other end. In March 1772, eight months after their ship had been due to sail, more than one paper reported that they had been spotted in England.[109] A further article suggested they had been involved in a mutiny on board a ship bound for Maryland. According to another the brothers had instigated the rebellion and had 'butchered the captain with remarkable instances of barbarity'.[110] The *Middlesex Journal* stated that if this was indeed true,

> there is no doubt that but such execrable monsters will speedily undergo that punishment due, though not equal, to their crimes, by which, from a most fatal partiality, they have been exempted in their own country, to the scandal of all law, humanity and justice.[111]

This prompted a letter from George Stevens, who claimed to have been onboard the *Scaresdale*. He assured the public that there had been no mutiny and that the brothers had behaved themselves impeccably. The captain had died of an illness he contracted, not from any violence offered by Patrick or Matthew Kennedy. The brothers had in fact safely landed at Virginia and he believed that some 'seditious, malicious, and evil-designed People' with ulterior motives had placed this erroneous news article.[112] Regardless of this attempt to silence the gossip, stories of the Kennedy brothers' escape from justice continued with claims of sightings and associations with violence. In August 1772, one of them was supposedly seen in Paris, dressed finely in 'suit of claret coloured cloaths [sic], trimmed with gold lace'. Apparently he was drunk and managed to start a riot before he was arrested and imprisoned, only to be released.[113] This story was embroidered with the news that the elder of the two men had joined the Irish Brigades (a French military unit formed in 1690 of Irish exiles) at Calais, 'a grateful return for the clemency shewn [sic] him by our amiable Sovereign', the report sneered. Clearly the campaign against the brothers (and the condemnation of Mansfield and the political elite that had spared them) continued with this most recent portrayal of them as at best ungrateful and, at worse, traitors.[114]

In mid-April 1770, a satirical letter reported that Matthew Kennedy 'who was hanged some weeks ago, received a respite during His Majesty's pleasure, for no other reason than that his sisters never had any connexions [sic] with the nobility'. The long piece by 'O'Connor' used the device of turning fact on its head (presumably to spare the writer or publisher from prosecution for libel).[115] What it implied was that the brothers were saved by the interventions of the nobility in answer to the wishes of their sisters. But exactly what were these connections, and what role did their sisters have at court or within the circles of government? In the months following the collapse of the appeal this began to become a little clearer.

In August 1772, the mercy shown towards a convicted sodomite gave one correspondent to the papers a further opportunity to condemn the king and his ministers for showing similar mercy to the Kennedy brothers. 'The Kennedies, for murdering a poor old man in the decline of nature, cruelly butchered as not being fit to crawl 'tween heaven and earth, [were] reprieved by the desire of the notorious Poll Kennedy, their sister'.[116] The Northampton Mercury stated that the 'truth' was that the first respite the brothers had received (in February 1770) had been issued on the strength of the jurors' retraction of their verdict based on the emergence of new evidence (this evidence being that it was McMahon that had given the blow that killed Bigby); the second followed afterwards with an instruction from the Secretary of State from the Northern Department, the Earl of Sandwich, to the keeper of Newgate to inform Matthew and Patrick Kennedy that the respites were, to all intents and purposes, a conditional pardon. However, at the king's council Lord Mansfield had apparently argued that at least one of the brothers should hang for the crime and so Matthew's name was included in the 'dead letter' (which decreed which felons awaiting execution should be taken to Tyburn). Matthew was only saved at the last minute by the intervention of the Secretary of State (Sandwich) who spoke to the king directly.[117]

George Selwyn also wrote to the king. The grounds for Selwyn's appeal was the doubt surrounding Matthew's conviction. In his letter to George III this is made quite explicit:

The fact against Kennedy, as stated to the jury, was founded on evidence doubtful in the nature of things, and very suspicious from circumstances of corrupt behaviour in the single witness who fixed it on him. But with great certainty it may be made clear to your Majesty, that Matthew Kennedy did not give the blow, by evidence which could not possibly be produced at the trial.[118]

Was this the case? The suggestion is that Bracegirdle had perjured himself in court. The evidence reportedly given in courts was as follows:

Bracegirdle: That is the person that struck Bigby, in the blue clothes, (pointing to Matthew Kennedy) and that is Patrick, in brown clothes, that struck me, (pointing to him.) . . . The tall one was beating of me; after he hit me with his cane he hit me with his hands. The other was following Bigby, and kept striking him at the same time, till the two men came up. One of them had something in his hand. Matthew Kennedy took it out of his hand, and struck Bigby with it.[119]

The doubt was planted at the trial itself with James Justice Culvertson's testimony and the suggestion, from St John, that Bracegirdle was open to a bribe. Moreover, McMahon's supposed confession that he was the guilty party (made, as noted earlier, after he had been cleared of the charge of murder by the Old Bailey jury and therefore safe from further prosecution) was supported by a member of that jury. James Sheridine signed an affidavit saying that had he and his fellow jurors been given that information during the trial they would have acquitted the Kennedy brothers. Sheridine added that he had been 'assured' by 'Messrs Selwyn and St John' that 'three creditable persons' had sworn to hearing McMahon's confession.[120] On the ground then it would seem Selwyn and St John were the Kennedys' key advocates, working all the channels they could to free the brothers. Were these indeed grounds for doubting the conviction or instead useful excuses to allow a plea for clemency? It would seem that where these well connected young men were concerned, Hay's explanation (of the provision of 'acceptable excuses' for pardons) is apposite.[121]

The campaign to save the brothers' lives was orchestrated from within government and parliament and closely connected to the court, and it became interwoven with the long running criticism of the incumbent regime by opposition radicals. At the heart of the matter were the lords of Weymouth and Sandwich, both of whom were unpopular figures in the eyes of the opposition. Thomas Thynne (Lord Weymouth) had been libeled by John Wilkes and the 4th Earl Sandwich had led the prosecution of the radical politician on charge of obscene libel in 1763. Wilkes' pornographic pamphlet 'An Essay on Woman' was dedicated to Sandwich's mistress, Fanny Murray. In doing so, Sandwich cemented his position in government but also alienated some sections of the public (being characterized as 'Jeremy Twitcher', Macheath's betrayer in a contemporary performance of John Guy's *Beggar's Opera*). Sandwich has often been portrayed as a man of lavish tastes; he enjoyed gambling and was a sometime member of the Hellfire Club (as was Wilkes), although more recently he has been somewhat rehabilitated as a hard-working politician.[122] Most important here is the fact that Sandwich was in government at the point that the Kennedy brothers were brought to trial and remained in a position of authority until the later 1770s. He was then ideally placed to assist them, but this still does not answer the question of why he would. In order to understand how the Kennedy brothers were able to marshal such high-powered figures to intercede on their behalf we need to look at the connections Weymouth and Sandwich had at Westminster and beyond.

One way to do this is to explore the anti-Wilkes coalition within parliament. In April 1769 the *North Briton* published the names of those MPs that had voted to expel Wilkes from the Commons in 1768, alongside the names of those that had supported him or had abstained. In doing so they were careful to draw the public's attention to the connections these men had.[123] Among those voting to expel Wilkes was George Selwyn; described therein as 'Surveyor of the Mint, paymaster of the Board of Works, and Register of the Chancery in Barbados', all sinecures that afforded him a considerable income. Lord Weymouth's brother, Henry Thynne, also voted against Wilkes and was listed as 'master of the King's Household'. This key role meant that Thynne was effectively in charge of all the king's servants from the kitchens to the bedchambers. However, it is another name on this list that really helps to explain the brothers' connections to power and influence. Grey Cooper MP was listed as a 'secretary to the Treasury'. Cooper's wife was named Elizabeth Kennedy and her two sisters were regular attenders at court. One of these two sisters was known as 'Poll' (suggesting her given name was Mary), and the suggestion made by the contemporary press was that they were notorious courtesans. Cooper and Sandwich were on close social terms, so now we have the connection that helps to explain why Matthew and Patrick escaped the noose: they had family in positions of influence within the closest circles of government. And it would seem that the 'notorious Poll Kennedy' might well have been intimately connected to Sandwich himself. It appears to have been an open secret that it was Sandwich and his 'political influence' that saved them from the rope. Was Poll Sandwich's mistress? This is the allegation laid by Renwick, which he attributes to contemporary commentators.[124] Nor was this the first time that the Kennedy sisters had influenced events; the *Whisperer* commented that the sister (who was described as being 'in very good keeping') had been able to intervene with 'the Russian, or some foreign ambassador' to procure a 'protection for one Samuel Phipps'. Phipps (a convict) had been allowed to stay at home while others had been forced into the Navy. This was achieved 'by the imposition of a common prostitute'.[125] Donna Andrew has written that the morality of politicians was increasingly under scrutiny in the late eighteenth century. 'Of course men in public life had always been chastised for various kinds of corruption' she writes,

> but, until this period, it was the sins of venality rather than those of immorality, that were seen as the most frequent, and attacked as the most nationally threatening vices of the ruling classes . . . what was new, however, was the focus on other kinds of personal and political vice.

This is in evidence in the Kennedy case where it is suggestion that corruption in high office is linked to sexual favours offered by 'Poll' Kennedy to ensure that her brothers escaped the lawful and proper punishment that had been prescribed for them.[126]

This helps explain the campaign of support for Anne Bigby and against the clemency shown towards the brothers. The critics of government led this and, more specifically, the critics of Mansfield and the corrupt judiciary he represented. The attempt to 'screen murderers from suffering' was evidence, one correspondent wrote, of corruption in high office.[127] Another complained that it demonstrated the 'weakness of [the] administration, who on many late occasions have known neither when to dispense with the law, nor when to put them in execution'.[128] So this was an example of how, as Stewart Jay has framed it, a 'cohesive opposition developed around a series of questions related to the central theme of the excessive power of the executive ministry'.[129] Thus the brothers owed their lives to the connections made, not by themselves but by their sister, who (according to Blackstone's report of the collapsed trial at King's Bench) 'was intimately connected with some Persons of Quality'.[130] By contrast, Blackstone described Anne's supporters as a 'set of persons in London, who were in violent opposition to the government' who acted 'merely to raise an Odium and popular Clamour'.[131] Clearly he meant Horne Tooke and the *Middlesex Journal*. Anne's appeal was allegedly financed by the Commissioners for Lighting and Watching in Westminster (who oversaw the watch and so had a vested interest in protecting their 'people'). However, the support for the Bigby cause was part of a wider attack on Mansfield, government, and the king, orchestrated by the anonymous writer of the *Letters of Junius* and others.[132] 'Junius' and others harked back to the Wilkes affair during their criticism of the government and king. The Kennedy case was used along with other infamous attempts to influence 'justice'. The pardoning of the Kennedys was linked with that of Edward McQuirke, an Irish chairman that had killed one of Wilkes' supporters during the election of Sergeant Glynn a few years earlier.[133] Sandwich was described in the *North Briton* as a 'constant companion of bawds and bullies'; the first a likely reference to Poll Kennedy and the second to McQuirke and the other so-called Brentford ruffians that had taken part in Sir William Proctor's campaign to contest the Middlesex seat with Glynn.[134] Crusovite condemned Weymouth and Mansfield within his list of 'persons obnoxious' in an open letter to the king in March 1770.[135] Similarly 'Junius' criticized George III for allowing men such as North, Weymouth, and Sandwich to hold positions of power. They were, he declared, a 'Satyr upon all government'.[136] Lord Mansfield was explicitly included in this 'cabal of elites' who were 'responsible for the evils of the kingdom'.[137] Mansfield, like Bute before him, was also a Scot, making him vulnerable as 'a target of English prejudice' but it was his position in the so-called secret ministry that marked him out for Junius' attention.[138]

However, this government was far from being as weak as the opposition suggested. Lord North was an 'able' politician and having ridden out the Wilkes affair the administration had emerged seemingly stronger.[139] Indeed it was the opposition that lacked strong leadership and the infighting between elements of Wilkes' original supporters helped North consolidate.[140] While there may well have been plenty of people who agreed that corruption in high office was a scourge on the nation state, the problem, as an early historian of the period wrote, 'was that the co-operation between these forces was imperfect'.[141] The 'Bloomsbury Gang' may have drawn criticism from commentators but they seem to have been all but untouchable in the early 1770s. This 'strength' or immunity to criticism ultimately benefitted those on whom they chose to help through their influence, in this case Matthew and Patrick Kennedy.

Conclusions

It seems then that a newspaper propaganda war was fought with the Kennedy case being used as a proxy for a political battle between those that supported the government and those that opposed it. Central to this was the argument surrounding corruption in public office and the transparency of decision-making. Hay has argued that for the pardoning process to work smoothly and successfully it had to retain its sense of mystery;[142] those involved had to remain in the shadows, away from public scrutiny. In this case, however, the whole process of seeking a reprieve and then a conditional pardon for the brothers took place in full view of an interested and well-informed reading public. The number of newspaper mentions of the case (in news items and correspondence) suggests that the fate of the Kennedys was a lively topic of conversation. The identities of those involved were hardly obscured and the legitimacy of the decision was widely challenged. So what does this mean for Hay's thesis?

Hay wrote that petitions for pardon 'were most effective from great men'.[143] The Kennedy case certainly conforms to this model but then so did that of Thomas Gordon (whose case is examined in Chapter 4). As will be seen there, Gordon's father had connections that enabled him to bring two major aristocratic houses into play in the attempt to save his son. He had a personal audience with George III and one of his supporters was a close friend of the Prime Minister. Yet the young Gordon was executed, and on far more flimsy evidence than that used to convict the Kennedy brothers.[144] It would seem that elite connections on their own were not enough; timing is everything. Matthew and Patrick Kennedy were condemned and pardoned in a period of relative political calm for the king and his ministers. They had survived 'Wilkes and Liberty', and the revolt of the American colonies was still around the corner. The brothers also had a powerful ally in their sister who was at court and intimately involved (in all senses of the word) with the decision-makers that mattered. The papers roundly criticized the king and his ministers for being influenced by 'a common prostitute' but Sandwich simply ignored this. After all, he was a known womanizer and gambler who kept a series of mistresses; this 'scandal' was hardly a revelation. Mansfield was widely criticized by his opponents but revered by his friends and he too could ride out any criticism of his decision-making in the case. He had probably conducted the King's Bench trial in such a way that was legal but likely to confound Anne Bigby's purpose by use of clever tactics. The odds were stacked against her from the start; she had support but it was not as rich or as powerful as that behind the killers of the watchman.

Hay argues that in the aftermath of the 'riots of 1760 and 1780, Wilkes and the French Revolution', the English ruling class was determined to 'repel any attacks on the mystery and majesty of the law'.[145] This case suggests that while they may have attempted to do this they sometimes failed. The pardoning process was dragged through the press for several years and was used as a political weapon to criticize an administration that was seen as corrupt and filled with placemen. There can hardly have been anyone able to read or to understand what was read to him that was unaware of the controversy surrounding Poll Kennedy and her relationship with Sandwich and other members of the ruling elite. There is little 'mystery and majesty' here. Possibly, as King and Ward have recently argued, the criminal justice system worked differently outside of the capital.[146] Perhaps in the provinces and on the periphery deference was in better shape than it was in the metropolis.

Peter King offered a constructive critique of Hay's thesis in 1984, suggesting that the pardoning process was more nuanced and based on a more pragmatic rationale than Hay allowed, but the reality is that neither thesis is wholly satisfactory.[147] Elite connections did matter but only so long as they were the right connections at the right time. The nature of the criminal and the crime were certainly important factors in saving thousands of property offenders from the gallows, as King argues, but in this case a very brutal murder of an entirely innocent victim was completely unjustifiable, and yet the brothers walked (or rather sailed) away to relative freedom. They were 'respectable' but their sister was anything but. Anne Bigby, spurred on by her politically motivated backers, came close to usurping the pardoning process but at the final hurdle she succumbed (very understandably it has to be said) to immense pressure exerted by powerful individuals. Her agency was undermined but she walked away a much wealthier woman than she started. This was hardly recompense for the loss of her husband, of course, but many would have seen it as a legitimate form of compensation. Horne Tooke refused to condemn her for this supposed avarice. He argued that the appeal was being used as it had been intended: to provide compensation for the loss of a family member. In this context perhaps it is necessary to re-evaluate the motivations of individuals who chose to pursue these sorts of legal actions.

What this case study demonstrates is that the English justice system was 'shot through with discretion', as King tell us, and that 'discretion' was exercised at all levels. One's ability to use discretion, however, was severely limited by access to money, political influence, and legal knowledge. This chapter has offered a glimpse into the workings of the Hanoverian justice system and its intersection with statue and common law in theory and practice. It demonstrates the importance of seeing the criminal law as a much less monolithic structure than Hay allowed for and one where discretion based on the nature of the crime committed and the age and status of the offender was perhaps less important than King has suggested. In the next chapter, we can explore a case that has strong similarities (at least in terms of the level of 'reasonable doubt' that surrounded the guilt of the key protagonist). However, here the outcome was very different: the person accused of murder was convicted and executed within days of the killing he was found responsible for. There was no appeal process, no attempts by 'persons of quality' to save his life. In fact the opposite was largely true – he was hanged because it was expedient to hang him, as an example to others.

Notes

1. *Middlesex Journal or Chronicle of Liberty*, 3–5 April 1770.
2. Hay, 'Property, Authority and the Criminal Law'.
3. Ibid., p. 45.
4. King, 'Decision-Makers and Decision-Making'.
5. Ibid.
6. Douglas Hay, 'Writing About the Death Penalty', *Legal History*, Vol. 6 (2006), p. 45; King, *Crime, Justice and Discretion*, pp. 315–19.
7. Gatrell, *Hanging Tree*, pp. 42–43.
8. King, 'Decision-Makers and Decision-Making'.
9. Gray and King, 'The Killing of Constable Linnell'.
10. David Lemmings, 'Negotiating Justice in the New Public Sphere', in David Lemmings (ed.), *Crime, Courts and the Press in Early Eighteenth-Century Britain 1750–1850* (Farnham, Ashgate, 2012), p. 302.
11. Hay, 'Property, Authority and the Criminal Law'.
12. The one exception being W. R. Riddell, 'Appeal of Death and Its Abolition', *Michigan Law Review*, 24 (8) (June 1926), pp. 786–808.
13. Junius, *The Letters of Junius* (London, 1804).

14. Gray and King, 'The Killing of Constable Linnell'.
15. Old Bailey Online [OBO], Matthew Kennedy, Patrick Kennedy, Michael McMohan, John Evans, Murder 21 February 1770, t17700221-44.
16. Ibid.
17. Ibid.
18. P. Clark, *The English Alehouse: A Social History* (London, 1983), pp. 257–58.
19. Ibid.
20. Ibid.
21. Ibid.
22. Reynolds, *Before the Bobbies*.
23. Ibid., p. 22.
24. OBO, t17700221-44.
25. Ibid.
26. *Bingley's Journal*, 23–30 May 1772.
27. OBO, t17700221-44.
28. Ibid.
29. *General Evening Post*, 22 February 1770.
30. OBO, t17700221-44.
31. Ibid.
32. Ibid.
33. Ibid.
34. Rabin, 'Drunkenness and Responsibility for Crime', p. 477.
35. *General Evening Post*, 22–24 February 1770.
36. Linebaugh, *The London Hanged*.
37. *Lloyd's Evening Post*, 23 February 1770.
38. *London Evening Post*, 24–27 February 1770.
39. Hay, 'Property, Authority and the Criminal Law'.
40. Beattie, *Policing and Punishment in London*, p. 452.
41. *London Evening Post*, 28 June 1770.
42. *London Evening Post*, 27 February 1770–1 March 1770.
43. J. Cannon, 'Montagu, George, 4th Duke of Manchester (1737–1788)', *Dictionary of National Biography*.
44. J. Cannon, 'Savile, Sir George (1726–1784)', *Dictionary of National Biography*.
45. *Gazetteer and New Daily Advertiser*, 2 March 1770.
46. P. Carter, 'Selwyn George Augustus (1719–1791)', *Dictionary of National Biography*.
47. P. M. Geoghegan, 'Howard, Frederick, 5th Earl of Carlisle (1748–1825)', *Dictionary of National Biography*.
48. www.historyofparliamentonline.org/volume/1790-1820/member/spencer-robert-1747-1831 [accessed 15 December 2015].
49. *General Evening Post*, 3–6 March 1770.
50. *Westminster Journal*, 10 March 1770.
51. *Independent Chronicle*, 14–16 March 1770.
52. See for example the work of Randall McGowen, John Beattie, V. A. Gatrell, and Simon Devereaux in discussing the end of the 'bloody code' in the early nineteenth century, as noted in the previous chapter.
53. Ibid.
54. *Lloyd's Evening Post*, 14 March 1770; *Gazetteer and New Daily Advertiser*, 18 May 1770.
55. *Lloyd's Evening Post*, 14–16 March 1770.
56. Hay, 'Property, Authority and the Criminal Law'.
57. *General Evening Post*, 12–16 April 1770.

58. *Northampton Mercury*, 23 April 1770.
59. *London Evening Post*, 13-16/4/1770.
60. Morgan and Rushton, *Eighteenth-Century Criminal Transportation*.
61. Ekirch, *Bound for America*, p. 119.
62. It would appear that it was common for agreements to be reached with individual captains of boats travelling to America to carry the convicts even after the practice of transportation was formalized under legislation passed in 1718. The placing of convicts on ships was negotiated by contractors who were paid around £5 each for their services by the borough; this was organized by the local justices. The carriers were supposed to return a certificate that declared they had successfully discharged their commission. Unfortunately these certificates rarely survive. D. M. M. Shorrocks, 'Transportation of Felons from Sandwich to Virginia, 1721–1773', *The Virginia Magazine of History and Biography*, 68 (3) (July 1960), pp. 295–300.
63. The Earl of Fife to George Selwyn, 28 April 1770 in J. H. Jesse, *George Selwyn and His Contemporaries, with Memoirs and Notes* (London, 1843), 389.
64. Fife had written a letter of introduction to a friend in Maryland 'who will be vastly good to him', in Jesse, *George Selwyn*, 389.
65. The Appeal was abolished in 1819.
66. Gregory Durston, *Crime and Justice in Early Modern England: 1500–1750* (Chichester, Barry Rose Limited, 2004), p. 631.
67. E.g., Christopher Slaughter (in 1709); James Clough (1729). The last was Abraham Thornton (1817). See E. A. Kendall, *An Argument for Construing Largely the Right of an Appellees of Murder to Insist on His Wager of Battle and Also for Abrogating Writs of Appeal* (London, 1818); R. V. Barnewall, *Reports of Cases Argued and Determined in the Court of King's Bench* (London, 1818).
68. Sir James Burrow, *Reports of Cases Argued and Adjudged in the Court of King's Bench During the Time Lord Mansfield etc.* (London, 1790).
69. Riddell, 'Appeal of Death'.
70. Kendall, *An Argument*.
71. Ibid., p. 9.
72. William Blackstone, *Commentaries on the Laws of England*, Vol. 4 (Chicago, University of Chicago Press, 1979).
73. Kendall, *An Argument*, p. 71.
74. Ibid., p. 49.
75. 'A man shall not be vexed twice for the same cause'. Renwick, 'Appeal of Death', p. 803.
76. Renwick, 'Appeal of Death', p. 793.
77. From Cobbett's *Parliamentary History*, Vol. XVIII, 1291 quoted in Kendall, *An Argument*, p. 302.
78. Renwick, 'Appeal of Death', p. 806.
79. Ibid.
80. 59 Geo III c.46 (1819) *An Act to Abolish Appeals of Murder etc.*
81. One in 1726 'when a French barber was tried at the Old Bailey for murdering his wife, whose brother brought an appeal' *General Evening Post*, 26 May 1770.
82. *Independent Chronicle*, 27–30 April 1770.
83. *Dublin Mercury*, 10 May 1770.
84. *Lloyd's Evening Post*, 23–26 February 1770.
85. *General Evening Post*, 26 May 1770.
86. Burrow, *Reports of Cases*, p. 2650.
87. Ibid., p. 2643.

88. 'As Chief Justice of King's Bench, Mansfield became involved in a number of prosecutions of interest to the Crown. He presided over a series of controversial seditious libel trials, most notably the trials in 1764 of John Wilkes (and the printers of Wilkes's manuscripts) and the 1770 proceedings against the publishers of the 'Junius' letters. During these cases Mansfield received unflattering notices in the press for insisting that the issues of whether intent and sedition had been proven were questions for the court – not the jury – to decide. Mansfield, however, regarded his service in libel cases as one means to arrest what he regarded as the "calamitous decline" of the nation'. Stewart Jay, *Most Humble Servants: The Advisory Role of Early Judges* (New Haven and London, Yale University Press, 1997), p. 38.

89. William Blackstone, *Reports of Cases Determined in the Several Courts of Westminster-Hall, from 1746. to 1779*, Vol. 2 (London, 1828), p. 715.

90. Arthur Lyon Cross, 'Judges in the British Cabinet and the Struggle Which Led to Their Exclusion After 1806', *Michigan Law Review*, 20 (1) (November 1921), p. 27.

91. John Horne to Mr. Wilkes, *Middlesex Journal*, 8–10 January 1771.

92. *Middlesex Journal*, 5–7 June 1770.

93. *Middlesex Journal*, 6–9 October 1770.

94. *Gazetteer and New Daily Advertiser*, 15 October 1770.

95. *Lloyd's Evening Post*, 31 October 1770–2 November 1770.

96. Renwick, 'Appeal of Death', p. 806.

97. Blackstone, *Reports of Cases*, p. 716.

98. *Dodsley's Annual Register*, 1770, 161.

99. *Middlesex Journal*, 26 May 1770.

100. *London Evening Post*, 13–16 April 1771.

101. *Whisperer*, 26 January 1771.

102. Ibid.

103. *Middlesex Journal*, 26–28 February 1771.

104. *General Evening Post*, 2–4 April 1771.

105. *Bingley's Journal*, 20–27 April 1771.

106. While convicts were sent to most of the American colonies during the late seventeenth and early eighteenth centuries, more were sent to Virginia and Maryland than to the other settlements. In the second half of the 1700s, more than 10,000 men and women were transported to Maryland alone (Butler. 1896. 19.) The reason for this was commercial: as producers of tobacco Maryland and Virginia had much more need for bonded labour and ship's captains had more incentive to travel to southern ports where they could fill their hulls with tobacco for the return voyage to England.

107. *Middlesex Journal*, 6–9 July 1771. James Davie Butler, 'British Convicts Shipped to American Colonies', *The American Historical Review*, 2 (1) (October 1896), pp. 12–33.

108. July 1770 Scarsdale under Captain Christopher Reed (London).

109. *Bingley's Journal*, 7–14 March 1772; *London Evening Post*, 10–12 March 1772.

110. *General Evening Post*, 7–9 April 1772.

111. *Middlesex Journal*, 7–9 April 1772.

112. *Middlesex Journal*, 14–16 April 1772.

113. *London Evening Post*, 8–11 August 1772.

114. *Middlesex Journal*, 11–13 August 1772.

115. *Independent Chronicle*, 16–18 April 1770.

116. *Morning Chronicle*, 19 August 1772.

117. *Northampton Mercury*, 23 April 1770.

118. Jesse, *George Selwyn*, p. 391.

119. OBO, t17700221-44.
120. *Gazetter and Daily Advertiser*, 18 May 1770.
121. Hay, 'Writing About the Death Penalty', p. 45.
122. N. A. M. Rodger, *The Insatiable Earl: A Life of John Montagu, Fourth Earl of Sandwich, 1718–1792* (London, Norton, 1993).
123. *North Briton*, 15 April 1769.
124. Sadly he provides no sources for this, however, 'Lord Sandwich, Grey Cooper and his wife, and the two miss Kennedies [sic] her sisters' and were reported to 'have supped together at Vauxhall'. *Middlesex Journal*, 6–9 July 1771.
125. *Whisperer*, 26 January 1771.
126. Donna T. Andrew, *The Attack on Duelling, Suicide, Adultery, and Gambling in Eighteenth-Century England* (New Haven and London, Yale University Press, 2013), pp. 136–37.
127. *Gazetteer and New Daily Advertiser*, 18 May 1770.
128. *London Evening Post*, 3–5 May 1770.
129. Jay, *Most Humble Servants*, p. 35.
130. Blackstone, *Reports of Cases*, p. 716.
131. Ibid.
132. W. Bird, 'Liberties of Press and Speech: "Evidence Does Not Exist to Contradict the . . . Blackstonian Sense" in Late 18th Century England?' *Oxford Journal of Legal Studies* (2015), pp. 1–25.
133. Watson, *The Reign of George III*, p. 133; George Rudé, *Wilkes and Liberty: A Social Study of 1763 to 1774* (Oxford, Oxford University Press, 1962), p. 59.
134. *North Briton*, 16 June 1770; Rudé, *Wilkes and Liberty*, p. 61.
135. *Middlesex Journal*, 6–8 March 1770.
136. *London Evening Post*, 31 March 1770–3 April 1770. According to T. H. Bowyer, the 'immediate objective of the young Philip Francis in the series of pseudonymous letters signed Junius and Philo Junius, which were published at intervals in the *Public Advertiser* between 1769 and 1772 when the author was aged between twenty-nine and thirty-two, was to encompass the downfall of the Grafton administration and, subsequently, the North administration, in anticipation of their replacement by a ministry drawn from the opposition'. T. H. Bowyer, 'Junius, Philip Francis and Parliamentary Reform', *Albion: A Quarterly Journal Concerned with British Studies*, Vol. 21, No. 3 (Autumn 1995), p. 397.
137. Cross, 'Judges in the British Cabinet', p. 28. Carolyn Steedman has questioned whether Mansfield really deserves his reputation as a staunch foe of radicalism. She suggests that such depictions owe more to Charles Dickens' characterization of him and the Gordon rioters' reaction to him (in *Barnaby Rudge*. 1841) than they do to the reality of the man. Carolyn Steedman, 'Lord Mansfield's Women', *Past & Present*, No. 176 (August 2006), p. 105.
138. Jay, *Most Humble Servants*, p. 36.
139. Watson, *The Reign of George III*, p. 131.
140. Rodger, *The Insatiable Earl*, p. 128.
141. Leslie Stephen, 'Chatham, Francis, and Junius', *The English Historical Review*, Vol. 3, No. 10 (April 1888), p. 234.
142. Hay, 'Property, Authority and the Criminal Law'.
143. Ibid., p. 45.
144. Gray and King, 'The Killing of Constable Linnell'.
145. Hay, 'Property, Authority and the Criminal Law', p. 59.
146. Ward and King, 'Rethinking the Bloody Code'.
147. King, 'Decision-Makers and Decision-Making'.

3 'There Goes Clarke, That Blood-Selling Rascal'

Murder, Revenge, and the Crowd in Early 1770s Spitalfields

Introduction

In 1771 a brutal and very public killing was committed in Spitalfields, East London that offers us another window into the nature of homicide and its prosecution in the late eighteenth century. Here too politics and access to patronage were arguably important factors but unlike in the case of Matthew and Patrick Kennedy the circumstances pertaining here made mercy impossible. Instead this homicide and its prosecution reveal the full and unbridled power of the Hanoverian state to use the criminal justice system to make examples of those that dared to transgress or challenge its authority. It also demonstrates the importance of controlling the narrative (something that was almost entirely absent in the case described in the previous chapter). Here there were large numbers of witnesses and multiple perpetrators but community solidarity and intimidation limited attempts to determine guilt, and the power of the state's actors ensured that the official version of events remained dominant. In the end the authorities framed a prosecution in a carefully constructed manner to ensure that examples could be made in a long running dispute within the weaving community of East London.

This chapter will follow a similar pattern to that which precedes it: it will start by outlining the events that took place in Spitalfields in mid-April 1771 before looking at the trial that followed and its outcome. In this case the narrative is much shorter because the key protagonist (the man accused of murder) was not able to marshal powerful forces to prevent justice from taking its course. Instead he was whisked off to Newgate Gaol and executed within days of conviction. Moreover, this hanging was carried out close to the scene of the killing, as a very visible statement of the criminal justice system's authority. The case produced a considerable amount of archival material (more indeed than that of the Kennedy brothers) but the nature of this material is quite different to that produced in the case of Thomas Gordon (in Chapter 4) in that it demonstrates the underlying reasons for executing the condemned, rather than pointing to reasons to spare him. These reasons will be discussed throughout this chapter and returned to at the end. They have much to do with local and London politics, with the nature of the justice system and the value (or otherwise) of informers, and the prevailing power of the state. Let us begin however by exploring the events that led to the deaths of three men in 1771.

The Killing of Daniel Clarke

Tuesday, April 16, 1771 was a bitterly cold day. Apparently it snowed 'very fast', forcing one of the key witnesses to events that day to retreat at some point and take shelter from the elements. The weather is significant because it may have increased the likelihood that the victim of this crime would have died of exposure, while also making the identification of his killers that much more difficult. This lack of clarity was useful to those in power at the time. The poor visibility, a chaotic scenario, and an overreliance on the testimony of selective witnesses probably contributed to obscuring the identities of the real perpetrators and suggests that the authorities were more interested in finding scapegoats for the murder than they were in discovering whom had committed it. As with the Kennedy case we are reliant on a constructed narrative of what happened that afternoon and so throughout this it is necessary to see where alternative interpretations of 'evidence' might lead us to quite different conclusions to that reached by an Old Bailey jury later that spring.

Various witnesses testified to seeing a middle-aged man named Daniel Clarke, a pattern drawer who worked within the silk trade in Spitalfields, running through the streets around Brick Lane pursued by a growing crowd of angry people. Clarke would have made a decent living as a pattern drawer, earning perhaps 25–30s a week.[1] He was certainly wealthy enough to wear a wig and own a brace of pistols because he lost the former on his head as he ran, and he called for the latter (and a spare wig) when he took refuge at the house of his friend Mr Snee, who lived nearby in Cock Lane. In the 1770s Cock Lane ran from Shoreditch church yard down towards Whitechapel before it turned sharp left and out on to the open fields to the east of Shoreditch and Spitalfields. The pursuit of Clarke had started in Half Nichol Street, where he had been accompanying Benjamin West (a master weaver) to examine some silk work. Clarke was initially attacked by two men who were part of a small group of locals who evidently had issues with the pattern drawer. As Clarke was punched and kicked and knocked to the ground, someone called out, 'There goes Clarke, that blood-selling rascal!', or words to that effect. Clarke recovered himself sufficiently to evade his assailants and ducked down an alley or passageway that led to Cock Lane. There he quickly found the home of Mrs Snee and banged on the door to be let in. Mary Snee helped him inside and then dispatched a servant to Clarke's wife to get her to bring the items he asked (his pistols and a spare wig) while Clarke looked for a safe way out of the house to avoid the 'mob'.[2]

Ultimately this all failed him however. By now upwards of a hundred men, women, and boys were chasing him and baying for his blood. Clarke had been identified as an informer in the trial of two Spitalfields weavers who had been executed on the evidence he had offered at their trial some 16 months earlier.[3] I will return to that case and its importance later but for now it is necessary to continue with the narrative of Clarke's murder.

Clarke was not safe at the Snees' home once the 'mob' that pursued him realized he was there. He had opened the door to face them down, threatening one man with his pistols. That failed to do any good; he may have got hold of his guns but when confronted by one of his pursuers he either baulked at using them or the weapons failed to fire. Clarke retreated inside and wondered what to do next. Meanwhile the crowd outside had started to throw things at Mary Snee's windows. With the shutters open there was a very real chance they would break in so Clarke needed to find an exit and Mrs Snee needed him to vacate as soon as possible. He begged her not to let the crowd inside and she held on as long as she could. Four windows were broken and cries of 'D–n him, turn him out!', ' burn him, or drown him', were heard outside before a loud thump on the front door indicated that the crowd was trying to force entry.[4] Finally Daniel Clarke went down into the cellar and got out into the garden behind the house. Mrs Snee opened the door and the incomers demanded she hand him over. A cry went up that he had escaped over into the gardens behind the house (not the Snee's but those belonging to a commercial gardener) and the hunting pack set off after him.

According to the confused witness statements heard by an Old Bailey courtroom three months later, Clarke was already battered and bleeding by the time he reached Mrs Snee and the abuse he suffered continued in the streets thereafter. He was chased south, towards Spitalfields market and Christ's Church, and was next identified by two separate witnesses at the corner of White Lyon Street (or Yard) and Wheeler Street. Here the crowd had managed to corner Clarke and forced him up against wall where he sank onto his haunches. As the crowd circled him at least one man pushed through them to attack Clarke with a horsewhip. This beating supposedly lasted for a minute and then the crowd was off and after the struggling man as he tried to run away from them. Eventually they chased or dragged him to the open space east of Brick Lane known then as Weavers' Fields where a pond had been dug out as a result of brick-making in the area for many years.[5] Lifting him onto a small bridge, the crowd pitched Clarke into the water and some men followed him in to hold his head under.[6]

What followed was chaos. Clarke had been stripped to his breeches and was bleeding from several wounds. Small boys and others in the group were throwing stones and brickbats at him; others were calling him names and accusing him of being a paid informer who 'would swear peoples lives away'.[7] Stones rained down on him and he periodically struggled to his feet before being knocked back into the water. On at least two occasions select sympathetic or concerned members of the watching crowd tried to affect a rescue and so periodically Clarke was pulled clear of the water only to be thrown, or dragged, back in again. The crowd partly dispersed when they heard that 'Mr Fielding's men' (the Bow Street officers or 'runners') were on their way, but resumed their violence when that rumour proved false.

At some point (and it is far from clear exactly when) Daniel Clarke died as a result of this abuse, probably expiring at sometime around four in the afternoon. His traumatic experience had therefore lasted at least four hours (as he was first placed in Cock Lane around midday by a weaver he drew patterns for, Benjamin West). He had probably died from exhaustion and exposure as much as from any individual killing wound he sustained (his injuries were multiple and the result of 'different' blows to his head and body).[8] It was mob violence at its worse and the authorities (with no professional police force) were impotent in the face of it and so unable to save his life. The local constables would have been ineffectual and deputies could not be arranged at such short notice; the watch were not called out to the evening and the only other option was for the area's magistrates to call for military backup. This was something they were certainly prepared to do when it came to saving their own skins but not, it seems, when it was required to protect the person of a local craftsman who had angered his own community. However, the authorities, in the person of one of the local justices of the peace, David Wilmot, were determined that someone would be held accountable for Clarke's murder. This did not prove that easy to achieve however, as the people of Spitalfields, and most importantly its working class silk weaving community, closed ranks against outside authority and refused to give up the culprits. At this point, it seems, it became less important to find and prosecute the murderer or murderers and more important to present the state with suitable persons that could be held accountable for the death. The search for scapegoats now began in earnest.

The Arrest of the 'Usual Suspects'

Of the four case studies with which this volume is concerned, only this one has a sheaf of prosecution case notes that survives.[9] These contain the recorded depositions of the main witnesses (which are also held in the sessions files for the Old Bailey)[10] and the 'notes' and 'observations' of the prosecuting counsel. This then allows us to reconstruct the prosecution case from the Treasury Solicitor's perspective and to see how this might have been put across in court. Coupled with the version of the trial as recorded in the OBSP, this offers us an interesting insight into what concerned the prosecutors and what evidence they felt offered the best chance of a conviction. This however was also potentially quite different from what actually happened that April afternoon, and who was responsible for it.

It took a long time before Justice Wilmot was able to provide the crown with three suspects for Daniel Clarke's murder. By the time the trial reached the Old Bailey, three months had passed and it was only towards the end of this that all three of the accused were in custody. The three persons suspected of responsibility for Clarke's murder were Robert Campbell (a man with strong connections to the weaver's struggle against the reduction in their wages and conditions), Sarah (or Antis) Horsford (whose husband William had been hanged in December 1769 for breaking looms), and Henry Stroud, a local gardener. What is immediately clear from the Treasury Solicitor's case notes is that while there is a very strong body of evidence gathered against Robert Campbell, there is much less affecting Henry Stroud and very little that concerned Antis Horsford. Nevertheless the recommendation of the prosecutors was that an indictment of murder be brought solely against Stroud, and that he and Campbell be cited as 'aiders and abettors'.[11] However, nearly all the witnesses who saw Clarke in Spitalfields (either being chased through the streets or surrounded in the pond at Hare Street Fields) testified that he was attacked by numerous persons, many of whom were young lads throwing stones. The surgeon's report into Clarke's death found that he had suffered multiple wounds ('eleven contused wounds on his head') and that 'the different blows he received on the head were the cause of his death, *no one in particular*' [my italics].[12] The evidence suggests quite clearly then that Daniel Clarke was killed by a mob with no one person being directly responsible. This would have been an uncomfortable and unsatisfactory conclusion for the Old Bailey petty jury to reach, however, and so the authorities needed to pin the blame for the murder on one or more individuals whom it could be shown had the means, opportunity, and motive to kill the unfortunate pattern dresser. Robert Campbell was wanted in connection with the attacks on Clarke's looms, Antis Horsford's husband had been hanged for his involvement in the weavers' riots, and Henry Stroud was related by marriage to William Eastman, an individual who had been executed as a direct consequence of Clarke's testimony. Moreover Stroud, as was revealed at his trial, had a previous conviction for violence, even if (as will be shown later) the circumstances of this rather supported his version of events, not that of those that gave evidence against him.

In the immediate aftermath of Clarke's murder the magistrates tasked with investigating it encountered a wall of silence.[13] A rotation office existed in the area (at Whitechapel, one of three established in 1763) where the three most active justices were David Wilmot, Mr Camper, and Mr Digby. Previous histories have explored the dissatisfaction contemporaries felt with the magistracy in London in the 1700s, especially those dubbed 'trading justices' in Middlesex.[14] At best many men like Wilmot were viewed as incompetent or inefficient while at worst they were seen as venal and corrupt. As Norma Landau has written, in London (or rather in Middlesex, as the City of London was quite differently organized and perceived[15]) 'justice was a business'.[16] This prevailing opinion is illustrated by a letter sent to the Earl of Rochford by an anonymous correspondent on April 27, just 11 days after the disturbances in Spitalfields that ended in Clarke's death. Rochford, a seemingly diligent and competent diplomat and minister, had taken over from Thomas Thynne, the 3rd Viscount Weymouth, as southern secretary of state in December 1770. Weymouth's frequent absences may have meant that Rochford (who by 1771 was in his early 50s) had been, in effect, overseeing both the northern and southern offices until Henry Howard took over the northern role.[17] Rochford was a busy man and his biographer describes him as a capable reformer who rewarded those that served him. As Southern minister, he had wide remit overseeing

> civil, church and military appointments, grants of office, petitions to the Crown, licenses, patents, inventions, passports, pardons for criminals and correspondence with the judges, orders to the Admiralty and the Secretary at War, and a great mass of miscellaneous correspondence.[18]

The person that wrote to Rochford was unwilling to give his name but assured the secretary that he was well qualified to comment. This suggests the author was local to Spitalfields and was probably a man like Lewis Chauvet, a master weaver who had suffered at the hands of the weavers in their dispute about pay and conditions. The letter writer declared himself astonished at the events of the April 16:

> An innocent man murdered with every circumstance of cruelty, the work of many hours in broad day light, Justices of the peace on the spot surrounded with all needful assistance and I doubt not aided by government and yet none of the guilty apprehended.[19]

He insisted that the 'cutters' (the weavers that attacked the looms of masters that they held responsible for their woes) were involved and that they were being protected by the silence instilled by intimidation and by the cowering of the local magistracy. There was some truth in this. It was notoriously difficult for the authorities to arrest weavers suspected of rioting or involvement in direct actions against masters. During riots, crowds prevented the magistrates' men and constables from coming close or fought them off and rescued those arrested. During the long week of rioting that broke out in June 1780 after Lord George Gordon rallied support against parliament's attempt to dilute laws designed to exclude Catholics from participation in public life, rioters tore down the homes of magistrates involved, set fire to several gaols (including Newgate), and attempted to secure the release of those arrested. At the trial of William Eastman for the attacks on his property, Daniel Clarke had testified to the threats he received to keep quiet and not press charges. As the men retreated from Clarke's house, one came close to him and said: 'if he ever heard such a report of me he would cut my ears off'.[20] While the letter writer said that he regarded Wilmot as 'a very honest man' he described him as 'terrified' and accused the local justices of neglecting their responsibilities in the days following the murder. He called for more action and for the arrest of numerous 'old offenders' still at large following the weavers' riots earlier in the year.[21] The secretary of state (or more likely Porten the under secretary) forwarded the letter to David Wilmot who responded two days later. Wilmot was keen to reassure the southern secretary that he was doing everything he could and things were not as out of control as the letter writer had intimated. However, his reply reveals his frustration with the lack of information he had thus far been able to gather as he commented: 'not one of the witnesses is now to be heard of or found'. He dismissed the suggestion made by the anonymous letter writer that he and his officers should simply round up everyone suspected of being involved previously as counterproductive and impossible. Even if he had been able to 'apprehend all the Old Cutters the principal evidence against them was missing':[22] The key witnesses to the past troubles were Thomas Poor and his wife, who had already fled to Ireland to avoid intimidation, and Daniel Clarke, who was of course dead because he hadn't. Wilmot nevertheless assured Rochford that the rotation office was sitting daily and he had sent out men to hunt down the suspects and gather information. In common with contemporary practice, he had placed an advertisement for information with the newspapers and was desperately trying to find Robert Campbell, who was mentioned as the 'principal actor' in the anonymous letter Rochford had shared with him.

Wilmot comes across as a local magistrate who was a little out of his depth but attempting to retain his position of (limited) power and influence. As the case unfolded, he sought to reassure the secretary that he was dealing with the issue while at the same time asking for help and involving his senior colleague Sir John Fielding at Bow Street. One of the considerations here then is the need that Wilmot had to find culprits that could be put on trial and convicted of Clarke's murder. Evidently very many people were culpable in the death of the pattern cutter but it seems that only Robert Campbell could be clearly identified as acting directly to cause Clarke's demise (by holding his head under water). For Wilmot and his fellow justices the very real fear of reprisals was also a factor that affected their ability to prosecute the case. Wilmot may have 'talked tough' in his letter to the secretary of state but the accusation that he was 'terrified' is supported by later actions that he took.

The Spitalfields Weavers' Dispute

It is impossible to remove the trial of Campbell, Stroud, and Horsford, and the ritualized and collective murder of Daniel Clarke, from the contextual history of silk weaving in London. The story of Clarke's death is directly interwoven with the narrative of work and the erosion of traditional forms of employment and remuneration in late eighteenth century England. Clarke's killing is also directly linked to contemporary concerns about the working class in the 1760s and 1770s in a period of labour tension and widespread disputes. This period has received considerable attention from social and economic historians, as well as historians of crime, but it is necessary here to refresh our memories and consider the context in which the murder of Daniel Clarke took place.[23]

Silk weaving had been a small but important industry in Spitalfields and, to a lesser extent, the wider East End, from the fifteenth century onwards. By the mid-1600s this had grown into a prosperous and significant industry that involved considerable numbers of people. A City of London company was incorporated as early as 1629 which excluded those outside of the area from joining, helping to make Spitalfields silk the dominant centre for silk production in the British Isles. By the early decades of the 1700s there were an estimated 10,000 looms in Spitalfields, providing employment that Leonard Schwartz has estimated at around 40–50,000 by the midpoint of the century.[24] Silk manufacture involved a number of processes, from 'throwing' the silk thread, to pattern making, to weaving. Middlemen and factors emerged, masters employed journeymen and apprentices, and a distinct hierarchy existed. The industry was jealous of its position and throughout the seventeenth and eighteenth centuries it fiercely defended its virtual monopoly against the threat of foreign and more 'local' competition that augured a fall in living standards for the Spitalfields weaving community. As a consequence of this, silk weavers were at the forefront of labour disputes from the late seventeenth century onwards, featuring prominently in riots in the capital.[25]

Most weaving took place in the homes of weavers, although some masters had workshops where several looms operated at once. Masters employed journeymen to work on patterns and factors bought up silk at low prices to sell on to wholesalers; both these practices helped to deflate wages and to bring the smaller weavers into dispute with their masters, and sometimes with each other. They also resisted the introduction of machinery such as the engine loom that undermined wage rates. Using the 'right of search' weavers were legally able to force entry to premises where they believed 'outsiders' (those not members of the City company, for example) were being employed at lower wages and even empowered to destroy work made by them. This traditional 'right of entry' was probably what empowered the men that broke into Daniel Clarke's home in 1769. Collective self-interest also blended with political radicalism and led the weavers to be exploited or engaged as a political faction by a number of prominent radicals, from John Lillburne in the 1640s to John Wilkes in the 1760s. Riots in 1668 (against the introduction of machinery) were put down by the military, a pattern established early in the history of the weavers' disputes. The radicalism of the weavers clearly seems to have unnerved the authorities and contributed to the identification of Spitalfields and the East End as a place of social and political unrest, and therefore of danger. As Peter Linebaugh has written, in the silk disputes of the 1760s 'a theatre of terror and counter-terror in the location and manner of capital punishment was grimly played out in the London streets'.[26]

The 1760s saw underlying tensions combine with a slump in trade, which resulted in over 7,000 looms lying idle. In 1762 silk workers drafted a 'Book of prices' in an attempt to set fixed rates for piecework and thus protect wages and individual livelihoods. The masters were not inclined to accept such direction from the weavers and sought to undermine rates by installing machine looms operated by untrained or lower skilled (and thus cheaper) workers, sometimes employing women and children. In 1763 the end of the Seven Years War brought matters to a head as the conditions of the East End's silk weavers reached a critical point. This caused 2,000 weavers to take direct action against the masters and those working for them at rates paid under those set out in 'the Book'. Once again the military had to be called out to put down the consequent rioting.[27] In the course of this some of the actions that can be seen in the Daniel Clarke case were deployed. Weavers organized collectively and took retributive action against anyone that opposed them or gave information about perpetrators to the authorities. Folk customs – such as threatening letters or the *charivari* or Skimmington – were used to punish employers and fellow weavers alike, as this report from November describes:

> In riotous manner [they] broke open the house of one of their masters, destroyed his looms, and cut a great quantity of silk to pieces, after which they placed his effigy in a cart, with a halter about his neck, an executioner on one side, and a coffin on the other; and after drawing it through the streets they hanged it on a gibbet, then burnt it to ashes and afterwards dispersed.[28]

Weavers deployed these sorts of tactics and others in their protests. In the early decades of the 1700s this 'also involved the public shaming of their victims', as Shoemaker has noted: 'Women's calico dresses were ruined in the streets, and their misbehavior was portrayed as a form of sexual immorality'.[29] This ritualized counter to the actions of the masters to deflate incomes and undermine craftsmanship (as the weavers would have understood it) is indicative of contemporary notions of legitimate protest, and what Edward Thompson famously addressed in his essay on custom and customary rights.[30]

The economic situation for silk weavers hardly improved and they were impacted by a poor harvest and rising food prices in 1765. In 1766, the government, in response to concerns about the condition of weavers and the trade, imposed a ban on imported silks, something it had been obliged to do in the late 1600s as well.[31] In the meantime in 1765 the government had also passed a piece of legislation which sanctioned the use of the death penalty for anyone convicted of breaking into a building for the express purpose of damaging silk work or destroying looms.[32] This new law thus overturned centuries of custom but as with many such changes in workplace relations in the period the existence of new legislation was not easily accepted by those that it was imposed on. In part this may been because under the post-1688 parliament a sheaf of laws were legislated into existence to protect private interest and many of these swelled the so-called bloody code that prescribed the death penalty for all manner of new offences against property. This particular new law was a direct consequence of riots that had seen the Duke of Bedford's Bloomsbury home surrounded by thousands of angry silk weavers who held him responsible for their plight as a prominent member of the East India Company, which was engaged in the importing of cheap textiles from the Indian subcontinent. In May 1765, Russell, the 4th Duke of Bedford, had opposed a bill that would have imposed high duties on imported Italian silk and soon afterwards an anonymous pamphleteer published a deeply scathing critique of Bedford which he dressed up as a polite letter. This letter (entitled 'from a Spitalfields weaver, to a Noble Duke') set out the desperate position of the silk weavers who existed on 10*d* a day (a sum the duke supposedly said he would find comfortable to survive on), noting that once food and clothing is taken away the weaver suggests he would be left with just under 2*d* a day. He adds that 'no provision is made for those imprudents [sic] wretches who have been indiscreet enough to get themselves married, and in consequence, some of them have six or seven children'.[33] The deep-seated ill feeling caused by Bedford's seemingly callous disregard for the welfare of the weavers and their families is highlighted by the pamphleteer's suggestion that the duke should help set up a market be at the Royal Exchange so the children of the poor can be sold to members of the aristocracy and wealthy class who need children, so that 'people of fashion and fortune may go and provide themselves with as many infants as they think proper, just as they might bargain for a quarter of lamb'.[34] Bedford was a hate figure for many in the 1760s, his pursuit of wealth and influence a byword for venality, and the duke found himself on the end of perhaps the most vicious of all Junius' letters in September 1769, who declared that as he had 'lived without virtue' he 'should die without repentance'.[35] Bedford did die soon afterwards, in January 1771.

The 1760s were extremely hard for the weavers whose industry had been in decline for more than a decade. By then upwards of 30,000 people depended on the trade in the eastern parishes of Bethnal Green, Norton Folgate, and Spitalfields and external competition had depressed wages to the extent that the community, which had never been wealthy, was increasingly hard-pressed.[36] Disputes continued into 1767 and saw clashes between journeymen and masters, and those operating single (or 'narrow') looms and machine looms in Saffron Hill. This occurred after an informal agreement had been reached to implement a book of piece rates. Weavers, forbidden from forming combinations, had little option but to try and organize themselves in secret. A club was created which met in local pubs such as the *Dolphin* in Cock lane, where groups of 'cutters' discussed tactics and sent threatening letters to masters.[37] The period 1760 to 1767 was turbulent but would be eclipsed by the events of 1768–69, which saw tensions ramped up and executions on the streets of Spitalfields. Following attempts by weavers to set the prices for foodstuffs in local markets in 1768 and fresh outbreaks of localized rioting, the summer of 1769 witnessed widespread collective action against the imposition of wage cuts by masters. They adopted methods familiar to later trade unions, raising funds by levying (or extorting) taxes from those owning looms. The ability of the weavers to organize themselves worried the authorities, and Linebaugh cites the example of Secretary of State Shelburne writing in vivid prose of the threat posed by organized labour in the East End. Linebaugh situates the weavers as part of an international challenge to the 'ancient regime'.[38] Threatening letters, intimidation of those working for lower wages, and direct violent action against property were all tools deployed by the weavers in the 1760s and this course of action set them at odds with masters like Lewis Chauvet (who was quite possibly the author of the anonymous letter to the Earl of Rochford in April 1771).[39]

Chauvet, who owned a workshop in Crispin Street close to Spitalfields market, refused to be cowed by the weavers, and banned his workers from joining or paying into the various clubs, and employed guards to protect his property. This resistance was met by force as weavers gathered on August 17 and 21, 1769 to attack Chauvet's looms. In the course of the action, over 150 looms had the work cut out of them and destroyed. Chauvet advertised a substantial reward for information leading to the capture and prosecution of those responsible and despite a culture of silence (engendered by a climate of intimidation as well as community solidarity) one minor master and his wife gave evidence that led to the arrest of William Horsford, John Doyle, John Valline, and a number of others. Thomas and Mary Poor testified before Sir John Fielding at Bow Street that seven of their looms had been cut by a group of weavers belonging to a club known as the 'Defiance Sloop'. The *Dolphin* tavern was later raided by Fielding's officers (the Bow Street 'runners') and three men died in the resulting firefight (one soldier and two weavers). Doyle and Valline were tried under the legislation passed in 1765 and convicted although the evidence against them was weak. Chauvet had offered a reward of £500 (a huge sum in 1769) to tempt the Poors to perjure themselves and this seems to have been a pattern that was repeated in the face of the difficulties the authorities encountered in determining exactly who was responsible for the crimes that had been committed. Doyle and Valline were processed through London from Newgate to Bethnal Green for three hours before they were hanged before an angry crowd. Before he died Doyle protested his innocence, rejecting the tradition of offering a few 'last words' that admitted his guilt and forgave his executioners: 'let my blood lay to that wretched man who has purchased it with gold and them notorious wretches who swore it falsely away', he declared before he was 'turned off'.[40] The crowd, which was angry at the perceived injustice done to members of their own community and not with the executed felons, proceeded to tear down the gallows and reinstall them in front of Chauvet's factory in Crispin Street in an act that can only be seen as one of defiance. This was not what the authorities had wanted; their goal was submission and obedience and must have hoped that the added terror of an on-site execution would have focused minds. The City had manipulated the report of the trial in the Proceedings deliberately to make the prosecution case appear stronger in the Proceedings than it did in court, as Robert Shoemaker has noted:

Notes taken by prosecution lawyers at the trial of John Doyle and John Valline reveal that one witness testified that Mrs. Poor, whose house they had allegedly entered order to carry out the attacks, had said that 'she knew Doyle, but not [that] was one of the cutters', and another reported that she had said of the attacks 'that she was not frightened, for the thing they were about would do her good. . . . She knew there were friends among them that would not hurt her'.[41]

A similarly careful presentation of the Proceedings may well have influenced public opinion following the Stroud trial, although here there is evidence that some at least recognized that the principal defendant was innocent. William Horsford, William Eastman, and John Carmichael were all tried a fortnight after Doyle and Valline hanged. Horsford was convicted on the evidence supplied by the Poors while Eastman was found guilty on the strength of Daniel Clarke's testimony. Clarke had allegedly also had his evidence bought by Chauvet. The trio was executed at Tyburn this time, as the authorities had no stomach to revisit the chaos that had followed Doyle and Valline's execution.

The Trial of Henry Stroud, Antis Horsford, and Robert Campbell: An exercise in Perjury and Legal Construction

The trial of the three persons arrested in connection with the murder of Daniel Clarke took place on July 3, 1771, at the Old Bailey.[42] It was a long trial by eighteenth-century standards, lasting fully 12 hours. As the papers reported there were a great number of witnesses to be heard and plenty of evidence for the jury to digest. In the end it still only took the jurors 20 minutes to find Henry Stroud and Robert Campbell guilty, whereupon the judge sentenced them to be publicly hanged and then dissected at Surgeons Hall.[43]

The key witnesses for events leading up to Clarke's death were Benjamin West and Mary Snee. West was a master weaver who had employed Clarke as a pattern maker. He testified to seeing the deceased being pursued by a mob up Half Nichols Street but while he saw some of the violence meted out to Clarke he identified no one precisely, either by name beforehand or in court. It was common practice for the prosecutor or the judge to ask witnesses to point to the culprits as they stood in the dock. The Old Bailey's lighting was poor by modern standards but a mirror positioned just over the dock helped reflect light from the windows onto the accused, making it easier to see their features during the trial. This helped the watching jury discern guilt or innocence but also made identification easier. In many cases where defendants had been taken up within 24 hours of a crime being committed they would most likely have been wearing the same clothes they were when arrested, even if those vestments would have been crumbled and soiled by several days of incarceration in Newgate Gaol. In this case however it had taken a while to capture the three accused and some doubts must have existed concerning their identification by witnesses.

Like the previous witness, Benjamin West, Mary Snee was able to swear to seeing Clarke in a parlous state and to helping him on West's instructions, but again she did not (and could not) point the finger at any of the accused in the dock. The evidence given here was emotive and shocking but it wasn't necessarily substantive in terms of determining who was responsible for the pattern drawer's demise. Similarly John Marsh picked up the story after Clarke fled the Snee household and ran across the gardens behind the property. He was inside his house at Norton Folgate and having just eaten he heard the row outside and looked from his window. All was confusion but he ran upstairs to get a better view and from this position he saw a group of people gathered around a prone individual. Marsh then said he saw a man horsewhip the victim, but he recognized no one in the dock as being involved that day. Indeed he made a point of saying 'I know nothing of the prisoners'.[44] He could have been under pressure or intimidation to keep silent of course, but regardless of that his testimony did nothing to advance the prosecution case.

There was one important and respectable witness who did see a lot that day and had tried to intervene to save Clarke's life, something few others seem to have done. This was Thomas Gibson, a silk dresser who resided on Norton Folgate. His trade was therefore in the preparation of silk for weaving, although it is unclear whether Gibson was a tradesman as such or someone who employed others to prepare thread. Gibson had a lot to say to in the trial and although he broke off from the initial incident of the mob's pursuit of Clarke to return to his shop in Blossom Street, he soon picked up the flight and was present at the capture and stoning of Daniel Clarke in the pond. He had first seen the crowd around Clarke at around 2 in the afternoon, so some two hours after West had (if we take eighteenth-century timings as accurate that is). He saw Clarke surrounded by a crowd of perhaps 100 or more people and watched as 'a man came by with a dray, and said, Clear the way; he took a whip and began whipping of him'.[45] This attack lasted just a minute or two while Clarke sat on the ground with his back to wall as the blows rained down on him. This was probably the same horse whipping that Marsh described seeing from above. Gibson's evidence allows us to map the progress that Clarke had made and the direction he took thereafter (see Figure 3.1 below).

Daniel Clarke had escaped into the gardens behind the Snee's house on Cock Lane. This probably means the space bounded by York Street (to the west), Club Row (to the east), and Anchor Street (to the south). Norton Folgate lies south west of here, running as it did from Shoreditch to Bishopsgate Street. Thomas Gibson quickly went to his workshop in Blossom Street (parallel to Shoreditch) perhaps to make sure it was locked up as a riot seemed to be unfolding around him. He did not stay there long, however, and soon picked up the trail of those pursuing Daniel Clarke. This pursuit now had all the hallmarks of a hunt, but without the doubt that the quarry would ever get away. The mob hounded Clarke in Wheeler Street where he fell again and was pounded with dirt and struck several times by different people. He rose and they chased him right into Quaker Street. There Gibson saw someone move close to him and thump him hard crying out 'D[am]n your blood'.[46] That pitched him over again but he was soon back up on his feet and running for his life. From there he turned north onto Brick Lane (Gibson calls it the 'Broad way')[47] where for a moment no one assaulted him. Clarke made it to Hare Street where he was knocked down again near some brewery buildings. There the crowd stripped him of all his clothes expect his breeches and stockings and dragged him off towards the open fields at the end of the lane beyond St Matthew's Church.

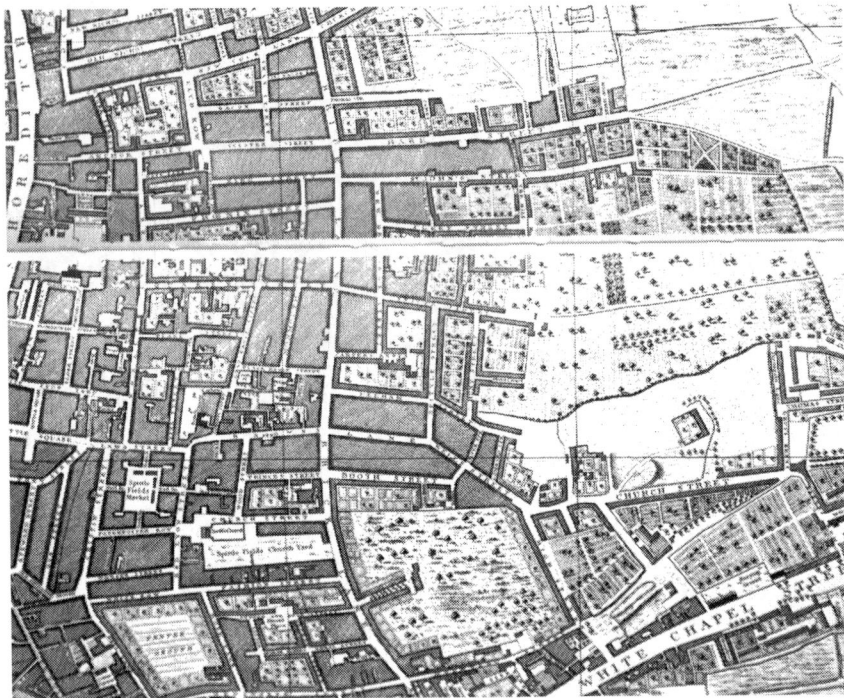

Figure 3.1 Spitalfields c.1750 from Rocque's Map. Hyde, *The A to Z of Georgian London*, pp. 12–13, reproduced with the kind permission of the London Topographical Society

Source: www.londontopsoc.org

This was the area that contained a pond created as the result of the digging of clay and brick earth to make tiles and bricks from the mid-sixteenth century. Gibson testified to there being a gathering of 2,000–3,000 people by the brick pond, many of them 'pelting him [Clarke] with earth and brick-bats, and anything they met with while he was in the water'.[48] At some point Gibson decided to intervene, a brave thing to do considering that he was acting against the community who were engaged in punishing someone they saw as an informer responsible for the death of a weaver. Nevertheless it was Gibson and another (unnamed) man that pulled Clarke out, with the silk dresser berating the 'the little brats' who were abusing the man. It did little good and Clarke was soon dragged back in. Gibson affected a second rescue but by now the pattern drawer was on the brink of death, exhausted as he was by his ordeal and bleeding from several wounds. In court Gibson was able to identify Robert Campbell as a man he had seen stride into the pond in just his shirt and plunge Clarke's head under the water. However, he was unsure as to whether it really was Campbell in all the chaos that afternoon; when the jury pressed him he said he thought it was him 'to the best of my knowledge' but because of the snow and the fact that he had left the scene of the crime (to see if he could get help or simply to avoid the awful weather and the possible anger of the crowd he was challenging is unclear, although he suggests he just took shelter for 20 minutes) made him a poor witness for the prosecution. Campbell's defence attorney was keen to press him on whether he had seen his client wade into the pond as he had suggested. There was a short discussion about the clothes that man was wearing – a buff or white coat, or a white shirt. Gibson was not prepared to swear to any identification of Campbell or anyone else for that matter. Importantly, he certainly did not identify Henry Stroud as playing an active role in Clarke's murder. At this stage, the principal witnesses brought by the prosecution had failed to provide conclusive evidence that any of the accused had played a direct part in Daniel Clarke's demise.

The next witness that the prosecution brought was Francis Clarke, a fruiterer who lived and worked on Gray Eagle Street, which runs south from Quaker Street and parallel to Brick Lane. He was at his front door having just had his dinner when he saw the 'mob' in Quaker Street. As two men approached him he asked them what was going on. They told him 'they had got Clarke that hanged the cutters'. He followed the crowd, collecting a friend (Mrs Hoe) on the way. Francis Clarke (who was no relation to Daniel) told the Old Bailey court that had spoken to the deceased while he was in the pond and had tried to offer some help, even if he seems to have been more concerned for his own safety (since he shared a name with him). He testified to seeing Henry Stroud that day but did not identify him as one of the individuals who were directly involved in the murder. He was there, but Clarke thought he was a brick maker, and he had not seen him involved in the hunting of Daniel Clarke through the streets. As for Campbell, to the best of his knowledge the first time he had seen him was at the committal hearing at Bow Street in front of Sir John Fielding. He added when asked that he had seen Sarah (Antis) Horsford at the pond but had not seen her 'do any thing'.[49] Instead he said he had seen a 'slim man' throw a cord over Clarke's head so he could be dragged back into the water after the second of Gibson's rescue attempts. He added that a 'boy, in a green waistcoat' had been very active in attacking Clarke but he could not swear to any of them being in the dock that day. He said he saw the man in the shirt and would recognize him if he was dressed properly. Again, then, another of the prosecution's key witnesses had failed to identify Stroud as the principal murderer of Daniel Clarke.

In an echo of the Kennedy brothers' trial, Francis Clarke now threw potential doubt into the proceedings. Clarke told the court that he had been approached in the aftermath of the events of that day by a 'gentle-man' who offered him 'fourscore pounds' (£80 – a considerable fortune) if he would swear evidence against Robert Campbell. He testified that the man had said: 'I see you are a stranger; if you will but swear to the man I will give you fourscore pounds'.[50] The man that approached him was in court, he said, but he could not (or would not) name him. He had served Clarke with a summons to appear at the Bow Street office, to give evidence against 'Bob' Campbell. According to Clarke the strange man then took him aside into an alley and said: 'you are the capital, or chief witness against the man; I said, what man: he said, Campbell, that was in prison; and said, if you will swear against him, you will have four score pounds, divided between you and the man that took him'. Clarke replied: 'God forbid I should go to swear against a person I do not know'.[51] If Francis Clarke was telling the truth then this was a clear attempt by someone to implicate Robert Campbell in the murder of Daniel Clarke.

The unnamed man remained unnamed in the Proceedings, being only referred to as 'the Man'. The court called the 'man' to the witness stand but when he was questioned directly he denied the attempt to bribe a witness and said he was simply a 'peace officer, a constable' employed by David Wilmot at the Whitechapel Rotation office. He had merely been dispatched to summons Clarke to give his evidence at a pretrial hearing conducted by Sir John Fielding at Bow Street. That hearing did not take place for several weeks and it seems Clarke was under pressure from two sides to testify or not. He may have been initially approached on the day after the killing and offered money but his testimony is vague enough to suggest that the approach might have been two or three weeks later, by which time Justice Wilmot would have been under considerable pressure to make an arrest. Meanwhile Francis Clarke was aware that he earned his living in Spitalfields (although he was not himself a part of the weaving community), so he was conscious that if he gave evidence against one of their own reprisals might follow. This helps explains his cautious approach in court. There may well have been an attempt to bribe him or at least to encourage him to testify that he had seen Campbell at the pond and active in Clarke's murder. Then again local intimidation might have warned him that he could face a very similar fate if he did so. Caught between these two opposing factions it is possible that Francis Clarke simply opted to tell the truth: he had seen Campbell, Stroud, and Horsford at the pond but had not seen them do anything that would have resulted in the death of Daniel Clarke.

However one chooses to view his testimony or his motives, Francis Clarke was another unreliable witness who claimed to have seen a lot but who was unable (or unwilling) to condemn Campbell and Stroud, let alone Sarah Horsford. The prosecution case was flimsy at this stage and given that the Old Bailey Proceedings has been found to minimize evidence that supported defendants and highlight that which was used to convict them, this is significant.[52]

Several other witnesses came forward to describe what they saw that wintry afternoon in April. Sarah Scales also saw what happened at the pond and was brave enough to condemn it at the time. In court she was reluctant to point the finger at anyone in particular though, saying: 'I was at the pond. I saw several pieces of bricks thrown at the deceased; and some hit him on the head; but I don't know any of the people that throwed'. She seemed nervous and the prosecution counsel told her not to be afraid. 'I am not afraid', she insisted, but since she could not or would not enlighten the court as regards to the defendants in the dock she was quickly stood down.[53] Susannah Hoe was similarly unhelpful although she too testified to seeing a man in just his shirt shove Clarke's head under water. She had gone up to the field with Francis Clarke and while she saw a number of people involved in drowning or stoning Clarke she could (or would) not swear to their identity. Indeed she told the court that identifying anyone from a distance was all but impossible: 'the day was so bitter', she argued, 'there could be no knowing a person without being pretty close'.[54] Elizabeth Breech was also clearly frightened as she sat in court to give her evidence. She had been standing next to Sarah Scales and her testimony was similar; she could not identify a culprit with any precision. Robert Baldwin was prepared to swear to seeing and hearing Campbell speak to Clarke as he was being dragged up Hare Street. He reportedly loomed over him and asked him 'if he knew Eastman' (the man who had gone to gallows as result of his informing on him). By now Clarke was pleading for his life. At the pond Baldwin watched as Campbell, divested of his coat and wearing just his shirt and breeches, ran into the pond and forced Clarke's head under water.

The key witness was Joseph Chambers, a brick worker. Chambers was crucial to the prosecution case because in all of the chaos and confusion, and despite the snow and cold, he saw Stroud clearly throwing bricks at the stranded man in the pond. He also saw a man in a shirt in the water (who may have been Campbell) but was unable to identify him because of being too far away. However there are reasons for doubting the veracity of Chambers' evidence. He said that he had known Stroud previously, which is how he recognized him at the pond. More importantly he admitted that he had been approached by another witness, James Knight, who urged him to testify against Stroud in court. According to Chambers, Knight had told him he knew Stroud was involved and was prepared to testify to Mr Wilmot. A reward had been offered by now and Chambers was quite open about this. On Wilmot's instruction, Chambers went to the gardens where Henry Stroud worked and under the pretence of buying some lettuces got enough of a look at Stroud to be able to say for certain that he was the man he had seen throwing stones at the Clarke in the pond. Wilmot backed this up in court saying that he had information that the wanted man's name was Stroud and discovered where he worked. Even then there was still some doubt as to Stroud's identification as the murderer, with doubts cast over what he was wearing that day.

Finally James Knight took the stand and pointed Stroud out in the dock. Knight worked with Stroud and his evidence neatly dovetailed with Chambers'. He was standing behind Stroud and saw him lob two or three stones towards the stricken victim. He also saw a man in a white shirt try to drown the pattern dresser but again he could not swear to it being Robert Campbell. This would seem to have been the vital identification that the prosecution required; someone that both knew Stroud and could place him at the scene and as active in the homicide. Given that Stroud was a relation by marriage to William Eastman (having married his sister) he also had an obvious motive for murder (or at least for involving himself in the ritual abuse of Daniel Clarke). However, this explanation is a little convenient given the recent history between Knight and his fellow gardener. As Knight was happy to admit in court, the pair had fallen out recently. Knight was drinking with a work colleague named 'Davy' (David Higgins) when Stroud walked into the same public house, the *Axe* on Hackney Road. As Stroud approached them Knight cried out: 'D–n it, here is the man I have been after all day; I will take him up; he is the man that murdered Clarke, and I will have the hundred pounds reward'. It was a joke, he said, or at least a joke that he had been looking for Clarke. Stroud told him he was 'a foolish sort of fellow'. Knight asked him to lend him a shilling but Stroud refused, leaving soon afterwards. Having said all this Knight performed a volte-face when questioned by the defence counsel. Their exchange went as follows:

Defence counsel.	After Stroud came in, did you ask to drink with him, or began talking of charging him and getting the hundred pounds?
Knight.	I asked him to drink first; I said first, when I saw him coming, this is the man that killed Clarke, &c.
Defence counsel.	What did he say to you?
Knight.	He said nothing to me in no shape.
Defence counsel.	Did not he call you a foolish fellow?
Knight.	No not that I remember.
Defence counsel.	You gave your evidence just now, that you charged him with being the man that killed Clarke; 'Stroud said I was a foolish of a fellow'.
Knight.	Not to my knowledge.
Defence counsel.	Did not you say so?
Knight.	Not to my knowledge.
Defence counsel.	Did not you tell him upon that day, If you will not give me a pot of beer, I will swear-it?
Knight.	I said, if he would not, I would take him up at once.

Defence counsel.	Did not he stay and drink his beer?
Knight.	He was not there above five minutes.
Defence counsel.	Did not you tell him, unless he would give you a pot of beer you would swear it against him, and take him up?
Knight.	Yes; he staid and drank the beer, and out he went.
Defence counsel.	Are you sure you was awake when he went out of the house, or drunk and asleep.
Knight.	As sober as I am now, and awake.[55]

It seems pretty obvious from this distance at least that there were serious problems with Knight's testimony and the defence counsel pressed him hard. His evidence was confused, contradictory, and quite probably driven by personal antipathy towards Henry Stroud. Another gardener named Bath (no first name was given) said he was with Knight all day on April 16 and so witnessed events just as Knight had. He swore that Stroud did not do anything wrong that day and also swore that he and Knight had left long before Clarke was dead. Someone was lying. Exactly whom was made a little clearer when David ('Davy') Higgins appeared to testify. He told the court that Knight had said he 'did not see any body throw any thing, but if he knew any body that could swear it, he would take him up'. Moreover in the weeks after the murder and notably after April 27 when the reward was posted Higgins said he was talking to Chambers who was very keen to give information against Stroud. Higgins said he knew Stroud but that it could not have been him that threw the stones because by Chambers' description the man he saw was quote different. He explained that: 'I told him it was not him, for Stroud was a great man, and cross-eyed'.[56] Every day following the posting of the reward Knight agitated at Higgins urging him to help him convict Stroud so they could all profit from the reward.

There were a considerable number of witnesses for the defence and very many of them gave more than just the usual statements about the defendants' character. John Rutter was a workmate of Stroud's and was with him at the pond. He said he threw nothing at all and merely commented that it was a sorry affair and that Clarke was a 'sad man'. John Winterson was another gardener who reported that Stroud was innocent. Both he and Rutter were closely examined by the prosecution who tried to make out that they were in some way complicit in the killing, having not stopped to help the victim. They stood their ground and maintained that Henry Stroud was innocent as charged. John Bailey had worked with Stroud for seven years and described him as 'a peaceable man; I hardly ever heard him have a word with a man in his life'.[57] This was not strictly true, however, as the court was later to hear. Mark Cole and a beer housekeeper named Lloyd both gave Stroud an alibi saying he was drinking quietly in the *King and Queen* pub when Clarke was finally killed. He could not, they argued, have dealt the man the blow that killed him.

The jury had plenty to consider but despite the weight of evidence that pointed to 'reasonable doubt' as to the guilt of any of the defendants both Campbell and Stroud were convicted of Daniel Clarke's murder. In reality there was little or nothing that would tie them to the murder. All of the evidence came from witnesses and most of that either exonerated one or other of them or at worst indicated that someone that looked something like them might have either stepped in to dunk Clarke or had been seen throwing stones at him. Only Chambers and Knight were certain they could identify Stroud and their evidence was extremely weak at best and, frankly, corrupt. Stroud was being set up by Knight because of a long-standing grudge between the two men; Chambers was hoping to profit handsomely, and the local magistrate needed a body to placate the government. Horsford was acquitted[58] as no one testified to seeing her do anything and several witnesses swore she simply stood by until a number of people urged her to go home before she was accused of something she had not done. Bob Campbell gave a long and impassioned defence but his complicity in Clarke's death is much harder to sweep aside. He may well have been the man in the white shirt sleeves that pushed Clarke under the cold water of the pond, leaving him half drowned afterwards. Yet even if he had dunked the poor man, he was hardly the only person responsible for Clarke's death that day. Loads of people – many of them small boys by all reports – were throwing stones, shouting abuse, hounding Clarke and forcing him to remain up to his waist in freezing water on a bitterly cold afternoon. This was a horrible way to die but it is very hard to pin the blame for it on any one person.

If one applies eighteenth-century law, as it was understood then, even here the killing of Daniel Clarke sits more easily within the definition of manslaughter rather than murder, although it can be seen how the interpretation could fall into one of murder as well. Manslaughter was killing 'upon a sudden occasion' rather than with 'malice aforethought'. Murder, while it contained malice, did not have to result in the instant death of the victim; so long as they died within a year then a murder charge could be brought. Moreover, Richard Burn notes that 'whenever it appears that a man killed another, it shall be intended *prima facie* that he did it maliciously, unless he can make out the contrary, by shewing that he did it on a sudden provocation or the like'.[59] Again, the fact that Stroud and Campbell, by their association with the weaver's dispute (however loosely), could be deemed to have grounds for malice towards Clarke, and so they fitted the profile of the sort of persons that might have been responsible for his murder. The facts were that multiple persons were actually responsible for the victim's death but the authorities could not hang the whole weaving community of Spitalfields. Justice Wilmot needed recognizable and suitable scapegoats and by offering money as a reward for information he ensured that local animosities and jealousies would provide the sacrificial victims he required. Stroud and Campbell were convicted and ordered to be executed and then dissected at Surgeon's Hall.

The Execution of Campbell and Stroud

The hanging of the two men deemed ultimately responsible for Daniel Clarke's murder has to be considered in the context of the execution, almost two years earlier, of two weavers condemned for their part in cutting silk from looms in Spitalfields. On Wednesday, December 6, 1769, John Doyle and John Valline were taken on a cart from Newgate Gaol to the crossroads at Cock Lane in Bethnal Green where a specially constructed gallows had been erected. The gallows had not been easy to assemble as a large crowd of 'inconceivable number' had gathered to thwart the authorities' purpose. The execution was carried out in haste and the pair only left hanging for 50 minutes (rather than the requisite hour) before they were cut down and their bodies 'delivered to their friends'.[60] The Middlesex sheriffs presided but did so reluctantly. The Recorder had sentenced the two men to death at Old Bailey with the stipulation that the execution should be carried out at the 'usual' place, which was Tyburn. When orders had come removing the execution to Bethnal Green to emphasize the rule of law to anyone amongst the weaving community who might be inclined to follow the 'cutters' example, sheriffs Townsend and Sawbridge (friends of Wilkes and thus sympathetic to the plight of the weavers) objected. They attempted to prevent the execution from taking place in the East End where it would inflame the community and, in their opinion, add ignominy to injury for the two condemned men. Ultimately they were unsuccessful although the execution was delayed while the king, Lord Weymouth, the Twelve Judges, Lord Mansfield, and John Glynn all considered the sheriffs' objection. The execution (and the attempt to hold it at Tyburn) prompted one pamphleteer to publish in full all the letters that had circulated between Townsend and Sawbridge, Weymouth and Glynn, such was the public interest in the case. The editor of the letters wrote a strongly worded postscript that condemned the attempt to usurp the 'civil power of this country'. He saw the sheriffs' attempt as entirely justified arguing that no one, not even the king (indeed, especially not the king), was able to increase a punishment handed down by the courts. Moreover, he viewed exemplary hanging as evidence of the oppression of 'the people', the weavers in this case, and hinted that Doyle and Valline were merely scapegoats. The civil power had, he concluded, been ordered into the area 'to *execute* the criminals it could not *apprehend*'.[61] Not only this but the East End of London had been rendered almost ungovernable by the authorities' mishandling of the weavers' dispute; 'a barrack has been therefore built, and soldiers have regularly mounted guard there for a long time past', noted, in contravention of English ideals of liberty and freedom from military power on the streets.[62]

As he was turned off, Doyle declared his innocence, and so omitted to make the expected 'last confession' (along with his peace with God) and told the watching crowd: 'Let my blood lie to that wicked man who has purchased it with gold, and them notorious wretches who swore it away'.[63] Valine did likewise, both dying 'game' but unbowed despite the state's determination to see them silenced and humiliated. The 'wicked man' was widely believed to be Lewis Chauvet and the crowd later surrounded his home and reigned down stones and insults on his household. Days later two more cutters were convicted at Old Bailey, William Horsford (Antis' husband) and William Eastman (Stroud's brother-in-law); both were sentenced to hang. Both protested their innocence. John Neale and Cornelius Chevalier were sent to prison for three months and a year respectfully, convicted of cutting Chauvet's looms. As the dust settled the weavers gathered together to discuss what to do and the military were dispatched to prevent more rioting. Sheriff Sawbridge interceded and calmed the situation, suggesting the weavers present a petition to the king outlining their grievances and in a peaceful way.

All of this set the background for the pursuit and ritualized murder of Daniel Clarke as the weavers' community settled into an uneasy peace for a few months. Not surprisingly, then, when the authorities finally got someone for Clarke's murder there was again a concern that the culprits be hanged quickly but publicly, to ensure the right message was received. Immediately following the close of the Old Bailey trial trouble had broken out outside the court. One of the men that had given evidence against Campbell was seen making his way from the Old Bailey. A crowd of weavers gave chase and it was only by the swift intervention of two City aldermen and marshalmen that he was saved from being lynched.[64] Justice Wilmot was worried that the events surrounding the execution of Doyle and Valline might be repeated and wrote again to Rochford asking for his support.[65] The Whitechapel magistrate feared for his own life and property and requested an armed guard. Not everyone thought that appropriate, however: John Wilkes, now Lord Mayor of the City, 'strenuously opposed the deployment of a military guard at the execution of two convicts, arguing that such a presence constituted an imposition of the military power where civil authorities were not only adequate but solely appropriate'.[66] The secretary of state, however, obliged David Wilmot, dispatching a letter to the secretary of war instructing him to send 'a colonel's guard' to attend the execution.[67] In the end the guard was unnecessary and Wilmot reported that the hanging passed off peacefully without 'the least disturbance', despite the 'vast crowd' that attended.[68] A grateful justice thanked his superior and provided suitable refreshment for the soldiery that had been dispatched to save him from the fury of the weavers. Like Doyle and Valline before him Henry Stroud went to his death protesting his innocence. Campbell, by contrast, had penned a message or sign (which has not survived), which he claimed were the 'ensigns of a society he belonged to' (perhaps the 'Bold Defiance') and met his end unrepentant.

Conclusions

It was unusual to hang felons at the site of their crimes rather than at Tyburn. The executions of Stroud and Campbell, and before them Doyle and Valline, represent, therefore, an attempt by the authorities to add ignominy to the sentence of death in keeping with earlier demands in the century that hanging was 'not punishment enough' for some murderers.[69] The last man to be hanged on site in London was John Dunn, executed in St Paul's Churchyard in 1795, over 20 years later.[70] Perhaps the selection of Henry Stroud and Robert Campbell as the only ones to pay with their lives for the collective ritual murder of Daniel Clarke is also reflective of contemporary views of the power of the imagination as expressed by Edmund Burke following the Gordon Riots of 1780. Rejecting the idea that the state should execute hundreds of guilty rioters, Burke argued instead that just six examples should be made, each 'hanged the same day in different parts of the city'. He wrote:

> The sense of justice in men is overloaded and fatigued with a long series of executions. . . . I have observed that the execution of one man fixes the attention and excites awe; the execution of multitudes dissipates and weakens the affect.[71]

It was of course vital that the authorities reestablish control over the silk weaving community of East London. This area had been synonymous with radicalism and proto-trade unionism from at least the seventeenth century. This community had been appeased or suppressed on a number of occasions from the late 1600s to the late eighteenth century but the events of April 1771 must have suggested to those in power that the correct lessons were not being learned. 'Cutters' had been arrested, tried, convicted, and brutally dispatched, but this had not dulled the community's enmity towards their 'masters' (defined both figuratively and actually). Daniel Clarke was a marked man and, while most of the time he merely had to run the gauntlet of verbal abuse when the opportunity presented itself, the community took revenge. This was no ordinary murder; it was a collective act that echoed other historical actions such as the murder of John Lambe in 1628. Lambe was considered a 'transgressive figure perceived to have breached common boundaries of religious and sexual decorum and [had] escaped punishment for his crimes'.[72] In the eyes of the community he was a legitimate target, just as Clarke was (albeit under different circumstances). As Alastair Bellany noted, Lambe's killing was 'a subversive political act (and understood as such at the time)' and it brought the wrath of the king (Charles I) down on the City fathers for allowing it.[73] Clarke's murder was equally subversive; it undermined the rule of law and the process of 'justice'. In these circumstances the state had to find someone guilty despite the best efforts of the community to shield the culprits. It did not matter then whether the persons executed were guilty or innocent, they were necessary sacrifices in the government's (and the capital's) battle for dominance over radical working class resistance to the inevitable march of capital. In the next chapter, politics and global events appear to have been more important than immediate domestic concerns, but the need to present a united front at home was never far from the minds of those making decisions on the lives of convicted criminals, just as today 'talking tough' on law and order is rarely a vote loser. Sadly, for one young man this reality cost him his life.

Notes

1. R. Campbell, *The London Tradesman, Being a Compendious View of All the Trades, Professions, Arts, Both Liberal and Mechanic, Now Practiced in the Cities of London and Westminster* (London, T. Gardner, 1747), pp. 115–16.
2. Old Bailey Proceedings Online (www.oldbaileyonline.org, version 8.0, 31 July 2019), July 1771, trial of HENRY STROUD ROBERT CAMBELL ANSTIS HORSFORD (t17710703-59).
3. This was the trial and execution of William Eastman and William Horsford in December 1769. Clarke had been the victim in the former case when six or more men broke into his property on Artillery Lane, where they proceeded to destroy silk work. Old Bailey Proceedings Online (www.oldbaileyonline.org, version 8.0, 31 July 2019), December 1769, trial of WILLIAM EASTMAN (t17691206-31).
4. Trial of Henry Stroud Robert Cambell Anstis Horsford (evidence of Mary Snee).
5. According to John Rocque's 1747 map of London, at the bottom of the fields there was a ducking pond (in a road that ran parallel to Mile End Road). It may be that the crowd took Clarke here although Rocque's map does suggest that other ponds existed that they may have deployed for the same purpose. Ralph Hyde, *The A to Z of Georgian London*, London Topographical Society Publication No. 126 (London, London Topographical Society, 1982).
6. As Shoemaker recounts, such public expressions of popular 'justice' were not uncommon in eighteenth-century London. In 1720 three pickpockets were seized and handed over to the 'mob', who dragged them to a pond and subjected them to a ducking. The trio had not committed a crime for which they could be indicted and tried, but were suspected of being thieves and so given the lesser punishment of public humiliation at the hands of their 'community'. Robert B. Shoemaker, 'The London "Mob" in the Early Eighteenth Century', *Journal of British Studies*, Vol. 26, No. 3 (July 1987), p. 288.
7. Trial of Henry Stroud Robert Cambell Anstis Horsford (evidence of Francis Clarke, fruiter).
8. TS11/169: Evidence of John Gibson, junior, Surgeon.

9. These are held in the National Archives at Kew. NA/TS11/169.
10. OB/SP/1771/07/001-028.
11. TS11/169: The King against Henry Stroud and Ann Horsford widow, upon an indictment for the murder of Daniel Clark.
12. TS11/169: Evidence of John Gibson, junior, Surgeon.
13. Hitchcock and Shoemaker, *London Lives*.
14. Norma Landau, 'The Trading Justice's Trade', in Norma Landau (ed.), *Law, Crime and English Society, 1660–1830* (Cambridge, Cambridge University Press, 2002), pp. 46–70.
15. Gray, *Crime, Prosecution and Social Relations*.
16. Landau, 'The Trading Justice's Trade', p. 60.
17. Trial of William Eastman (Clarke's evidence).
18. Geoffrey W. Rice, *The Life of the Fourth Earl of Rochford (1717–1781) Eighteenth-Century Anglo-Dutch Courtier, Diplomat, and Statesman. Book 2* (Lewiston, Queenstown, Lampter, Edwin Mellen Press, 2010).
19. NA/State papers [96] 1771 April 27: Anonymous letter to Lord Rochford relative to the murder of Daniel Clarke by the rioters of Spitalfields.
20. Shoemaker, 'The London "Mob"', p. 287.
21. NA/State papers [96] 1771 April 27: Anonymous letter to Lord Rochford relative to the murder of Daniel Clarke by the rioters of Spitalfields.
22. NA/State papers [97] 1771 April 29: Wilmot to Rochford.
23. See for example George, *London Life in the Eighteenth Century*; Hay, *Albion's Fatal Tree*; Linebaugh, *The London Hanged*; Thompson, *Whigs and Hunters*.
24. L. D. Schwartz, *London in the Age of Industrialisation: Entrepreneurs, Labour Force and Living Conditions, 1700–1850* (Cambridge, Cambridge University Press, 1992), pp. 35–36.
25. Shoemaker, 'The London "Mob"', p. 280.
26. Linebaugh, *The London Hanged*, p. 270.
27. Ibid., p. 271; Gerald B. Hertz, 'The English Silk Industry in the Eighteenth Century', *The English Historical Review*, Vol. 24, No. 96 (October 1909), pp. 710–27.
28. *The Gentleman's Magazine*, November 1763.
29. Shoemaker, 'The London "Mob"', p. 296.
30. E. P. Thompson, 'Custom, Law and Common Right', in *Customs in Common* (London, Penguin Books, 1991).
31. Schwartz, *London in the Age of Industrialization*, p. 204.
32. The so-called Spitalfields Act, (5 Geo. III c.48), see Hitchcock and Shoemaker, *London Lives*, p. 275.
33. Anon, *Letter from a Spitalfields Weaver, to a Noble Duke* (London, 1765), p. 9.
34. Ibid., p. 12.
35. Junius, *Letter XXIII: To His Grace the Duke of Bedford*, 19 September 1769.
36. A. K. Sabin, *The Silk Weavers of Spitalfields and Bethnal Green, with a Catalogue and Illustrations of Spitalfields Silks* (London, Board of Education, 1931), p. 11.
37. Schwartz, *London in the Age of Industrialization*, p. 204.
38. Linebaugh, *The London Hanged*, p. 274.
39. *A List of the Society for the Encouragement of Arts, Manufactures and Commerce* (London, 18 August 1766), p. 16.
40. Quoted in Linebaugh, *The London Hanged*, p. 281.
41. Shoemaker, 'The Old Bailey Proceedings and the Representation of Crime', p. 569.
42. Trial of Henry Stroud, Robert Cambell, Anstis Horsford.

43. *Bingley's Journal*, 6–13 July 1771.
44. Trial of Henry Stroud, Robert Cambell, Anstis Horsford (evidence of John Marsh).
45. Ibid. (evidence of Thomas Gibson).
46. Ibid.
47. Brick Lane was notably wider than the streets and alleyways around it but it while it was described as a 'great thoroughfare' in 1772, it was not paved and was considered to be 'much out of Repair and incommodious'. Survey of London: Volume 27, Spitalfields and Mile End New Town. Originally published by London County Council, London, 1957. www.british-history. ac.uk/survey-london/vol27/pp123-126 [accessed 1 August 2019].
48. Trial of Henry Stroud, Robert Cambell, Anstis Horsford.
49. Ibid. (evidence of Francis Clarke).
50. Ibid.
51. Ibid.
52. Shoemaker, 'The Old Bailey Proceedings and the Representation of Crime'.
53. Trial of Henry Stroud, Robert Cambell, Anstis Horsford (evidence of Sarah Scales).
54. Ibid. (evidence of Susannah Hoe).
55. Ibid. (evidence of James Knight).
56. Ibid. (evidence of David Higgins).
57. Ibid. (evidence of John Bailey).
58. Although this is actually far from clear in the record of the case at the OBO and in the Digital Panopticon.
59. Burn, *Justice of the Peace*, Vol. 2, pp. 507–8.
60. *The Cambridge Magazine: Or, Universal Repository of Arts, Sciences, and the Belles Letters* (London, Thomas Evans, 1769), p. 522.
61. Anon, *Genuine Copies of All the Letters Which Passed Between the Right Honourable the Lord Chancellor and the Sheriffs of London and Middlesex and Between the Sheriffs and the Secretary of State Relative to the Execution of Doyle and Valine* (London, R. Davis, 1770).
62. In one letter, the sheriffs were at pains to state that by amending the terms of execution after the event, and without proper authority, the government and crown were opening a legal can of worms. 'If the crown can in one instance, contrary to the sentence, appoint a different place of execution', they argued, and 'change the *usual* place of execution to *Bethnal-Green*, it may to Newgate-street, or even to Newgate itself: and thus our boasted usage of public execution (not less necessary to the satisfaction and security of the subject than public trial) may make way for private execution, and for all those dreadful consequences with which private executions are attended in every country where they have been introduced'. This is of course exactly what eventually happened after the Tyburn procession was ended in 1783, executions moved to Newgate and then inside prisons from 1868 onwards. Anon, *Genuine Copies of All the Letters*.
63. *The Annual Register, or a View of the History, Politics, and Literature, for the Year 1769* (London, J. Dodsley, 1770).
64. *Gentleman's Magazine*, 6 July 1771.
65. *Letter from Mr. Wilmot to Lord Rochford Requesting a Colonel's Guard to Attend the Execution of Robert Campbell and Henry Stroud*, 7 July 1771.
66. Devereaux, 'The City and the Sessions Paper', p. 486.
67. 7 July 1771, *Draft of a Letter to the Secretary at War Directing Him to Order a Colonel's Guard to Attend the Execution of Robert Campbell and Henry Stroud for the Murder of Daniel Clarke in Spitalfields*.

68. *Bingley's Journal*, 6–13 July 1771.
69. Anon, *Hanging Not Punishment Enough* (London, 1701).
70. Devereaux, 'Recasting the Theatre of Execution', p. 168.
71. Quoted in Wilf, 'Imagining Justice', p. 65.
72. Alastair Bellany, 'The Murder of John Lambe: Crowd Violence, Court Scandal and Popular Politics in Early Seventeenth-Century England', *Past & Present*, No. 200 (August 2008), p. 44.
73. Ibid., p. 44.

4   The Royal Duchess and the Apothecary's Son

Homicide, Communal Prejudice, and Pleading for Pardon in Provincial England*

Introduction

So far all of the case studies chosen for this volume have been closely focused on London. The murder of John Bigby took place on Westminster Bridge, while the killing of Daniel Clarke occurred in Spitalfields, in the east. Both cases were critically affected by the prevailing political winds of the day with the outcome in part decided not by evidence offered in court but instead by political expediency and the machinations of the pardoning process. In this chapter some of these same issues will be explored but from a slightly different perspective. Here the central crime in question – the murder of parish constable – took place far from the capital in a very small and previously quiet village in the Northamptonshire countryside. Nevertheless this case touched London society directly as it resulted in a long drawn out attempt to save a young man from the gallows which was played out in the pages of the London press. So, like the Kennedy case some 18 years earlier, the case of Thomas Gordon offers us a rare window into the way in which the pardoning process was made visible to the English reading public, once again questioning Hay's assertion that it operated in secret.[1] There are clear differences in the political circumstances surrounding this case and that of Henry Stroud and Matthew and Patrick Kennedy, however. This case was overshadowed by one of the most important European, indeed global, events of the eighteenth century – the French Revolution, and this undoubtedly affected Gordon's chances of avoiding death by hanging.

Prosecutions for homicide in Northamptonshire were rare in the eighteenth century. As the opening chapter of this volume demonstrated, there were just four persons hanged for murder in the county in the period 1770–1799. In total there were only 32 hangings altogether in nearly 30 years, and given that four members of the Culworth gang were hanged collectively in 1787 alongside two other felons, this means there were several years without a hanging at all.[2] Contrast this with the capital where throughout the 1780s (and indeed across the longer period) public execution was commonplace. Pattishall, where these events took place, was a small village situated close to the main transit route (Watling Street) taking goods and people through central England. It was close (less than four miles) to the large market town of Towcester and a centre for commerce and a rival to Northampton. Pattishall was home to around 500 people, many of whom were employed in occupations typical across Northamptonshire, such as labourers, farm servants, farmers, tradesmen, and small craftsmen – including shoemakers, weavers, and stockingers.[3] Pattishall had been enclosed in the 1770s, peacefully it seems (by contrast to the unrest that had blighted the nearby village of West Haddon which had seen anti-enclosure rioting in 1765).[4] The village was an open parish and no one landed family dominated.[5] This small English village came to the attention of newspaper readers in the capital's several coffee houses as a result of a series of loosely connected, but ultimately important, events which also go some way in explaining why any history of those events has survived at all. These events helped define precedent in law and exposed the workings of the pardoning system as it operated outside of London.

This case study of one unusually well-documented murder in a small and largely rural community offers opportunities to tap in to debates about xenophobia in rural communities, the use of judicial discretion, the nature of the criminal trial, and the wider political influence on judicial proceedings in the late 1700s. It also gives an insight into the creation of narratives that influenced trial outcomes, especially when, as in this case, those contributing to the narrative were overwhelming on one side of the argument. Here competing definitions of murder or justifiable homicide, while they can be seen from outside with the distance of history, were quickly closed down and reframed in the interests of local participants. Just as the authorities in Spitalfields were keen for their version of what happened at Weavers' Fields to be accepted as the dominant 'truth', so the community of Pattishall were determined that they controlled the narrative of events in July 1788. Here though there was little doubt that the person accused of murder had been the cause of the victim's death, but there was substantial (in hindsight at least) evidence that points to his actions being either accidental or justifiable. This case began, however, with a much more straightforward assault charge and the issuing of a warrant to appear before a magistrate. This is really where the case should have stopped and, had it played out as so many of these must have done on the 1700s, we would most likely never have heard of it. County justices issued tens of thousands of warrants for assaults in the eighteenth century, the majority of which ended in settlements brokered between the warring parties.[6] This one ended in a murder charge, two assize hearings, a death sentence, referral to the Twelve Judges, an appeal to the King's Bench court, and a widely-reported petitioning campaign involving highly prominent members of the aristocracy and King George III.

Local Tensions and the Assault on Haynes Pratt

In 1786, Francis Gordon acquired land on the edge of Pattishall, on Watling Street, and close to the coaling depot at Foster's Booth (a small hamlet), where travellers often stopped for refreshments and to water or change their horses.[7] It was much less isolated then than its location might at first suggest, and for Francis – an old man with a wife and late teenaged son – it seemed like the perfect place to set up in business. Francis Gordon had been a surgeon in the armed forces, giving more than 30 years service to the crown and travelling the world. In 1785, his regiment (the 66th foot) was posted to the Caribbean island of St Vincent, and, at this point, the elderly medical man decided the time was right to retire. It was a wise and well-informed decision. The Caribbean was notoriously rife with disease and the 66th had suffered there before, losing 102 men to 'putrid fevers and dysenteries' in just one year, 1764.[8] Instead of going with them, the 63 year-old surgeon chose to establish a shop selling 'grocery and drapery goods' along with 'with mercery and drapery goods', all fashionable items for the period and things that the women (and men) of Pattishall, Towcester, who passed by would covet and part with good money for.[9] The shop would be run by his wife, Winifred, and his son, Thomas, while Francis enjoyed his retirement.

The enjoyment of his retirement seems partly to have taken the form of occupying a seat in one of the local taverns and regaling his audience with stories of his military adventures. While an affable old man telling tall tales might not seem to be threatening to anyone, it is possible that, as an outsider, he ruffled a few local feathers. Moreover, by setting themselves, physically and figuratively, outside of Pattishall, it seems that the Gordon family made some important enemies and, more generally, were viewed as unwanted 'foreigners' in what was a close-knit and insular society. As Keith Snell has noted, xenophobia was a core feature of the attitudes of many local people in eighteenth-century England. Those that arrived from outside the parish or county were to be treated with suspicion.[10] Not only were the Gordons 'foreign' in a very local sense, they were almost certainly foreign in other ways. Francis, and possibly Winifred, were Scots, more likely hailing from the north-east coast. Tension between Scotland and England remained prevalent in the late 1700s, as memories of the invasion of England by 'Bonnie' Prince Charlie (Charles Edward Stuart) in 1745 were still relatively fresh in English minds. Perhaps more to the point, the Gordons were relatively wealthy by comparison to many of the locals they interacted with: Francis identified himself as 'rich' and described his family as being 'in elegant circumstances'.[11] Alongside this the Gordons were religious dissenters and there is a suggestion in the archival material associated with the case that they looked down on the local community as beneath them.[12] All of this, coupled with the fact that they had set up a competing business on the edge of the village, makes it quite understandable that the local community should view them with, at the very least, suspicion and, at worst, outright dislike. This enmity probably manifested itself in harsh words and cold distance for the most part, but in July 1788 things took a turn for the worse.

'On the 22nd of July 1788', Leach's *Cases in Crown Law* records,

> Mr Francis Gordon being at a public house at Towcester, about four miles from Pattishall, a quarrel arose between him and one Haines [sic] Pratt, a Blacksmith of Pattishall; and after a long and violent altercation, Pratt struck Mr Gordon on the head with his fist; upon which Mr Gordon drew a long sword from a cane which he had in his hand, and pointing it at him told him to keep off; but whether Gordon ever touched Pratt with its point did not appear. Pratt however, on the ensuing day, procured a warrant from Mr Eccles, a justice of the Peace, to apprehend Mr F. Gordon.[13]

The public house in question was not in Towcester but, as that was the nearest town, it is not surprising that such a mistake was made in the record. Instead it is much more likely that the alleged assault occurred at the *Boot* inn, in Eastcote, one of the other hamlets in the parish of Pattishall.[14] Haynes Pratt was the Pattishall blacksmith. He came from a well-established local family in the village who lived on in the village for at least another century.[15] They were not wealthy, certainly not as wealthy as the Gordons, and did not pay the rates. Haynes Pratt was almost certainly in his late 20s or early to mid-30s in 1788 and a fit, strong man, as blacksmiths needed to be.[16] The term 'assault' covered a wide range of actions in the 1700s, as even a casual glance at legal handbooks will confirm.[17] It is doubtful whether the elderly former army surgeon even touched Pratt, let alone did him any serious injury. Nevertheless Pratt decided this was opportunity to humiliate the old man and probably gain some financial compensation as well.[18] Pratt obtained a warrant from a local magistrate named Eccles and wasted no time in making sure it was served. The blacksmith first approached Thomas Hart, the Thirdborough (or Constable) of Pattishall – a carpenter who held responsible positions within the village community as an overseer as well as a constable.[19] Hart pointed out to the blacksmith that Mr Eccles had made the warrant out to a fellow constable, the recently appointed George Linnell, and so the blacksmith would have to now find him if he wanted the warrant to be delivered. Since Pratt undertook all of these journeys himself, it seems unlikely that Francis Gordon's assault had done any real damage at all.

George Linnell was a farmer with a considerable investment in the parish and whose social status was even higher than that of the Gordons. This is evidenced by the fact that the Linnells paid higher rates. Indeed one London paper later described George Linnell as 'the Governor' of Pattishall.[20] Pratt took his warrant to Linnell's house later that morning and asked him to execute it. This now set in motion a series of unfortunate events that would end in the deaths of two individuals and touch the highest corridors of power in the land. Without a detailed independent account of the events of July 1788 we are largely reliant on the assizes judge's report of what happened in court and, therefore, how the prosecution case set out the sequence of events that led to George Linnell's killing.[21]

The Murder of Constable Linnell

Thomas Linnell set off from his home, accompanied by his servant Thomas Burton, and carrying his constable's staff of office. He arrived at the Gordons' house at about eight o'clock in the evening, when it would have still been fairly light, this being the summertime. He knocked on the Gordons' shop door, which was answered by Winifred Gordon. Linnell enquired as to whether her husband was at home and explained the purpose of his visit. On learning that Linnell intended to serve her husband with a warrant for an assault on Pratt, told him that her husband was not in the house and flatly refused to 'let him in to see whether Mr Gordon was at home or not'.[22] The other occupant of the house, Thomas Gordon, supported his mother and insisted that his father was out. This gave the newly appointed constable a problem; his authority was being challenged in what was probably one of the first occasions he had been required to exercise it, and he was under pressure from Pratt and his supporters to act as the law expected. Linnell pressed his intention to serve the warrant, reiterating that he had been informed that Francis was at home and wished to see for himself. The situation now deteriorated rapidly as, and according to the villagers' account, Thomas Gordon threatened Linnell, declaring that 'the first man that enters my door or my ground I will end his life'.[23] Winifred then closed the door in the constable's face, and mother and son locked up the shop, before going upstairs and peering out of the windows. The constable deliberated for a few minutes and then knocked again. He got no response but the witnesses at the scene said they saw a gun being pointed out of the upstairs window.

At this point Linnell decided to turn to Thomas Hart for advice. As a more established authority figure and someone Winifred and the Gordons perhaps knew much better, Hart agreed to try and talk Winifred and Thomas round.[24] Winifred insisted on talking to Hart from her window, possibly wary that the constable might force the door if she opened it at all, and she repeated her claim that her husband was not at home. This was an important moment in the case and suggests that the Gordons were already adopting an entrenched position against the outside world. Why do this unless they felt threatened in some way by the constable's presence? While it is hard, given the one-sided nature of the sources available, to be sure of what really happened that summer evening I think we can reasonably assume that Hart and Linnell were not alone when they had gone to the cottage. The depositions of others (and the material accounts supplied in the subsequent petition papers for mercy) would suggest that not only were they accompanied by Burton (Linnell's servant) and a handful of others (presumably including Pratt) but that a significant part of the community had made its way up the Pattishall lane towards Foster's Booth. Hart repeated Linnell's statement that they had information that Francis was at home and that unless they were allowed in to speak to Francis it might become necessary for the constable to use force. Winifred then delivered a further warning: 'Let him at his peril, he or any other that attempts the door shall be a dead man for we . . . have plenty of ammunition in the house'.[25] Once again Hart tried to persuade her to relent but Winifred insisted her husband was 'not at home' and suggested they return the next morning between seven and nine if they wished to see him.[26] She added that her husband was 'a man of property and would not run away for so paltry affair and desired him to desist and not to be led on by a parcel of ignorant foolish people'. After some discussion Linnell and Hart agreed this was the best course of action, and Linnell told the Gordons that this arrangement 'would suit him well'.[27] After Thomas had also assured him that his father would appear at the agreed hour next morning, Constable Linnell headed off down the lane towards his own house.

And there this whole affair might have rested until the following day. Heads would have cooled and with villagers heading off to their daily tasks there would have been less of a crowd to make trouble or gawp outside the Gordons' property. Winifred may have feared for her husband's safety or simply wished to avoid the embarrassment of seeing him taken away in front of the whole community. However Linnell did not stick to this agreement. Hart probably went home at this point, believing his work to be done, but George Linnell returned to the Gordons' house. Why did he do this? Thomas Burton, Linnell's servant, gave the following reason. 'Some time after his master being told he ought to execute the warrant on Gordon or he might go away his master agreed to return to Mr Gordon's and took Thomas Percy, James Wilding, Thomas Sherman and this informant'. The other accounts are less clear, and this is one of the few points when the testimonies given by the prosecution witnesses diverge. One simply says that 'the constable went away and returning charged this informant and others to assist him'. Another talks of 'the deceased then drawing off but some little time afterwards he returned again with the informant who carried an iron bar'. Another describes the way 'the deceased went from door to door' and at the instigation of 'some persons' from the village, charged a group of people to assist him. What is clear however is that Linnell returned to the Gordons' house with at least four men chosen and then deputized by him for that purpose. These were Percy, Wilding, Sherman, and Burton. We can be sure of this because these four – plus Job Kerton who 'was in the street when the constable was going towards the house' and joined them then – constituted the main trial witnesses.[28] It is also evident that Linnell returned because he was under pressure from the villagers, perhaps orchestrated by the angry blacksmith Pratt, to so do. His authority had been challenged and, moreover, challenged in public by a woman and a mere youth. He could not let his new term of office begin with such a humiliating climb-down; he had to execute the warrant and trust that the villagers' information (that Gordon was at home) was reliable.

So he returned and tried once more to execute the warrant. According to one account Linnell 'was determined to get into the house'.[29] He went to the front door and tried the latch, but Thomas Gordon once again threatened Linnell with his gun and the constable withdrew. By then there was a large crowd gathered outside the Gordons' house. Many of them followed Linnell as he took his chosen helpers, including Thomas Percy with his iron bar, down the lane and entered a close that adjoined the garden at the back of the Gordons' house.[30] Having instructed the crowd not to encroach upon the Gordons' land (an instruction that was almost universally ignored) Linnell and his chosen assistants then climbed a wall and got into the garden. His intention seems to have been to gain access to the house through the door on the garden side. As Linnell scaled the low wall into the garden Thomas spotted him from the chamber window and aimed his gun. As Linnell made his way towards the back door a number of witnesses reported that hearing Winifred say 'Fire Tom!' and 'kill them' although others denied hearing her say anything of the sort. George Linnell was only between seven and ten yards from the house when Thomas' gun discharged a single bullet that struck the constable in his groin and brought him down. The wounds extended to 'a part of the penis, the right testicle, and a small portion of the right thigh' and the bullet having also lacerated an artery, he died soon afterwards. According to the prosecution witnesses it was at this point (rather than before the shooting) that the local inhabitants began to assail the windows of the house with stones and to attack it with other weapons. Francis, who had been at home all the time, appeared and he, Thomas, and Winifred Gordon all surrendered themselves to the authorities.[31]

The Defence of Justifiable Homicide

As with the case of Henry Stroud there is more than one way to view the events of that July evening in Pattishall. Although the prosecution's version of the story dominates the surviving sources, the Gordons presented a very different version of events, arguing cogently that the killing of Constable Linnell was in fact a case of justifiable homicide and not of murder. While it seems possible that these were presented at the subsequent trial we have no record of this and in fact the judge's report of the proceedings hints that the defence largely failed to offer a coherent and convincing alternative. Instead we must rely on the pardoning process and the records that generated to try to see events from the perspective of the Gordons. Several of the key arguments are set out in Francis Gordon's later petition for a pardon for Thomas. 'My most unhappy son', he wrote,

> is under sentence of Death, occasioned by a Wicked and malicious people, who got a vile man to Gitt [sic] a warrant by Purgery [sic], and at eight o'clock at night to essemble [sic] to the number of one Hundred people with iron bars and Bludgeons then sent for the Constable to Serve the warrant. When the constable came he agreed to come in the morning and Went his way. The mob being disappointed some of them followed him and by threats obliged him to return and to go into a Field at the Back of the House and to Gitt [sic] over the Garden Wall with forty of more of the mob. Those in the yard were breakin [sic] the Lower windows and Doors with an iron Bar and others throwing stones to the upper windows it was past Nine oclock at Night when my unhappy son went to the window with a Gun which he laid on the window. The stones being throwing so fast one struck him on the Breast and the gun went off – he never thought that the constable was their [sic], as having agreed to come in the morning, he thought the mob wanted to Gitt [sic] into the house to murder us and to rob the House, as some of them said bring them out and we will murder them.[32]

The defence version challenges the prosecution on several counts in that it attempts to show that the 'murder' was a tragic accident (or manslaughter) or at worst a justifiable homicide caused by the actions of an unruly mob who had besieged the Gordons' house and were threatening their lives. The central argument involved the role of the hostile group of villagers who had gathered around the house. In this alternate version a large, armed, and riotous crowd of about a hundred or more people – i.e., about a third of the adult population of Pattishall – had already gathered about the house before the constable came to serve the warrant. They had not only used Pratt as a pawn to create a false accusation of assault but had also sent for Constable Linnell demanding that he serve the resulting warrant. When, after talking to the Gordons, Linnell and Hart agreed to defuse the situation by returning the next morning, they followed Linnell back into the village and threatened him, forcing him to return and serve the warrant. In the defence's version of the story the crowd also played a much more proactive role just prior to the shooting than the prosecution witnesses were prepared to admit. Crucially, in

Francis Gordon's account, they were already smashing the lower windows and doors and stoning the upper windows of the house before the fatal shot was fired. In addition, the defence argued that it was considerably later in the evening than the prosecution had admitted—past nine o'clock, and as darkness began to fall the defenders of the house could not see that it was the constable who had returned. They thought themselves under attack from an illegal mob that was specifically threatening to murder them. The shooting was not intended to harm an officer of the law; instead it was accidental, and done purely in self-defence.[33] The legal definition of justified homicide required that the killing 'must be owing to some unavoidable necessity' and the justice's manuals specifically stated that

> if anyone attempting feloniously to rob or murder any person in a dwelling house . . . or attempting to break any dwelling house in the night-time shall happen in such felonious attempt to be slain, the slayer shall . . . be acquitted and discharged.[34]

According to the defence's version, therefore, this was very definitely a justifiable homicide.

Arguably this was no accident; the Gordons' claim that the gun went off accidentally is difficult to believe, but many of the defence's other arguments have considerable force. By the time of the King's Bench hearing it was widely agreed that Pratt had been the main aggressor in the original fight at the *Boot* – which is in line with the Gordons' defence and indeed with common sense. Why would an elderly infirm man pick a fight with someone half his age that he knew to be the local blacksmith, a trade almost synonymous with physical strength? Moreover, Linnell's sudden decision to return unannounced to the Gordons' house after setting a watch on the house and agreeing to return the next morning also makes most sense if the Gordons were correct in arguing that he did so because the crowd insisted on it. Even if he had arrested Francis as planned at that time of evening he would not have been able to get him to Justice Eccles' house in Stoke Bruerne before nightfall. It was six miles or more and would have been a very difficult journey in the dark to a magistrate who might well have been unwilling to hear such a routine case between 10 and 12 at night. Linnell could have held Francis overnight but he could just as easily have kept an eye on him till the next morning by continuing to keep a watch on the house. To make a decision such as this and take a line of action that would have meant that he had to either imprison Francis for the night or undertake a long dark journey with his prisoner in the presence of a hostile crowd, Constable Linnell must surely have been under huge pressure from an angry group of Pattishall inhabitants (or alternatively to have himself felt great antipathy towards the Gordons and been part of the conspiracy).

Further doubts as to the veracity of the prosecution case are revealed by the account of the murder that appeared in the *Northampton Mercury* three days after the incident and subsequently in some London papers:

On Thursday the following shocking murder was perpetrated at Pattishall in this county: George Linnell, the constable of that parish, went to the house of – Gordon in order to execute a warrant on him for an assault upon a blacksmith of Pattishall; but finding the doors of his house fastened, Linnell and a number of people who had collected together about the house attempted to force their way in. They were frequently threatened to be fired upon by the man's wife and son if they persisted in their attempt; notwithstanding which, they began to demolish the windows; when the son fired upon them, and killed Linnell on the spot.[35]

By highlighting the fact that *before the shot was fired* the crowd had already tried to force their way in and had demolished some of the Gordons' house, this account supports a keystone in the Gordons' defence and, for that reason perhaps, it was later contested by the villagers. The following edition of the *Northampton Mercury* published a very different story, one which fitted much better with the prosecution's case by stressing that 'not a pane was broke nor any force used till the fatal catastrophe took place'. Caught between the two stories, the editor of the Northampton paper eventually took a neutral stance, asking his readers in view of 'several contradictory reports' recently published to suspend their judgement till a legal investigation had taken place.[36] We might, to use a modern phrase, suggest that he 'was got at' by 'interested parties'. However, this does not alter the fact that there were clearly some witnesses (one of whom later gave evidence at the trial) who not only saw the events of July 23 very differently from the way they were portrayed by the prosecution but also wished to make their views public. We therefore have two very different interpretations about what happened on the evening of July 23. There was definitely a case to answer. A local constable undertaking a legal duty had been shot dead. Yet at the same time the defence's arguments raised many questions about whether an indictment for murder was appropriate. Much of the prosecution's evidence was far from incontestable. Did those questions create sufficient doubts about the prosecution's case to enable the accused to avoid the gallows?

The first place where these competing versions of events played out was the coroner's hearing, which began the day after the killing and took place at the *George* inn (just up the road from the Gordons' house). Almost all of the members of the coroner's jury, the key decision-making body at this point, lived in Pattishall. Although they came from a fairly wide spectrum of social groups, the majority of the jurors can be traced as owners or tenants of land in the enclosure records or in the

1780s Land Tax assessments of either Pattishall or the neighbouring parish of Cold Higham.[37] Some were men of considerable substance. William Waite, for example, was a land tax assessor and endowed a charity that continued to benefit the children of the parish well into the nineteenth century.[38] The witnesses who appeared at the coroner's inquest (and were then bound by recognizance to give evidence at the assizes) came from a rather less wealthy cross-section of the village than the coroner's jury. Thomas Burton (Linnell's servant) and Job Kerton were listed as labourers, and both of them had been involved in the attempt to gain entry to the Gordon's home; Thomas Sherman was a tailor; James Wilding a framework knitter; only Thomas Percy, who was a butcher, followed a trade that usually required the possession of some capital.[39]

The coroner's inquest was effectively (if not deliberately) constructed so as to oppose any version put forward by the Gordons. All the witnesses and all of those serving as jurors were local inhabitants and so it was never likely, given what we know about the antagonism that many locals felt towards the Gordons, that the coroner's jury would be sympathetic. Meeting as it did in Pattishall itself the day after a local man of considerable substance had been killed by an outsider, the verdict was never in doubt. Though some individuals may have dissented from the final decision, 'the jury', as the *Northampton Mercury* briefly reported, 'brought in their verdict of wilful murder; upon which Thomas Gordon and Winifred his mother were committed by the coroner to the county gaol, to take their trial at the next assizes'.[40] At this initial stage of the judicial process, therefore, local witnesses from a community whose xenophobic attitudes are all too clear had managed to shape the trial around the charge of murder rather than justifiable homicide. However, the assizes court – given that it was held in Northampton and thus at a distance from Pattishall and with a jury that was not packed with those prejudiced against the Gordons – presented a much deeper test of the power of local feeling to shape the legal process. As a result the family may well have felt that it would give a more sympathetic hearing to their side of the story. This belief may have made them complacent; it was certainly misplaced.

The Northamptonshire assizes convened in March 1789. Thomas Gordon was charged with murder and Winifred Gordon was indicted as an accessory, and both would have spent the preceding months following the incident in Northampton Gaol, in desperate conditions. Both crimes carried the death penalty on conviction, although if the defence could argue that the shooting was justifiable then both might avoid hanging. As was noted in the introduction, homicide cases in Northamptonshire were rare in the late 1700s; this was one of only four between 1770 and 1800, so it is reasonable to imagine that the trial was followed closely in Pattishall and the county as a whole. Following the grand jury's private hearing (of which we have no record), the indictment was declared a 'true bill' and the case sent on for public trial – as the vast majority of murder indictments were in the late eighteenth century – before a petty jury of 12 middling men drawn from throughout the county. However, if the Gordons were hoping for a balanced trial in which they had equal opportunity to present their version of events they were to be sadly disappointed. The judge's trial report and the depositions of witnesses taken at the coroner's hearing and then sent to the assizes leave the impression that the Gordons' side of the story was poorly represented and largely dismissed. In the account of the trial written by Judge Baron Thompson in response to the Gordons' later petition, the focus is almost entirely on the evidence presented by the posse of Pattishall men who assisted Constable Linnell that evening. Baron Thompson spent nearly six pages outlining the prosecution case in factual language and never once suggested that any of the evidence might be problematic or concocted. Having effectively rubber-stamped the decision made by the jury in his court, he then spent less than a page on the defence's alternative view and on describing a crucial point in the trial – the dismissal by the court of the main defence witness' evidence, the reasons for which he did not feel it necessary to record.

'On the part of the prisoners', he wrote,

> it was alleged that they were ignorant of the constable's return, having understood that he had agreed to wait till the next morning and that the house being beset on the back by a large mob, who had broke the windows with stones, and appeared to be endeavouring to force the house, what the prisoner Thomas did was in resistance to such an attack; and one witness for the prisoner swore that before the gun was fired two men (one of whom was a witness for the prosecution) stood at the garden wall shaking their fists at Thomas Gordon, abusing him and telling him to shoot if he dare, and that in fact stones were thrown by the people, which broke Gordon's windows, before the gun was fired; but he gave his evidence in a way which did not gain him credit with the jury; and Francis Gordon, the father, who admitted that he was at home when the constable first came and continued there, swore that before the gun was fired, the windows on the back of the house were broke by large stones and that the mob was beating on the kitchen door: but the witnesses for the prosecution positively denied that there was any riot or disturbance or violence offered to the house before the gun was fired although it was admitted by them that after the deceased was shot the windows were broken by stones thrown by the people. . . . The jury found both the defendants guilty . . . I see no circumstances in his case which I conceive will warrant me in recommending him as an object of the Royal Mercy.[41]

Judge Thompson may have remained neutral during the trial – this is what judges were supposed to do, acting in effect as the defence for the defendant[42] – but his report clearly favours the prosecution version. The short report about the trial that was published in several London and provincial newspapers (but not in the *Northampton Mercury* whose editor had decided to remain neutral) presented a rather different reading that showed much more sympathy for the Gordons' alternative narrative. The facts were 'rather singular' the report noted.

> The father, mother and son retiring to this county . . . became obnoxious for no other reason than that the country people considered them as foreigners, and not being born in the county. There were frequently little quarrels between their neighbours and them, till at last a justice's warrant was obtained for a supposed assault made by the father.

The report then noted that the fatal shot was fired *after* the stoning of the house had begun and not before it as the prosecution alleged, and pointed out that the constable knew all along that Francis was at home, thus casting doubt on the reasons given by the prosecution for his sudden and unannounced return.[43]

The newspapers' willingness to raise these questions about the conviction made no difference to the verdict, however. Faced by the defence's attempts to establish doubts about the validity of their version of the story, the villagers succeeded in undermining the credibility of the key defence witness and responded to the Gordons' defence with a concerted rebuttal which persuaded the jury that the killing of Constable Linnell was definitely murder rather than justified homicide. Given that both stories seem credible and that the Gordons' counter-case raised enough questions about the prosecution to make it difficult to assert that it had been established beyond reasonable doubt that this was a murder, the question naturally arises of why this defence failed? Thomas Gordon was a young man with 'an irreproachable character' and there was no evidence that he bore any previous malice towards the victim. The explanation may, in part at least, rest with the quality of the defence at the trial. Some of the later correspondence suggests that the Gordons did not feel they were 'fully heard' at the trial and in reflecting on the trial the highest judge in England – the Lord High Chancellor (Edward Thurlow) – privately commented that given the coherent alternative story available, a better defence might well have produced a different outcome.

> A boy of nineteen, by the encouragement of his mother, protecting an aged father, a circumstance fit to engage pity. The representations that the old man was oppressed by a malignant confederacy and attacked by an enraged mob, would have been a perfect Defense. But

no part of this Defense was made out at the trial where it would have been alleged more properly. The attempt to make it out failed by the discredit of their only witness produced to prove it.[44]

In other words the Gordons were ill served by the team of lawyers they had hired. Was this a result of a paucity of funds, of ignorance, or perhaps because they fundamentally believed that their story was so obviously credible that the jury could not fail to believe them? Again there is an echo here of the Stroud case: Henry Stroud knew he was innocent, knew he had tried to save Daniel Clarke and had not participated in his stoning and drowning, but brought few witnesses to court to counter the orchestrated claims of those that wanted to do him ill. Moreover the authorities needed a quick conviction and execution in order to quell (or to attempt to subdue at least) the tensions amongst the weaving community of Spitalfields. In 1789, in Pattishall, Northampton, and indeed the wider country, the Gordons' actions could also be read as a direct threat to authority and one that needed to be quashed. While Thomas Gordon's conviction represented a triumph for the Pattishall villagers and their insular hatred of strangers, the odds were also stacked against them because one of the defence's two chief witnesses, Francis Gordon, had lied to the authorities in order to avoid arrest, and – most importantly – because the dead man was a parish constable. These factors, coupled with the poor quality of the defence team hired for the purpose, effectively condemned young Thomas to death.

There was a possible twist to the case as the Gordons attempted to use a legal loophole to avoid the inevitable. It was suggested that George Linnell had not been officially confirmed as parish constable, which would mean that he did not have the authority to execute the warrant. This would undermine his status and support a defence of justifiable homicide. After all, when Mr Eccles had issued the warrant to Haynes Pratt, the blacksmith had taken it to Thomas Hart, not to Linnell. Clearly then there was some doubt as to who Pattishall's constable actually was. This issue, and some technical doubts about the indictment against Winifred as an accessory, led the assize judge to defer sentencing in March 1789 and refer the case to the Twelve Judges in London.[45] No defendant convicted at assizes had any right of appeal, but if the circuit judge believed that a case required further examination he could reserve it for consideration by the Twelve Judges, who met between circuits for this purpose. As John Langbein has noted, the decisions of the 12 in selected cases such as this could have long-lasting consequences as they set precedents in law.[46] This was a rare occurrence, which again affords us an opportunity to look at the usually secretive pardoning process. On average only 8 cases a year were referred to the 12, but it was the only remaining avenue of review.[47] The judges would discuss the case based on the trial judge's report and the presentations of crown and defence counsel (if they were offered),[48] and overall about 40 per cent of convictions were overturned or amended as a result. However, this only happened if either new evidence was introduced or there had been a clear misapplication of the law by the original trial judge and jury.

When the judges met in the Exchequer chamber on June 24, 1789 the first question they discussed was whether George Linnell 'had been duly elected into the office' of constable for the parish of Pattishall.[49] 'If he had not been constable', several London papers reported, 'it would have been justifiable homicide'.[50] All parish officers had to be formerly sworn in by a magistrate, and it seems that Linnell had not been sworn before he served the warrant on the Gordons. Anyone serving a warrant or attempting to arrest another had to 'be a legal officer for that purpose', but crucially in reviewing this case the Twelve Judges ruled that 'if he be a constable or other known officer *de facto*, acting within his district, it is sufficient without proving his appointment and swearing in'.[51] Since some of the prosecution witnesses had made a point of observing that Linnell was carrying his staff of office as he approached the Gordons' house and so could be clearly recognized as the constable, the judge's ruling confirmed that Thomas Gordon had shot and killed a legal officer carrying out his duty and thus finally eliminated any possibility that his crime could be redefined by this means as justifiable homicide. The fact that Mrs Gordon had never met him must, therefore, have been deemed irrelevant. Hart would also, presumably, have told her that the warrant was lawful and that Linnell was constable so, as a legal attempt to save Thomas it was of limited use and almost certainly doomed to fail. Once again it seems the Gordons were being badly advised. A month later, on July 23, 1789, Judge Hotham announced at the Northamptonshire assizes that 'by the unanimous opinion of the twelve judges . . . the case was fully and properly proved' against Thomas Gordon. He then 'passed sentence on the son to be executed on Saturday. It was the most affecting scene that was ever held in a court of justice to see the distress of the mother when sentence of death was passed on her son'.[52]

However, Winifred was spared because the Twelve Judges had grave doubts about the validity of her conviction. 'The case of the mother', several London newspapers reported, 'was that she, being indicted as accessory before the fact, the evidence turned out she was principal . . . the twelve judges . . . were of the opinion that the indictment was bad'. This second and quite complex point of law occupied the Twelve Judges for much longer and East's report suggests that this case established a new legal precedent. The key issue seems to have been that 'one indicted as accessory before cannot be convicted on evidence proving her to have been present aiding and abetting at the fact' and, after much argument, the judges therefore decided that Winifred should have been indicted for murder rather than as an accessory, but that her conviction for the latter charge was unsafe.[53]

This did not lead to Winifred's immediate release. Anne Linnell, the wife of the murdered constable, 'preferred an appeal of murder' against Winifred at the Northamptonshire assizes,[54] just as Anne Bigby had done over a decade earlier in the search for justice for the murder of her husband, John. Mrs Gordon seems to have remained in prison for at least another eight months (on top of the year she had already spent in Northampton Gaol). It was therefore her ageing husband Francis who bore the main burden of attempting to obtain a pardon for their son. The next crucial stage of Thomas Gordon's journey through the English criminal justice system began almost immediately after he was sentenced to death. As we have noted earlier, murderers were supposed to be hanged within three days of their conviction but before he left Northampton at the end of the assizes Judge Hotham ordered a temporary respite for Thomas until Monday, August 3 – 'with a view', the *Times* noted 'of giving him an opportunity of applying for mercy'.[55] Francis Gordon was now involved in a frantic attempt to mobilize various members of the eighteenth-century elite to help him to obtain a conditional pardon for his son.

The Attempt to Save Thomas Gordon's Life

The petitioning process began almost immediately after the Twelve Judges' ruling. Francis Gordon did not need to wait until the death sentence was officially pronounced on Thomas at the Northamptonshire assizes, he would have known what that outcome would be and have recognized that the clock was ticking if he was to save his son's life. Home Office records indicate that a petition from Winifred and Thomas Gordon accompanied by one from some of the freeholders of Pattishall had already been received by July 12—nine days before the assizes.[56] Francis Gordon had clearly already begun rallying support and had managed to persuade some of the middle ranking men of Pattishall to sign a petition asking for leniency. Unfortunately that petition has not survived. However, it was only when the death sentence had been formally passed on Thomas that the appeal process entered its final most intense stage. As had been the case with Matthew and Patrick Kennedy, Francis Gordon had somehow been able to make some very powerful connections. In particular he was able to mobilize the Duke and Duchess of Gordon – probably through his connection with the Duke's uncle, Lord Adam Gordon, Colonel of the 66th Regiment and so someone under which Francis Gordon may well have served – and the Duke and Duchess of Gloucester. Both families wrote letters and approached key government figures in person on Thomas' behalf.

These were no minor members of the British aristocracy. Alexander, fourth Duke of Gordon, was described by Lord Kames as 'the greatest subject in Britain in regard not only to the extent of his rent roll, but also to the number of people dependent on his protection'. Alexander Gordon, the fourth to hold the title, was a man who preferred the comforts of his estate and country sports to the cut and thrust of politics. His grandfather had been a Jacobite sympathizer but his father had played an important role of the field at Culloden. He had raised two regiments to fight the Americans and the French in 1776 and would do so again in 1789.[57] Although he was elected as one of the 16 representative peers of Scotland in 1767 and later became an English peer in 1784, he was more interested in his estates than in parliamentary events.[58] These estates were in north-east Scotland, in Moray and above Aberdeenshire – the same area from where the Gordons had come. He was buried at Elgin cathedral, the spiritual centre of that part of the Highlands. Alexander Gordon was drawn into politics by Henry Dundas to support Pitt and was apparently well thought of at Westminster as well as being popular in polite society.[59] He had, then, the right sort of connections to be a useful ally for Francis Gordon and his family. London society was even more impressed by Jane, the Duchess of Gordon. She went to London for the season throughout the 1780s and her intellect was 'much admired' by William Pitt, the prime minister, for whom she canvassed very heavily in 1784. Pitt described her as 'the first whipper-in of the Tories' and the extravagant dinners she gave for members of his government turned her London home into the social centre of the Tory party in the same way that Devonshire House in the time of the Duchess of Devonshire was the focus of the Whigs. She was a society beauty possessed of considerable charm, as her portrait in the national Gallery in Edinburgh suggests.[60] It is alleged that she once helped her son (George, Marquess of Huntly) to recruit a regiment by 'offering the king's shilling from between her own lips'. The story may have been embellished but Jane was clearly a woman of charm and influence. More importantly for Thomas Gordon, the Duchess was very close to the unmarried Pitt. She acted as his hostess at Downing Street throughout the crucial period 1787–1789 and later referred to this as the period when she 'lived with' him. In the late 1780s she unsuccessfully attempted to pair him up with her eldest daughter, and on at least one occasion in 1788 it was observed that Pitt's performance in the House was affected by the fact that he had got drunk the night before with Dundas and the Duchess.[61]

While the Duke and Duchess of Gordon were intimately linked with those in positions of power within parliament and the government, the Duke and Duchess of Gloucester were arguably even better positioned, close as they were, at the heart of the royal family. William Henry, the Duke of Gloucester, was the king's favourite brother. Although the Duke's relationship with the king had been badly affected by the revelation in 1772 that six years earlier he had secretly married a commoner, Maria, the widow of the second Earl Waldegrave, by 1780 George III was allowing him (if not his wife) back into court life.[62] Unlike the king's oldest sons, the Duke was supportive during George's bout of insanity in late 1788 and early 1789, and in the summer of 1789 the Duke not only placed his house in Weymouth at the king's disposal, after the latter had taken the Duke's advice and gone there to convalesce, but also joined him there at a key moment in the petitioning process.[63] So, just as was the case with the Kennedy brothers, Thomas Gordon's petition for a conditional pardon had powerful supporters.

This study has already established that in the later eighteenth century, the pardoning process was rarely seen by the public. The letters and judges' reports that survive in the Home Office records were private transcripts, many of which were written between members of the social elite who did not expect their contents to become public. 'Pardon-dealing', Douglas Hay has observed, 'went on at the highest levels only, well concealed from the eyes of the poor'. The largely private nature of the petitioning process made the records it created immensely useful to historians, but it also protected the participants in vital ways. 'Failing to get a pardon', as the same author has recently pointed out, could involve 'embarrassment, a loss of status'. If the efforts of elite petitioners were unsuccessful, it was extremely helpful that their failure would not usually become known to the general public.[64] However, those involved in attempting to get a pardon for Thomas Gordon did not enjoy this immunity from public scrutiny. The London newspapers, many of which covered the story both sympathetically and in some detail, not only announced that every effort was being made by the 'first characters of the country' but also told their readers who the key players were.[65] A number of them noted that Francis Gordon had the backing of the Duke of Gloucester and several other noble personages[66] and others made it clear at a crucial stage that 'Their Royal Highnesses the Duke and Duchess of Gloucester and the Duchess of Gordon humanely interested themselves in the fate of young Gordon'.[67] This was to be a very public test of the ability of leading aristocratic figures to influence the pardoning process.

The role of elite connections in the pardoning process has been the subject of much debate amongst historians. Hay's statement that 'the claims of class saved far more men who had been left to hang by the assize judge than did the claims of humanity' has been subjected to extensive critical scrutiny, as systematic research has revealed the important role played by such factors as youth, gender, previous good character, reformability, etc.[68] However, while Peter King's detailed work on Essex has suggested that 'aristocratic support was not an automatic ticket to mercy',[69] few historians would disagree with Hay's view that 'It was the greatest good fortune to get the attention of a sympathetic peer. In a system which gave first weight to those with the most power their influence was naturally greatest'.[70] The debate on this issue is therefore a subtle one. It is not about the potential power of aristocratic connections – few would disagree that they could be important – but about the extent and limits of that power and about the context and timing of appeals.

This case, which has left more documents in the eighteenth century Home Office archives than almost any other petitioning campaign, especially by comparison to that of the Kennedy brothers, offers an excellent opportunity to investigate this issue. What precisely were the limits of aristocratic influence within the pardoning system? If, as Hay has argued, 'Petitions were most effective from great men', a case such as Thomas Gordon's, in which there were clearly major questions about the evidence against the prisoner and in which several great men (and women) were involved would surely be most likely to end in a conditional pardon or even a free pardon.[71] Even though this was a murder case, and involved the killing of a constable, it also centred on a family that was highly respectable – another factor pinpointed by Hay as important and whose household head could boast 30 years of service as an army surgeon. Given that the counter-case advanced by the petitioner was acknowledged by the Lord Chancellor himself as having considerable power – thus creating a vital potential bargaining space – this provides a marvellous opportunity to study aristocratic power in action within the eighteenth-century criminal justice system. Moreover, it also offers a means of extending our understanding of the eighteenth century pardoning process in a new direction. Because the judge announced a ten-day respite immediately after sentencing Thomas Gordon – a rare event which is itself an indication either that he believed that there was a good case for a pardon and/or that Francis Gordon's connections were already at work – and because Francis then gained another respite at the end of that period, the Pattishall case offers a opportunity to explore pardoning procedure as it was applied to homicide.

The first recorded petitioning initiative that was undertaken on Thomas Gordon's behalf after the death sentence was announced was a letter written by the Duke of Gordon on July 25, 1789 to Evan Nepean, the Under Secretary of State at the Home Office,[72] pointing to the 'many alleviating circumstances in favor [sic] of the young man, who is only 19 years of age' and asking for Nepean's 'good offices in procuring a pardon for that unhappy young man, which will not only confer a very particular favor [sic] upon me, but be the means of extricating a wretched family from misery and disgrace'. Enclosed with this letter was Francis Gordon's own petition. 'Permit an old man bourn [sic] down with the Heavey [sic] Affliction, after serving my King and Country for thirty years to Humbly implore your Goodness towards my most unhappy son who is under sentence of Death, occasioned by a Wicked and malicious people' he wrote, before eloquently laying out the defence's alternative version of events (already discussed) and pointing out that 'the unhappy Boy never committed any crime before and was urged to this as protecting his aged Parents'. Francis did not attempt to get a free pardon, pleading instead that his son should be transported 'to save a Life that may become a useful member to Socialty [sic] in this world'.[73]

Although this initial intervention by the Duke of Gordon was very positive in tone and Francis' letter was both moving and well argued, the Duke received a polite but far from optimistic reply from Nepean. The trial judge had sent him a very 'full and circumstantial' account of the evidence and his report, Nepean pointed out, stated expressly that he saw no circumstances that would warrant a pardon. 'I cannot but concur in this opinion', Nepean wrote, before adding 'particularly as almost all the favourable points relied on in the petition are contradicted by the evidence given at the trial' – a phrase that indicates just how effective the Pattishall anti-Gordon trial witnesses had been in getting their version of the story over at the expense of that of the Gordons. The Duke of Gordon seems to have been greatly discouraged by this negative response. In a subsequent letter he wrote about 'being ashamed to give you this further trouble after receiving your answer about Gordon several days ago'.[74] However Francis Gordon had by this time managed to obtain the help of other powerful allies. Armed with 'recommendations from the Duke of Gloucester and several other noble personages', he obtained a personal audience with the king.[75]

Since the London press clearly recognized this as a dramatic 'human interest' story, many now carried reports of Francis' desperate journeys to save his son. On the last day of July 1789, three days before Thomas was due to hang, Francis arrived at Weymouth where King George III had been staying for some time. The Duke of Gloucester almost certainly helped to set up this meeting, which probably took place at the Duke's Weymouth residence, Gloucester House, where the king was staying. It may not have been a coincidence that the Duke arrived in Weymouth on the same day that Francis Gordon reached the town and that Francis almost immediately obtained an audience with the king.[76] According to the press King George showed the elderly Francis great respect. 'His Majesty received him with the greatest condescension and took him by the hand, and desired him sit down and refresh himself', the *Whitehall Evening Post* reported. The king then 'read the recommendations with great attention and seemed much affected. After considering a few minutes he told Mr Gordon that the necessary forms would not allow of an immediate pardon, the time being too short, as he perceived the execution of the unhappy youth was fixed for the next Monday, but he would grant him a respite'.[77] The newspapers reported that Francis was delighted with the outcome and that 'he ran over the town publishing the joyful news' while the local notables congratulated him on his success. They then reported that Francis caught the earliest coach for London to present the king's messages in person at the Home Office and, reaching there at noon on the Sunday, was able to get dispatches made out to stay the execution.[78] He then set off riding overnight to Northampton. Meanwhile the arrangements for Thomas' execution had begun. On the Sunday night the condemned sermon was preached and the press reported that Thomas 'behaved with great fortitude, in full expectation of the awful event'. However, 'on Sunday evening he expressed much anxiety to see his father, and bid him a last farewell. His father was not to be found, at which information his fortitude left him, and he wept bitterly'. Francis arrived in Northampton at 3 a.m. but he was refused entrance to the gaol until six. Once inside, the newspapers reported, he 'flew to his son, and found him fervently employed in prayer, not being acquainted with the happy turn of his fate'.[79]

> The father, in a flood of tears, embraced his child, and announced, in a voice scarcely intelligible, the happy tidings of a respite; and the son, upon hearing the joyful news, fainted away in his parent's arms. This scene was heightened by the arrival of Mrs. Gordon, the mother, who became almost frantic with joy.

The relief was only temporary, however. The Home Secretary Grenville had postponed Thomas' execution for only 14 days and the final outcome still remained in the balance.[80]

The apparently warm reception Francis had received from the king suggested there was a real possibility that a conditional pardon would be granted but the private correspondence of the king and key members of the cabinet indicates that matters soon took a different and more negative turn. On the same day that Thomas received his respite, the Home Secretary, William Grenville, wrote a letter to the king stressing the role the Duke of Gloucester and the Duke of Gordon had played in obtaining it, enclosing 'the papers relating to the case', and requesting 'your majesty's command upon it'. Precisely what papers he enclosed is unknown but presumably they included the judge's report, the petitioning papers, the now missing petition from Pattishall worthies, and quite probably (and if so crucially) a letter from Pitt that also survives in Grenville's papers and which (though undated) was filed immediately before his letter to the king – implying it was written previous to that letter. Pitt's letter made it clear that the Prime Minister saw no reason to pardon Thomas.

'I have read the report', Pitt wrote.

> I can discover no grounds for mercy: as the sort of defence set up for the prisoner appears to have been disbelieved both by the judge and the jury; and it seems not to be disputed that the constable was shot in a situation in which it is hardly possible for the prisoner not to have known him. The deliberate intention to obstruct the execution of the warrant . . . is confirmed . . . by denying that the father was at home.[81]

Pitt does not seem to have met Francis Gordon and as a hard-headed and deeply pragmatic politician with a lawyer's training his default position seems to have been a legal one, which allowed the Gordon's counter-narrative no room for manoeuvre. The King's response to the papers sent to him by Grenville, which was written the next day, made it clear he was taking the same line as Pitt, his letter very matter of factly commenting in the midst of other business that ' I cannot see any reason to prevent the law taking its course on the convict at Northampton'.[82] Thus, only four days after he had given Francis great hopes of a conditional pardon for his son, and granted a 14-day reprieve, the king had changed his mind. Why? This change may have been simply a reaction to the judge's very negative report. The king certainly had a reputation for following the letter of the law and for rarely going against the judge's advice. Equally the king may have been influenced by Pitt's opinion. In the summer of 1789, the king was exhausted and still convalescing and Pitt's standing was higher than it had ever been. Although Pitt and George III had a guarded working relationship, the king trusted Pitt and gave him a relatively free hand, especially after the Regency crisis, when the king talked of stepping back from active involvement in government.[83] However, whether the king came to this view independently or under the influence of Pitt and his ministers, the net effect was the same. The key people Thomas Gordon most needed to persuade were clearly against a further reprieve or a conditional pardon at this point.

The story was not over, however. First the Duke and Duchess of Gloucester and then the Duchess of Gordon took up the reins and worked hard for Thomas' cause. With just over a week to go before the new date for the execution, the Duke and Duchess of Gloucester wrote a series of letters to all the three key players – Thurlow (as Lord Chancellor), Grenville, and Pitt. In an intensive period of activity between August 10 and 14 they also obtained interviews for Francis Gordon or for his lawyer with Thurlow and with the Grenville, while in addition the Duke of Gloucester arranged meetings between himself and these influential men. Maria, the Duchess of Gloucester, meanwhile played a slightly different role, writing heartfelt letters designed to appeal to the emotions of various government ministers. Not all her letters have survived and some are undated but her appeals were both direct and emotional:

> if the poor young man could get another respite, as such things have been oftener for very worthless criminals, his provocations might be mentioned to the judge in a recommendation for mercy, which could not be in the form of trial mentioned in the court. These unfortunate people have been punished more than our laws allow for. For they, that is mother and son, have been in prison upwards of a year – and the poor old father from elegant circumstances is reduced to poverty – all criminals are not so severely punished. And although

the young man has killed a man, he bore him no malice; he thought his father's house attacked at an undue hour after the mother had promised her husband should appear the next morning. – Think then dear sir, how it must aggravate the poor old man's affliction to think it was his refusing to deliver himself up to the justice's warrant which has brought his son to an ignominious and cruel death: with the additional misery of a triumph to those malignant people who had vowed their ruin from the moment they settled in the town. . . . Perhaps the constable may have left a wife – I dare say if I promised to take care of her she will not wish to go on to further vengeance – such people as those can commonly be comforted with money.[84]

Although the Gloucesters received some initial encouragement, they met with only very limited success. The Lord Chancellor wrote on August 11 saying that at their request he had 'seen the poor man whose story interests your benevolence and compassion', and since his letter also included his very positive remarks (already quoted) about the Gordons' side of the story being a perfect defence if made out at the trial, Francis may well have persuaded him of the potential validity of the Gordons' counter-narrative. However, Thurlow's letter bluntly pointed out that despite all these potential mitigations, the offence was still 'an impudent defiance of the Law of the land, a deliberate murder of an officer of justice in the execution of his duty' and although Thurlow also said that he had talked to Grenville, and that the latter was 'ready to hear with favour anything which can be urged materially in favour of the convict', Grenville's subsequent correspondence made it clear that no real progress had been made. The Duke of Gloucester had written to the Home Office on the 10th asking for a further reprieve and for help in 'getting a favourable report from the judge' so that 'this poor man may be transported', but the reply he received from Grenville the next day was not sympathetic. The Home Secretary respectfully informed him that he had 'transmitted to His Majesty, unaccompanied with any remarks from me' both the petitions and the trial judge's 'very full' report of the evidence given at the trial, 'which differs in several very essential particulars from the representations of the case as contained in the petitions'. After 'very careful and attentive perusal of this report' Grenville clearly saw no grounds for a pardon, and he claimed that although he 'did not presume to state this opinion to his Majesty' the king had agreed that he too 'did not see any grounds for altering the sentence'. The following day the bad news Grenville had communicated was confirmed by a letter the Duchess of Gloucester received from Pitt. After thanking her for her letter and making the usual routine references to the case exciting compassion, the Prime Minister stated regretfully that now that the king had made his decision he could not trouble him again unless fresh circumstances had come to light with which 'His

Majesty had been unacquainted at the time of his considering the case'. Since, Pitt then pointed out, 'none such have appeared nor can I see any ground for thinking it is at all likely that any such can be brought forward at this time', this was, he felt, 'an insuperable obstacle to the prolongation of the present respite'.[85]

At this juncture, with less than a week before Thomas' current respite would end, the key players in the government – Thurlow, Grenville, and Pitt – were presenting a united and extremely pessimistic front. While claiming neutrality and stressing the king's central role, they were all clearly against offering even a conditional pardon. Their claims that they had not influenced the king in any way are difficult to evaluate and should not necessarily be taken at face value. The king's sudden change of heart at the beginning of the previous week may or may not have been influenced by Pitt's negative stance at that point, and we have found no written record of any later discussions that may have taken place between the king and his ministers. However, should they have wished to do so, Pitt (and to a lesser extent Grenville) would certainly have had several opportunities during the weekend of the 8th and 9th to quietly make their views clear in person. Pitt arrived in Weymouth on the night of Friday the 7th and spent much of the weekend with the king. A Privy Council, at which four cabinet ministers (including Grenville as well as Pitt) gave advice to the king, met at Gloucester House (the king's Weymouth residence) at midday on the Saturday. Pitt then dined with the king that evening and accompanied him to church the following day. It certainly seems very likely that the subject would have come up since, according to the *Whitehall Evening Post*, Francis Gordon also returned to Weymouth on Saturday the 8th to 'solicit a further respite' from the king. Not surprisingly, given what we know from the private correspondence and given the fact that Frances' main royal supporter, the Duke of Gloucester, was no longer present (being now back in London), Francis does not seem to have received any positive response from the king on this second visit, and the *Post*'s observation that 'there is reason to suppose he will not succeed' may well have been based on inside information.[86]

Thus, as the final week before Thomas was due to hang began, those working on his behalf would have been all too aware that they were facing an uphill struggle. The very negative letters received by the Duke and Duchess of Gloucester on August 11 and 12 from the men in the three key government positions offered little hope and the Duke of Gloucester, never the strongest of characters, was clearly wavering. In response to his letter to the Home Office, the Duke had finally been sent a copy of the judge's original report, and when returning this document he admitted that although he had previously 'entertained the most sanguine hopes of success', having read it he was now inclined to feel that 'here my interference must end'. In fact, however, he continued to be very active on the

Gordons' behalf. He had already been to see the Lord Chancellor that day and had suggested to him that, as the judge himself had entertained some doubts as to whether the Gordons had been able to properly present their defence in court, there might be hope of getting him to change his line on the case when he returned from the circuit on the 20th. On the 11th, the Duke had an encouraging interview with the Lord Chancellor who was 'so kind about the unfortunate man' that the Duke wrote to him the following day asking him to give the Gordons' attorney, Mr Groves, an audience.[87] The rest of the letter makes it clear that once they realized that the king would not be consulted again – and the execution would not therefore be any further delayed – unless fresh evidence came to light, the hopes of Thomas Gordon's supporters focused mainly on two issues. First, could they get the judge to modify his report – this would require a further respite as the judge was not due back in London from his work on the circuit until three days after the current respite ended. Second – a more distant hope – they could delay until after Winifred's case came up again and hope that evidence that could be brought at that trial might be used to 'soften the fate of the son'.[88] The two letters written by the Duchess of Gloucester that have survived were both written at about this point (although we know from the replies she received that she had already written others). Her letter to Grenville, quoted in detail previously, certainly reflected the more pessimistic mood of Gordons' supporters by the middle of this final week. 'If it is impossible to gain a reprieve let me entreat you to grant me one fortnight more, and give your orders that the poor old man may be allowed to see his unhappy wife and son every day, and not to be insulted by the jailer', she wrote. 'Let your first act in office be saving a life . . . perhaps if there was time to write to the judge, he might be prevailed upon to look down with pity – nobody can like to hang if they can find an excuse, however slight, for mercy'.[89] The other letter that survives from the Duchess shows her frantically networking on Thomas' behalf, referring to the Lord Chancellor's sympathetic responses and his hints (however vague) that the Home Secretary was also sympathetic. This letter once again pleads for further respite so that the Gordons might 'find things to urge which would assist', while stressing that 'the life of a young man, who has ever been an irreproachable character is of too much consequence not to make it a duty . . . to try every method'.[90]

The newspapers, which may well have been able to keep up with events so well because they were being supplied with information by those working on Thomas' behalf, were also pessimistic at this point. On the 12th, the *Public Advertiser* reported that 'their Royal Majesties, the Duke and Duchess of Gloucester, and the Duchess of Gordon, humanely interest themselves in the fate of young Gordon, under sentence of death at Northampton, for whom His Majesty, at the personal intercession of his father, was pleased to grant a respite a few days ago. It is much doubted, however, whether the law must not take its course' – an article that was repeated in the *Bath Chronicle* the following day.[91] However, everything suddenly changed on the evening of August 13. Several London evening papers, including the *General Evening Post* and the *St James Chronicle*, announced that 'another respite is granted to Mr Gordon of Northampton, which it is expected will be followed by the King's free pardon, and a discharge of Northampton Gaol' and the *Morning Post and Daily Advertiser* published almost exactly the same story the following morning. The press coverage then became even more optimistic. On August 14 both the *Diary or Woodfall's Register* and the *Morning Star* were apparently certain of the outcome and were now predicting a full pardon. 'Young Gordon of Northampton', they announced, 'has had a second respite; which will be followed by the King's free pardon'. For a brief moment, the Gordons' hopes suddenly seemed to be coming to fruition.[92] The same story was later repeated in several tri-weeklies.[93] What brought on this sudden optimism? Although it must remain a matter of conjecture, the answer may well be related to 'the first whipper-in of the Tories', the beautiful and determined Jane, Duchess of Gordon. The Duchess was close to the Prime Minister and was extremely active in Tory circles more generally. 'After the breaking up of the House on Wednesday', the *Public Advertiser* reported on July 3, 'Mr Pitt and a party of friends were entertained at the Duchess of Gordon's in St James's Square'.[94] Given that the press explicitly named her on August 12 as one of those using their influence on the Gordons' behalf and given that she was so close to the centre of the governing party, it is somewhat surprising that no letters from her survive in the pardoning archive. However, since she was in personal and quite intimate contact with many of the key players she would not have needed to write to them. As Pitt's Downing Street hostess, who 'was a great help to him socially and politically' in that role, she could lobby him and other key players in person and this appears to be what she did. On August 13 she organized a party. 'Yesterday', *The Times* reported on the 14th, 'the Duchess of Gordon gave a grand dinner to Mr Pitt and several nobility in St James' Square' – an event which was also discussed in the *Morning Star* the next day. 'The Duchess of Gordon remains in town', it reported, 'on Thursday she gave a turtle feast to Mr Pitt'.[95] This could be seen as an eleventh hour attempt by the duchess to persuade Pitt to take a different line. The timing is immensely persuasive and the method, a turtle feast, very well chosen. Despite the expense involved, Pitt had a great love of turtle. Pitt was also becoming increasingly partial to drink and the Duchess already had a history of heavy drinking bouts with the Prime Minister and his friend Dundas.[96] It is more than possible that Pitt may have dropped hints during this convivial gathering which gave the Gordons ground for hope. The press certainly caught wind of an immensely hopeful rumour at precisely this point and a stray unascribed and undated document that has survived in the Home Office archive, and which seems to have been written at almost exactly this point (i.e., on August 13), suggests that for a moment at least the authorities wavered. It reads as follows:

> Mr Pitt has carefully read over the Report and the letters from the Duke of Gloucester; The inclosed [sic] note will explain Mr Pitt's sentiments upon the case. (no note survives). If Mr Grenville means to send to the king no time should be lost; His Majesty will leave Exeter on Saturday morning, and if he does not get Mr Grenville's note in the course of tomorrow the answer will not perhaps be obtained in time to save the man's life. The king might not wish to be stopped on his way from Exeter. . . . The execution stands for Monday next.[97]

For a brief period of time on the day of the party at the Duchess' house and on the day that Grenville received the Duchess of Gloucester's most emotional appeal, it seems that someone in the Home office was seriously considering getting a message to the king in time for a further respite. This was never done, however.

Mr Groves, Francis Gordon's attorney, did gain a further audience at the Home Secretary's house in Wimbledon on the 14th, where we know Pitt also visited Grenville that day,[98] but Groves was not successful in getting a further reprieve. 'Having attentively considered everything which Mr Groves could alledge [sic] upon the subject of this unhappy convict I see no fresh circumstance which I could submit to His Majesty', Grenville wrote in a letter to the Duchess of Gloucester on the 14th. 'To direct a further respite . . . would . . . be an act of cruelty towards the convict himself by raising in his mind expectations which must in the end prove delusive'. He was more positive about Maria's suggestion that she could bribe Linnell's widow not to pursue Winifred any further,[99] but for Thomas the brief moment of well-publicized optimism was over. By the 15th the newspapers reflected this change. 'A paragraph has appeared in most of the London papers stating that another respite has been granted to Thomas Gordon', the weekly *Northampton Mercury* (which came out that day) and the *Whitehall Evening Post* reported. 'No official information, however, of this kind had been received at the Gaol when this paper went to press, so that at present his execution remains fixed'. By this time, Francis and his attorney seem to have realized that Thomas was going to hang. On Saturday the 15th they wrote to his mother to warn her that they had failed to get another respite and that the execution was almost inevitable, and Francis then set off for Northampton to be with his son in his final two days.[100] If, as seems likely, the Duchess had made one last effort, it had failed.

The Execution of Thomas Gordon

Thomas' execution took place on Monday, August 17, and was widely reported, although some London newspapers published only short accounts.

> Young Mr. Gordon, for whom a respite had been lately obtained, was executed last Monday morning, at Northampton. He behaved with the fortitude, which Religion only can inspire. The same was in the highest degree affecting. He was but nineteen,

being the full extent of the *General Evening Post's* report. Other newspapers contained much more extensive accounts. The *English Chronicle*, for example, published a long paragraph. *Oracle Bell's New World*, the *World*, the *London Chronicle*, and the *Whitehall Evening Post* devoted about half a column to 'a letter from Northampton' which by its pious tone seems to have been written by the chaplain of the Gaol.[101] Francis, who was described in the newspapers as 'the poor wretched grey-haired old father', had arrived back in Northampton on Saturday the 15th and on the Monday morning he was there when Thomas, 'went to the chapel, and received the Sacrament with his mother, calling on the Almighty to forgive every one who had injured him'. His mother remained in prison and could not accompany him to the gallows. 'The last parting between them cannot be described', the papers reported, 'he walked with manly fortitude to a mourning coach waiting at the prison door, accompanied by two clergymen; who seemed highly to admire his pious behaviour'.

A huge crowd was there to see him die. 'The concourse of spectators on this occasion was extremely numerous', the *English Chronicle* recorded, 'and his fate greatly lamented'. It also praised him for his conduct, observing that 'though only nineteen, he died with a fortitude that did honour to manhood'.[102] The *Northampton Mercury*, which contained the most detailed report, was equally positive about Thomas' demeanour in his final moments. 'Dressed in a light drab-coloured coat with a black collar, a ruffled shirt, white waistcoat, buff breeches, white stockings and large shoe-Bows', it recorded, 'Throughout the whole of this most trying scene he never was observed to show the least mark of fear, but met his fate with the greatest fortitude imaginable'.[103] In his final speech on the gallows he tried to protect his mother. 'After being tied up by the Executioner, he addressed the spectators', the Northampton paper recorded

> 'I am now going to suffer for the Murder of this man; and my mother is shortly to be tried again for the same offence. I declare in the presence of God . . . that she never ordered me to fire, nor was she in the room with me at the time – That's all I have to say'. The usual

matters then being adjusted he gave the signal by dropping a hat and was launched into eternity.

Thomas Gordon died, it was reported, 'without a groan or struggle' and 'after hanging the usual time, his body was cut down and put into a hearse'.[104]

By this point there was clearly much sympathy for the Gordons. 'At the execution all eyes were bedewed with tears and every heart beat with sympathetic sorrow, as he lost his life for his affection to his father', several London papers wrote. 'Never was an object more pitied, or more deserving of pity, nor such universal wishes for his majesty's mercy to be extended to him', *Oracle Bell's New World* concluded. Thomas' body should, in accordance with the Murder Act of 1752, have been either anatomized or hung in chains but after it had been cut down 'the surgeons', the newspapers reported, 'with great humanity gave up the body to the old man and the hearse brought it to the inn where Mr Gordon resides when at this town'.[105] If nothing else the pardoning campaign had enabled Thomas to avoid dissection and receive a decent burial.

Winifred Gordon was acquitted of the charge of accessory to Linnell's murder after the Twelve Judges had found the conviction against her to be unsound, but she was not released after the assizes of July 1789. Instead she remained in gaol, 'an appeal of murder having been lodged against her', by George Linnell's wife and family. This kept her in gaol until the following assizes in March 1790 when various papers recorded that

> Winifred Gordon, appealed of murder at the last assizes, was brought to the bar, and a writ of certiorari being produced to remove the appeal against her into . . . King's Bench, returnable in fifteen days from Easter, she was remanded by due course of law.[106]

No further record of her journey through the criminal justice system has yet been found, but we can be sure that after the Twelve Judges review she was effectively acquitted as an accessory to murder and that she was never retried, as she could have been, for murder itself. Although it seems unlikely that the case against her continued beyond the spring of 1790, her punishment was hardly a light one. Even if she was released around Easter 1790 she would have spent nearly two years in prison in Northampton where the gaoler was frequently described as particularly hostile towards the Gordons. The death of her only son on the Northampton gallows was an immense punishment in itself. The final meeting 'between wife, father and son wrung every spectators heart', the newspapers reported, 'the father bewailing his wife and son's afflictions, the mother in deepest agony, and the son . . . on his knees praying for God's blessing and protection on his distressed aged parents'.[107]

By choosing to indict Winifred only as an accessory, those who put together the original prosecution accidentally created a legal loophole, but once the Twelve Judges had reversed her conviction as an accessory as 'bad',[108] she could have been retried for murder.[109] Given that female murderers tended to get relatively lenient treatment from the courts in the late eighteenth century, it is tempting to suggest that this decision not to re-indict her was related in some way to the fact that the offender concerned was a woman.[110] The key question here is if it had been a man shouting 'kill him' at the window would he have only been indicted as an accessory and, if he had been, would a further prosecution as principal have been mounted once the accessory charge had failed. Unfortunately we are left, as so often in such cases, with a bald fact – that the man hanged and the woman did not – but have insufficient evidence to evaluate the precise role that the gender of the offenders played in the outcome.[111] The final question remains, however. Why, given the prominent elite figures that petitioned for him, did Thomas still go to the gallows?

Conclusions

The case against Thomas was undoubtedly questionable and the alternative narrative the defence put forward even caught the Lord Chancellor's imagination for a while, when Francis Gordon told it to him face to face. Despite the fact that this was a murder case, and the murder of a constable at that, it could be argued that the Dukes and Duchesses of Gloucester and Gordon were sufficiently powerful and connected to the social and political relations at the heart of the government to enable them to obtain at least a conditional pardon fairly easily. They clearly had direct access to the main political players and when their involvement became known several press reports certainly assumed they would succeed. Yet despite a period of quite intense activity, of interviews, letter exchanges, and strategic dinner parties involving key government figures, they failed. As Edward Barry put it in his 1792 account of Thomas Gordon's case in his *Practice of a Justice*, 'Great interest was made to secure a pardon, but he was executed pursuant to his sentence'.[112]

This may have been partly due to the fact that at least some of the particular individual members of the high aristocracy that were involved brought with them severe impediments when it came to games of high patronage such as these. Maria, the Duchess of Gloucester, certainly carried a heavy payload of negative equity. The king had never acknowledged her marriage[113] and was still excluding her from the court in 1788.[114] Without this recognition she was a lightweight with a problematic background – a commoner and the illegitimate daughter of a milliner who had attracted the eye of one of the Walpoles. Moreover by 1788 her marriage to the Duke was in very severe difficulties and he had developed a well-established relationship with her lady-in-waiting.[115]

Pitt's letter to her, while polite, implies that he did not regard her highly. It refers to your Royal Highnesses 'interference' – a word that was rarely used to describe the activities of other aristocratic petitioners. He also politely but summarily dismisses her request about 'my coming up to town tomorrow'.[116] Maria was adrift and increasingly marginalized even in her own home. This may help to explain why she took up the Gordons' cause so passionately, but it made her a very poor petitioner from the Gordons' point of view – especially where the king was concerned, since he continued to request that his brother avoid even mentioning her in conversation. She also fell ill on August 14 – a vital moment in the petitioning process.[117]

The Duke of Gloucester had much more potential as an ally in the Gordons' cause. Despite the damage done to his relationship with George III by his secret marriage, by early 1789 his stock was as high as it ever been with both the king and his ministers. During the Regency crisis he had stood resolutely by the king, being praised in *The Times* at the height of the crisis in January 1789 for 'resisting every connection with the conspirators'. In May 1789 the same paper reported that his loyalty had been greatly 'distinguished by the King' and in June it noted that his 'affectionate conduct towards the King' had also ensured him the 'love and gratitude of the nation'.[118] The problem here, from the Gordons' point of view, does not seem to have been the Duke's lack of clout but his reluctance to use it. The Duke was of a 'quiet and retiring disposition' and although George III was staying in his house at Weymouth and the Duke was regularly reported to be promenading, bathing, and worshipping with him during the first week of August,[119] when the case was being discussed, he 'did not think it proper', one of his letters reveals, 'to make direct application'. He seems to have other matters he wished to obtain the king's help with and he had neither the nerve nor, perhaps, the commitment to risk discussing the issue of Thomas' pardon directly with his brother.[120]

The Duke of Gordon, by contrast, seems to have been committed to helping his uncle's ex-surgeon. He was in the capital at the beginning of August and probably introduced Francis to the Gloucesters. However, he was not particularly at home in the London political world and he had his own problems in August 1789. His brother Lord George Gordon – famous for instigating the 1780 Gordon Riots – was once again in gaol and in the news, for, amongst other things, libeling the Queen of France and later petitioning the National Assembly for help.[121] The Duchess of Gordon was much more engaged in the political world. In late July she was still in Edinburgh, but by August 10 she was back in London where the press remarked on her appearance with her three beautiful daughters when reporting a play enacting the fall of the Bastille.[122] Three days later she nearly pulled off a major reversal of Thomas' fortunes and she and the Duke of Gordon may well have stayed in the capital partly in order to see the case through. They left London to return to Scotland four days after Thomas went to the gallows.[123]

In trying to explain why the Duchess, her husband, the Gloucesters, and several others failed to save Thomas, despite the Duchess' many contacts in the highest government circles, attention inevitably needs to be directed to the four key political players. Their roles are, however, extremely difficult to unravel. Was the king too concerned with notions of hierarchy or legality, at a time when revolution was threatening the very foundations of royal and aristocratic power elsewhere in Europe, to let the killing of a constable go without sacrificing a life? As Devereaux has observed in considering the way in which 'public justice' was presented in the capital in the later 1780s, the French Revolution dominated the political agenda. He writes that

> the concern about the portrayal of justice in the Sessions Paper after 1787 can be viewed as an aspect of a broader concern about the portrayal of authority in general at a time when events across the channel were bringing an uncommon pressure to bear on questions of the legitimacy of established authorities and the potential power of the press in encouraging people to question them.[124]

Was Grenville in his first months at the Home office, and with his mind much occupied with other events, such as the escalating crisis in France and the trial of Warren Hastings, unwilling to challenge or even trouble the judges?[125] Was Pitt's attitude decisive? Some contemporaries clearly believed his lack of energy was responsible for the outcome. The day the Duke and Duchess of Gordon left for Scotland, the *Morning Post* announced that:

> The execution of Gordon at Northampton after the flattering circumstances that seemed to promise a pardon to this unfortunate young man, is a reproach to the Minister, as the cause was in the highest degree honourable to the feelings of the unhappy victim. Mr. PITT should have taken [the] matter up, as the crime was the result merely of filial affection. It is possible, however, that what implied so much sensibility, was the very thing that prevented the stoic virtue of our Minister from interposing in his behalf.[126]

Though this comment is opaque and the evidence is patchy, Pitt may well have played a central role. At the Duchess' party on the 13th he may well have hinted that he would be willing to go back to the king for a further respite, but, when it came to it on the 14th, he and Grenville, following the final meeting with Groves, made no further attempt to stop the execution. There is of course another way to look at Pitt's decision-making that summer. In the spring of the previous year the king was incapacitated by his illness and, as Simon Devereaux has shown, this meant that four sessions at the Old Bailey passed without the committee sitting in judgement on the Recorder's Report. This left a large number of convicts waiting to hang and presented the very real problem that there would 'not be a gallows large enough to hang them all on a single occasion. Nor could the government see any merit in an execution display (or a sequence of them!), which would surely detract from the public joy at the monarch's recovery'. Pitt insisted that any reduction in execution in 1788 was only a temporary one, occasioned as it was by a 'technical' problem.[127] Therefore, one way we might interpret this is that Thomas Gordon was also awaiting his execution at a time when the government was aware that in London at least they could not execute huge numbers of felons. Nevertheless the rule of law needed to be upheld. This might explain Pitt's reluctance to support a plea for clemency.

Thurlow was also out of the picture by the crucial days of the 13th and 14th. He left London for Scarborough on the 12th. However, he was close to the king and as Lord Chancellor his role may well have been more important than this suggests. His letter to the Duchess of Gloucester certainly reminds us how unwise it can be to assume that the eighteenth-century criminal justice system was in any sense fair. Having just heard Francis' story and described it as a 'perfect defence' he had no qualms in still concluding that without more evidence 'it will be impossible to appeal or indeed to wish for His Majesty's intervention'. Politically Thurlow was a trimmer who had secretly hedged his bets during the Regency crisis and made preliminary approaches to the opposition, and whose relationship with Pitt was extremely strained in August 1789.[128] While recognizing intellectually the power of the Gordon's counter-narrative, Thurlow showed no inclination to let notions of justice get in the way of practical realities and his attitude sums up the deeply pragmatic nature of the English pardoning system in such cases. Pardons were quite frequently granted if the judges believed that the jury had mistakenly found the defendant guilty. However, if the judge upheld the verdict and recognized no mitigating circumstances, it would take a powerful combination of forces to overpower that decision, especially in cases such as this where a figure of authority, however lowly, had been the victim. The aristocracy not infrequently achieved this in routine cases but in this case where the offence was a serious one, there might often be what Hay has termed 'a conscious weighing up of the avoirdupois of class'.[129] In these situations the key players were going to have to be not only powerful and well connected but also deeply motivated. In marginal cases they might also need to find a way to touch the emotions of the very highest figures in the political world whose attention and interests often lay elsewhere. Pardoning cases such as this created a delicate balance of forces and were played out in a unique conjunction of circumstances, which were partly shaped by general social attitudes and established political practices but were not wholly determined by them.[130]

In the end the killing of Constable Linnell, which seems to have arisen mainly out of a situation created by the deeply xenophobic and local-ized attitudes of many of Pattishall's inhabitants, resulted in two deaths rather than one not only because the narrative of the local men who accompanied Linnell that night was sufficiently powerfully presented by the villagers to persuade both the jury and the judge of its validity, nor simply because, once written, the judge's report exercised a very powerful influence on all involved but also because an array of the 'first characters in the country' failed to persuade those in charge of the pardoning pro-cess of the validity of the Gordon's counter-narrative. In the process, the case demonstrated not only the limits of aristocratic power and the many contingencies that might block or facilitate the use of that power but also the reason why the elite preferred to keep the pardoning process as private as possible. This very well publicized failure of some of the most powerful and well connected members of the aristocracy, including one of the richest men in Britain and the member of the Royal family closest to the king (not to mention the Prime Minister's public hostess), was a very public demonstration of the limits of their influence, as well as a very powerful demonstration of the potential impact of local xenophobia on those who had the misfortune to become its targets.

There was a clear alternative narrative in this case but it was over-whelmingly quashed by a local conspiracy to obscure the truth from 'outsiders'. Moreover the political atmosphere in which the events of July 1788–August 1789 occurred were unfortunate for Thomas Gordon and his family. It could be said that, along with the villagers of Pattishall, events also conspired to see him hang. At least he was spared the igno-miny of anatomization at the hands of the surgeons, although this would have been little comfort to his grieving parents. Finally, then, let us con-sider the fourth case study of homicide in the late eighteenth century and one that is perhaps more unusual than the three that precede it but which has several themes that link it to them.

Notes

* A version of this chapter first appeared as an article in *Family & Community History* in 2013. I am very grateful to Peter King and to the editors of the journal for permission to recycle that article in this volume. All subsequent mistakes are of course my own. Gray and King, 'The Killing of Constable Linnell', *Family & Community History*, Vol. 16, No. 1 (2013), pp. 3–31.
1. Hay, 'Property, Authority and the Criminal Law'.
2. For the Culworth Gang see Jack Gould, 'The Culworth Gang', *Northamp-tonshire Past & Present*, Vol. 53 (2000), pp. 38–48.
3. V. A. Hatley (ed.), *Northamptonshire Militia Lists, 1777*, Vol. 25 (North-amptonshire Record Society Publications, 1973), p. 194.

4. J. M. Neeson, *Commoners: Common Right, Enclosure and Social Change in England, 1700–1820* (Cambridge, Cambridge University Press, 1993).

5. Richard Moss and Iris Illingworth, *Pattishall: A Parish Patchwork* (Northampton, Millcop Publishing, 2000), p. 24.

6. Gwenda Morgan and Peter Rushton, 'The Magistrate, the Community and the Maintenance of an Orderly Society in Eighteenth-Century England', *Historical Research*, Vol. 76, No. 191 (2003), pp. 54–77; Peter King, 'The Summary Courts and Social Relations in Eighteenth-Century England', *Past & Present*, Vol. 183, No. 1 (2004), pp. 125–72; Gray, 'Making Law in Mid-Eighteenth-Century England', pp. 211–33.

7. E. Barry (Rev.), *A Supplement to the Present Practice of a Justice of the Peace; And Complete Library of Parish Law* (London, 1792), p. 2.

8. 'The 66th regiment . . . has been recruited three times since it left England, and . . . there are only 15 out of 550 that have lived to return to their native shore'. (*The Annual Register for the Year 1773*, p. 141); Edward Long, *A History of Jamaica, or, General Survey of the Antient and Modern State of That Island: With Reflections on Its Situation, Settlements, Inhabitants*, Vol. 2 (London, 1774), p. 190.

9. T. Leach, *Cases in Crown Law, Determined by the Twelve Judges; by the Court of King's Bench; and by Commissioners of Oyer and Terminer, and General Gaol Delivery* (London, 1792), p. 413.

10. K. D. M. Snell, *Parish and Belonging: Community, Identity and Welfare in England and Wales 1700–1950* (Cambridge, Cambridge University Press, 2006), pp. 32–42.

11. Petition of Francis Gordon on behalf of his son. TNA HO47/8/51-56.

12. Winifred supposedly described them as 'a parcel of ignorant and stupid people'. TNA/KB1/26: James Wilding's deposition. I have found no conclusive evidence that the Gordons were dissenters but the *Northampton Mercury*, 22 August 1789 reported that Thomas Gordon was accompanied to the gallows by a 'dissenting clergyman' so this makes that suggestion at least probable.

13. Leach, *Cases in Crown Law*, p. 413.

14. By late nineteenth century there was a *Boot* inn there. *Kelly's Directory* (1894), p. 220.

15. There is a picture of Haynes Pratt Burrows, a direct descendant of the blacksmith, taken some time in the early twentieth century, in Moss and Illingworth, *Pattishall*, p. 58.

16. His presence in both the 1777 and 1796 Militia lists (where he was described as a blacksmith) means that his minimum age in 1788 would have been 27 and his maximum age 37 assuming there were not two Haynes Pratts, such as son following father. 'Liability to serve in the militia rested on able-bodied men between the ages of 18 and 45 years'. Hatley, *Northamptonshire Militia Lists*, p. ix.

17. Burn, *Justice of the Peace*, Vol. 1, pp. 111–13.

18. It was common for magistrates to broker settlements in cases of common assault. The most likely outcome – if an allegation of assault was upheld – was for the aggressor to pay the victim's costs (for a warrant or summons and his other legal fees) and to hand over a small sum by way of compensation or to cover any medical treatment that might have been required. Drew D. Gray, (2007) 'Settling their differences: the nature of assault and its prosecution in the City of London in the late eighteenth and early nineteenth centuries' in K. D. Watson (ed.) *Assaulting the Past: Violence and Civilization in Historical Context.* (Newcastle-upon-Tyne, Cambridge Scholars

Publishing, 2007); King, 'Punishing Assault'; Morgan and Rushton, 'The Magistrate'.

19. A Thirdborough was a constable, Joseph Shaw, *Parish Law or a Guide to Justices of the Peace, Ministers, Church-Wardens, Overseers of the Poor, Constables, Surveyors of the Highways, Vestry-Clerks, and All Others Concerned in Parish Business*, 3rd ed. (London, 1736).

20. *Public Advertiser*, 11 July 1789; the term 'governor' is an unusual one in a rural context. Linnell does not appear to have owned any land in the area but he did occupy a considerable amount of land – (NRO Church rates, Pattishall) – and was described as a farmer in the Pattishall hamlet of Ascote in his will – (NRO Will of Geo.Linnell).

21. This account is based primarily on the coroner's inquest depositions (TNA KB1/26) and Judge Thompson's report (TNA HO/8/51-6) and the write-ups of the case in Leach, *Cases in Crown Law*; and Barry, *A Supplement*. There are some inconsistencies between the accounts of five witnesses (Burton, Wilding, Sharman, Pearcy, and Therton) but the core of story remains the same in each.

22. HO/8/51-6.

23. Burton said he tried to reason with Thomas saying 'Sir, it is to be hoped that you would not end any man's life but Thomas merely repeated his threat adding "D–n my soul, the first man that enters the door loses his life"'. HO/8/51-6.

24. Perhaps because, according to the judge's report, Hart, unlike Linnell, was known to Winifred. HO/8/51-6.

25. HO/8/51-6.

26. Ibid.

27. KB1/26.

28. Ibid.

29. Barry, *A Supplement*, p. 2.

30. The close and garden wall are still visible in the 1880s Ordinance Survey map and the house exists to this day on the A5 at the corner of Foster's Booth Lane, which was previously known as 'Pattishall Lane'.

31. KB1/26; HO47/8/51-6.

32. —Ibid. Petition of Francis Gordon.

33. HO47/8/51-6.

34. William Dickinson, *A Practical Exposition of the Law: Relative to the Office and Duties of a Justice of the Peace*, Vol. 1 (London, 1813), p. 805.

35. *Northampton Mercury*, 26 July 1788; *London Chronicle*, 31 July 1788; *Whitehall Evening Post*, 29 July 1788.

36. *Northampton Mercury*, 2 and 16 August 1788.

37. William Pinchard, John Winckles and John Pell, for example, had all gained land in the Pattishall enclosure in 1771 and Pinchard was described as a farmer in the Parish's Militia List of 1777. The same document gives the occupations of three other jury members. Richard Wrinckles was a butcher, and the two John Pells found on the jury were given the occupations of labourer and weaver – NRO X270-1V; Land Tax 1788 and Militia List Pattishall 1796; Hatley, *Northamptonshire Militia Lists*, p. 193.

38. NRO 1788 Land Tax; Francis Whellan, *History, Gazetteer, and Directory of Northamptonshire; Comprising a General Survey of the County, and a History of the Diocese of Peterborough* (London, 1849).

39. KB1/26; By 1849 Pearcy's family were combining the sale of alcohol with butchery and had a retail outlet at Eastcote (Whellan, *History, Gazetteer, and Directory of Northamptonshire*).

40. *Northampton Mercury*, 26 July 1788.

41. HO47/8/51-6.

42. Beattie, *Crime and the Courts*, p. 343.

43. All suggest that the Gordons' home was under attack *before* the gun was fired. *Whitehall Evening Post*; *General Evening Post*, both 29 July 1789; *London Chronicle*, 31 July 1789.

44. HO47/8/51-6.

45. The five cases reserved in that year were: 'Pegge, Downes, Gordon & wife, Rickman & Wilkins'. D. R. Bentley QC (ed.), *Select Cases from the Twelve Judges' Notebooks* (London, 1997), appendix 1, p. 185; Randall McGowen, 'Forgery and the Twelve Judges in Eighteenth-Century England', *Law and History Review*, Vol. 29, No. 1 (February 2011), pp. 221–57.

46. Langbein, *The Origins of the Adversary Criminal Trial*, pp. 212–13.

47. Bentley, *Select Cases from the Twelve Judges*, p. 9; McGowen, 'Forgery and the Twelve Judges'.

48. In many cases they were not represented. As Bentley has noted, 'If the prisoner was not represented the judges would usually decline to hear counsel for the Crown. In the case of Thomas and Winifred Gordon the crown did present evidence so it is possible that the Gordons were also represented'. Bentley, *Select Cases from the Twelve Judges*, p. 16.

49. Leach, *Cases in Crown Law*, p. 416; *Whitehall Evening Post*, 27 July 1789.

50. *Whitehall Evening Post*; *London Chronicle*, both 23 July 1789; *Morning Post and Daily Advertiser*; *Diary or Woodfall's Register*; *Public Advertiser*, all 27 July 1789.

51. Edward Hyde East, Esq of the Inner Temple, *A Treatise of the Pleas of the Crown*, Vol. 1 (London, 1803).

52. Barry, *A Supplement*, p. 4; *London Chronicle*, 30 July 1789; also *Northampton Mercury*, 25 July 1789; *Morning Post and Daily Advertiser*; *Public Advertiser*, both 27 July 1789.

53. *London Chronicle*, 23 July 1789; *Diary or Woodfall's Register*, 27 July 1789; *Morning Post and Daily Advertiser*, both 27 July 1789. East highlighted the fact that '[if] two be indicted as principals, and it appear that one of them were accessory before, he shall be discharged of that indictment. This was the case of Winifred Gordon, who together with Thomas Gordon were indicted, for that *they* on the 23 July 1788 *made an assault* on George Linnell, a constable, in the execution of his office. . . . After argument in the Exchequer-chamber, it seemed to be the opinion of all the judges, though they differed in other respects, that this indictment only amounted to a charge against Winifred Gordon of being an accessory before, though it charged her, as it should seem improperly, with having joined in the assault on the deceased. . . . But it was the opinion of all the judges that she might be indicted again as principal; in which the four concurred, if, as the others thought, she could not be convicted upon this indictment charging her as accessory before'. East, *A Treatise of the Pleas of the Crown*, pp. 350–52.

54. *Morning Post and Daily Advertiser*, 27 July 1789. The Linnells came from the nearby village of Whittlebury where family members were frequently churchwardens. Anne buried her husband at Whittlebury rather than Pattishall and one of George Linnell's Whittlebury relations offered his bond on the indictment against Winifred Gordon.

55. *Whitehall Evening Post*, 27 July 1789; *St James Chronicle and British Evening Post*; *General Evening Post*; *London Chronicle*, all 30 July 1789; *Public Advertiser*, 3 August 1789; *The Times*, 4 August 1789.

56. HO13/7.

57. On Colonel Adam Gordon, see Barlow (1775 2:462). Alexander Gordon's grandfather was a Jacobite sympathizer but his father played an important role for the King at Culloden (Johnson 1798:143).

58. H. M. Chichester, 'Gordon, Alexander, Fourth Duke of Gordon (1743–1827)', in Michael Fry (Rev.), *Oxford Dictionary of National Biography* (Oxford, Oxford University Press, 2004), www.oxforddnb.com/view/article/11023 [accessed 25 January 2010]; Rosemary Baird, *Mistress of the House, Great Ladies and Grand Houses* (London, Weidenfeld & Nicolson, 2003), p. 216.

59. Chichester, 'Gordon, Alexander'. His association with his namesakes in Pattishall is less clear however. Francis Gordon had served in the 66th foot that had been stationed in Aberdeen in 1770 where it recruited from amongst the local population. It is possible that Francis was a Scotsman and joined the regiment in Scotland. Given his surname, he may even have been seen by Gordon as a 'clan' member.

60. Jane Maxwell, Duchess of Gordon, c 1749–1812. Wife of the 4th Duke of Gordon (With her son, George Duncan, 1770–1836. Marquess of Huntly, later 5th Duke of Gordon. General) by George Romney (1778).

61. Baird, *Mistress of the House*, pp. 220–21; Derek Jarrett, *England in the Age of Hogarth* (New Haven & London, Yale University Press, 1974), p. 100. Ehrman records that with Pitt bereft following the death in 1786 of his previous hostess – his sister Harriet – the Duchess 'moved in on' Pitt in 1787 and reached her height of association (and presumably influence) with him in 1789. J. Ehrman, *William Pitt: The Years of Acclaim* (London, Constable, 1969), pp. 582–84.

62. John Brooke, *King George III* (London, Constable, 1972), pp. 418, 432–47, 540; Matthew C. Kilburn, 'Royalty and Public in Britain: 1714–1789', Thesis submitted for the degree of Doctor of Philosophy (Oxford University, 1997).

63. George III's acute mental disturbance became so grave between December 1788 and February 1789 that it provoked a major political crisis about the possibility of Regency. When the king, after his recovery, studied the parliamentary debates about the possibility of a Regency he chose to confide his anger to the Duke of Gloucester. Ida Macalpine and Richard Hunter, *George III and the Mad Business* (New York, NY, Pantheon Books, 1970), p. 92; Jeremy Black, *George III: America's Last King* (New Haven and London, Yale University Press, 2006), pp. 275–84; Stanley Ayling, *George the Third* (New York, Alfred A. Knoff, 1972), pp. 346–51; Brooke, *King George III*, pp. 538–40; *English Chronicle or Universal Evening Post*, 4 August 1789; *Diary or Woodfall's Register*, 5 August 1789.

64. Hay, 'Property, Authority, and the Criminal Law', p. 47; Hay, 'Writing About the Death Penalty', p. 50.

65. *Oracle Bell's New World*, 21 August 1789.

66. *London Chronicle*; *Whitehall Evening Post*, both 1 August 1789.

67. *Public Advertiser*, 12 August 1789; *Bath Chronicle*, 13 August 1789.

68. Hay, 'Property, Authority, and the Criminal Law', p. 44; King, *Crime, Justice, and Discretion*, pp. 297–320; Hay, 'Writing About the Death Penalty', pp. 41–42.

69. King, *Crime, Justice, and Discretion*, pp. 318–19.

70. Ibid.; Hay, 'Property, Authority, and the Criminal Law', p. 46; John Beattie, 'The Royal Pardon and Criminal Procedure in Early Modern England', *Historical Papers/Communications Historiques* (1987), pp. 16–17.

71. Hay, 'Property, Authority, and the Criminal Law', p. 45.

72. Nepean, the son of a Cornish innkeeper, undertook a number of duties at the Home office including advising on the conviction or pardoning of convicts. E. Sparrow, 'Nepean, Sir Evan, First Baronet (1752–1822)', in Fry (Rev.), *Oxford Dictionary of National Biography*, www.oxforddnb.com/view/article/19894 [accessed 25 January 2010].

73. HO47/8/51-6.

74. Ibid.; Simon Devereaux has argued that Nepean rarely seemed to have any significant impact on the actual decision-making process but it remains unclear whether this was entirely the case here. Simon Devereaux, 'The Criminal Branch of the Home Office 1782–1830', in G. Smith, S. May, and S. Devereaux (eds.), *Criminal Justice in the Old World and the New: Essays in Honour of J.M. Beattie* (Toronto, Toronto Centre of Criminology, 1998), p. 279. The Duke of Gordon was also unwell at this time (*The World*, 15 July 1789).

75. *London Chronicle*; *Whitehall Evening Post*, both 1 August 1789. Why the Duke and Duchess of Gloucester took up the case of Thomas Gordon is hard to explain. Like the Duke of Gordon, the Duke of Gloucester had military connections.

76. *English Chronicle or Universal Evening Post*, 4 August 1789; *Diary or Woodfall's Register*, 5 August 1789.

77. *Whitehall Evening Post*; *London Chronicle*; *English Chronicle or Universal Evening Post*, all 1 August 1789.

78. *The New London Magazine*, Vol. 50, 18 August 1789; *Whitehall Evening Post*, 1 August 1789.

79. *General Evening Post*; *London Chronicle*; *St James' Chronicle or the British Evening Post*, all 4 August 1789; *Public Advertiser*, 6 August 1789.

80. *London Chronicle*; *General Evening Post*; *St James' Chronicle or the British Evening Post*, all 4 August 1789; *Public Advertiser*, 6 August 1789; HO13/7.

81. A. Aspinall (ed.), *The Later Correspondence of George III, Volume 1: December 1783 to January 1793* (Cambridge, Cambridge University Press, 1962), p. 436. This letter implies that Grenville had already given instructions for a temporary reprieve on the basis of letters from the two Dukes before Francis Gordon arrived with the news from Weymouth. See also *The Manuscripts of J. B. Fortescue Esq, Preserved at Dropmore*, Vol. I, Royal Manuscripts Commission Thirteenth Report, Appendix, Part II (1892), p. 488.

82. *The Manuscripts*, p. 488; E. Evans, *William Pitt the Younger* (London, Routledge, 1999), p. 3.

83. Brooke, *King George III*, pp. 491–92, 542; Black, *George III*, p. 289; G. Ditchfield, *George III: An Essay in Monarchy* (Basingstoke, Palgrave MacMillan, 2002), p. 159; Beattie, 'The Royal Pardon', p. 18. The so-called Hanging Cabinet would of course have given Pitt and key ministers such as Grenville regular experience of making pardoning decisions with the king about Old Bailey cases. What is less clear, however, is exactly how involved the king was, and how any disagreements were resolved since only cryptic records have survived – Beattie suggests that while the monarch continued to preside over such meetings, nevertheless the system 'gave the king's ministers considerable influence', Beattie, *Policing and Punishment in London*, pp. 346–62, 350. This influence was almost certainly greater than usual in the immediate aftermath of the king's illness which had interrupted the system earlier that year. Hay, 'Writing About the Death Penalty', p. 43.

84. HO47/8/51-6. Undated Letter from Maria, Duchess of Gloucester. Although giving no direct indication who it was sent to, the letter says 'let your first act

in office be saving a life' thus indicating it was written to Grenville who had recently been appointed Home Secretary. Although dated simply 'Thursday' it was almost certainly written on the 13th of August.

85. HO47/8/51-6. Letters to Duchess of Gloucester from Thurlow, 11th August 1789, and from Pitt, 12th August 1789. Letter from the Duke of Gloucester to the Home Office, 10 August 1789; Letter to the Duke of Gloucester from Grenville, 11 August 1789.
86. *London Chronicle*, 8 August 1789; *Diary or Woodfall's Register*, 10 August 1789; *World*; *The Times*; *Morning Star*, all 11 August 1789; *Morning Post and Daily Advertiser*, 13 August 1789; and on Francis's visit – *Whitehall Evening Post*, 8 August 1789.
87. HO47/8/51-6, Duke of Gloucester to Lord Chancellor, 12th August 1789.
88. Ibid.
89. HO47/8/51-6. Undated letter from Maria, Duchess of Gloucester probably written on the 13th August 1789 – see note 100.
90. HO47/8/51-6. This was dated Wednesday and therefore written on the 12th of August though it arrived at the Home Office on the 13th and is was labelled there – TNA HO47/8/51-6 Maria, Duchess of Gloucester 12th August 1789.
91. *Public Advertiser*, 12 August 1789; *Bath Chronicle*, 13 August 1789.
92. *General Evening Post*; *St James Chronicle or British Evening Post*, both 13 August 1789; *Morning Post and Daily Advertiser*, 14 August 1789.
93. The same story was later repeated in tri-weeklies such as the *London Chronicle*; *Whitehall Evening Post*, both 13–15 August 1789 and in provincial papers such as *Bath Chronicle*, 20 August 1789. On a Free pardon see *Diary or Woodfall's Register*, 14 August 1789; *Morning Star*, 15 August 1789.
94. *Public Advertiser*, 3 July 1789; on Jane's beauty and energy see Baird, *Mistress of the House*, pp. 215–18.
95. *The Times*; *Morning Star*, both 14 August 1789; Jarrett, *Pitt the Younger*, p. 100.
96. After giving a turtle dinner at Downing Street, he had been criticized in the *Morning Post* for this extravagant taste. 'Mr Pitt gives TURTLES [capitals in the original] to his political associates rather too often', it observed. 'It is extraordinary that he should be addicted to such high feeding'. *Morning Post and Daily Advertiser*, 5 August 1789; *Morning Star*, 3 August 1789; *World*, 4 August 1789; Ehrman, *The Younger Pitt: The Years of Acclaim*. pp. 100, 108, 454, 582–85, 586 on drink killing Pitt in the end.
97. TNA HO47/8/51-6, Untitled internal note – the time of writing was '45 past 4 pm'.
98. TNA HO47/8/51-6, Grenville to Duchess of Gloucester, 14 August 1789. *The Morning Star*, 15th August 1789 reported that 'yesterday Mr Pitt set off from his house in Downing Street for Mr Grenville's seat at Wimbledon'.
99. 'As the appeal which is lodged against the mother is a proceeding in the nature of private satisfaction only and one in which the public is in no aspect concerned, there can', he suggested, 'be little doubt that your Royal Highness' interposition with the widow of the constable would prove effectual'. TNA HO47/8/51-6, Grenville to Duchess of Gloucester, 14 August 1789.
100. *Northampton Mercury*; *Whitehall Evening Post*, both 15 August 1789; *World*, 21 August 1789.
101. *General Evening Post*; *English Chronicle or Universal Evening Post*; *Whitehall Evening Post*, all 18 August 1789; *Oracle Bell's New World*; *London Chronicle*, 20 August 1789; *World*, 21 August 1789.

102. *English Chronicle*, 18 August 1789.
103. *The Northampton Mercury*, 22 August 1789.
104. Ibid. Similar if shorter accounts appeared elsewhere. 'His last words', the *World* reported (21 August 1789) were 'My mother was not in the room when the gun was fired'.
105. *Oracle Bell's New World*, 21 August 1789; *London Chronicle*, 20 August 1789; on the Murder Act – *London Gazette*, 7 April 1752; *London Evening Post*, 21 March 1752.
106. *Oracle Bell's New World*, 21 August 1789; *Northampton Mercury*, 6 March 1790; *St James' Chronicle or the British Evening Post*, 9 March 1790; *English Chronicle or Universal Evening Post*; *London Chronicle*, both 11 March 1790.
107. *St James' Chronicle or the British Evening Post*, 9 March 1790.
108. *Diary or Woodfall's Register*, 27 July 1789.
109. Dickinson, *A Practical Exposition*, p. 12.
110. Peter King, 'Gender, Crime and Justice in Late Eighteenth and Early Nineteenth-Century England', in M. Arnot and U. Usborne (eds.), *Gender and Crime in Modern Europe* (London, UCL Press, 1999).
111. It is also possible that the prosecution wished to avoid a retrial of Winifred because it would give the Gordons a chance to put forward their counter-narrative more powerfully than at the original trial.
112. Barry, *A Supplement*, pp. 3–4.
113. Kilburn, 'William Henry, Prince, First Duke of Gloucester'.
114. *The Times* modern index says Maria was not invited to the Windsor ball on the 27th of August 1788 because the marriage was 'not acknowledged at court'.
115. Kilburn, 'William Henry, Prince, First Duke of Gloucester'.
116. TNA HO47/8/51-6, Pitt to Duchess of Gloucester, 12 August 1789.
117. *Morning Star*, 15 August 1789.
118. New Index to *The Times*, January–December 1789.
119. *English Chronicle or Universal Evening Post*, 4 August 1789; *Diary or Woodfall's Register*, 5 August 1789.
120. Christopher Hibbert, *George III: A Personal History* (Houndmills, Penguin, 1998), p. 167; TNA HO47/8/51-6, The Duke of Gloucester. The *Morning Post and Daily Advertiser* reported in the middle of the key week on the 5th of August 1789 that 'The Duke of Gloucester has prudently bent his course again to Weymouth. There is something very flattering in the notice of his Majesty, besides which, it may lead to matters more substantial'.
121. His brother did not always get a good press, one paper called him the 'mad bigot'. *Bath Chronicle*, 6 August 1789.
122. *World*, 10 August 1789.
123. They set off on Friday the 21st of August according to the *Morning Star* (22 August 1789) and *The Times* new index (22 August 1789).
124. Devereaux, 'The City and the Sessions Paper', p. 496.
125. It remains possible that Grenville could not afford to upset the judges, although it should be noted that Judge Thompson was a very recent appointment and was anything but a senior judge at this point (Foss 1848–64:374).
126. *Morning Post and Daily Advertiser*, 22 August 1789.
127. Devereaux, 'England's "Bloody Code" in Crisis and Transition', p. 90.
128. TNA HO47/8, Thurlow to the Duchess of Gloucester, 11 August 1789; Edward Foss, *The Judges of England with Sketches of Their Lives, Volume VIII, 171–1820* (London, John Murray, 1864), p. 383. Several newspapers

made much of the open split between the two men – *World*, 30 July 1789; *Morning Star*, 1st August 1789 which also describes Pitt as supported by 'the benign countenance of a great Lady' – could this be the Duchess of Gordon? *Morning Post and Daily Advertiser*, 3rd and 14th August 1789, finally persuaded the king to get rid of Thurlow in 1792.

129. Hay, 'Property, Authority, and the Criminal Law', p.46.
130. King, *Crime, Justice and Discretion.*

5   Sex, Scandal, and Strangulation

The Strange Case of Francis Kotzwara and Susannah Hill

Introduction

In September 1791, a murder trial took place at the Old Bailey courthouse in the City of London. The accused, Susannah Hill, was one of the capital's many prostitutes; the victim (Francis Kotzwara) was her unfortunate client. Susannah was acquitted of the murder and the lesser charge of manslaughter on the grounds that there was insufficient evidence to prove her guilt. She had been charged with causing Kotzwara's death by hanging him from a cord in her rooms in Vine Street. However, it quickly became apparent (to the press, court, and the author of an obscure printed pamphlet) that her 'victim' had been engaged in an act of autoerotic asphyxiation.

In some respects this is an example of unproven homicide or misadventure, but not perhaps worthy of great attention. However, the case was unusual and the details of the crime were salacious, and, as a consequence, the court forbade any reporting of them. Fortunately, this dictum was ignored by at least one person present and this led to the publication of a fascinating pamphlet (entitled *Modern Propensities*)[1] that explored not only the case itself but several contemporary concerns about the hanging of criminals and one little known form of deviant sexual practice. While this pamphlet and trial are not unknown, they have not previously been subjected to detailed analysis. This chapter will explore the strange case of Francis Kotzwara and Susannah Hill and attempt to show how it fits into the wider themes of this book and its concentration on the discretionary nature of decision-making in regards to capital punishment. Unlike the stories that have preceded it this did not play out in the contemporary press; instead there was a clear and determined attempt to stifle any commentary on the affair. Yet that attempt was in vain and the survival of information about the case allows us to investigate the ways in which some contemporaries engaged with debates about hanging as a form of execution. As was noted in the introduction, while executions were frequently described in print culture, the act of hanging was rarely, if ever, the focus of these publications. If there was any unquiet about the physical act of execution and its effect on the viewing crowds, then most sources were silent about it. This then offers an alternative view of hanging and perhaps a new perspective on attempts to restrict access to the execution ceremony.[2]

The pamphlet itself is a commentary on the state of society and on what constitutes appropriate, and inappropriate, forms of sexual activity. It may also be a carefully disguised form of erotica or pornography. Julie Peakman notes that such writings have been 'labeled [by later commentators on these works] somewhat indiscriminately as pornography, erotica, smut, obscenity, clandestine or forbidden texts, sexual fiction and libertine literature'.[3] This makes *Modern Propensities* quite hard to classify. The eighteenth century certainly witnessed a growth in the publication of all sorts of printed advice, discussion, and entertainment associated with sex, as Tim Hitchcock has noted.[4] Sarah Toulalan, Julie Peakman, and Karen Harvey have similarly described and analyzed the development of a large market in erotica and pornography in the seventeenth and eighteenth centuries.[5] Roy Porter noted the proliferation of sex manuals and argued that such manuals were deemed (by their authors) to be a necessary counter to perceived ignorance and misconceptions concerning sex, impotence, infertility, and sexually transmitted diseases.[6] Hitchcock suggests it is much less clear how these manuals were received or whether the information they provided was used. Thus, while sex manuals such as *Aristotle's Master-piece: or, the Secrets of Generation Displayed in the Parts Thereof*, (1684) or Dr Nicholas Venette's *Mysteries of Conjugal Love* (published in English in 1703) or Dr Graham's *Lecture on Generation* (1783) all provided their readership with 'a possible source of knowledge about sex', both McClaren and Hitchcock note that readers might have used the information to indulge in activities unlikely to result in conception.[7] Historians of sex appear to agree that the authors of these manuals had the intention to establish sex aimed at procreation as the only respectable form of sexual activity.[8] Onanism, homosexual sex, and even casual heterosexual sex were not normal and were proscribed or frowned upon. Moreover, as Toulalan has written, these works 'reveal a culture in which heterosexual, penetrative sexual intercourse, completed by orgasm, was the form of sexual activity that was considered most acceptable and capable of delivering complete sexual gratification for both partners'.[9]

Once again the timing of this trial is important, occurring as it did in the immediate aftermath of the French Revolution and at a time of considerable political debate and social change. Katherine Binhammer sees the 1790s as 'critical moment in the history of sexuality', linking together as she does the various political and philosophical movements of the period, 'the birth of the modern feminist movement, the social enforcement of compulsory heterosexuality, the strengthening of an intricate juridical structure of surveillance and censorship, the advancement of a concern with population control, and the invention of pornography'.[10] Nick Rogers points to an increasing contemporary interest in the publication of cases of 'criminal conversation' (divorce) and the trade in 'aristocratic erotica' across the eighteenth century.[11] Nor was it unusual for political satire and sexual misbehaviour to be interconnected in texts from the seventeenth century.[12] Indeed Michel Foucault argued that

> the very idea of sexuality is an essentially bourgeois one, which developed as an aspect of the self-definition of the [middle] class against the decadent morals of the aristocracy and the rampant immorality of the lower classes in the course of the eighteenth and nineteenth centuries.[13]

This chapter opens a new dialogue on these issues by using this case of alleged homicide to comment on contemporary attitudes towards deviant sexual practice and an interesting coalescence of eighteenth-century print culture, advice manuals, and the publication of one scandalous (and pornographic) novella as well as to explore underlying concerns about the public execution of felons. It will suggest that one particular aspect of capital punishment, largely overlooked by historians of crime, may have influenced attempts to remove the execution of offenders from sight. Finally, it will argue that concerns about deviance and sexuality coalesced in the early 1790s with wider anxieties about sex and allowed the author of the pamphlet an opportunity to exploit this for commercial gain. Once again timing and prevailing political and social issues affected the course of a homicide prosecution in ways that went beyond a simple presentation of the facts of the case. For Susannah Hill, this worked in her favour and saved her from almost any consequences of the actions she took in the early autumn of 1791. Unlike Henry Stroud, Thomas Gordon, or the two Kennedy brothers, the prosecution against Hill for homicide was not carried through to a conclusion. She walked away from the Old Bailey with her life and her freedom even though she was ultimately responsible for the death of another human being.

The chapter is organized into three parts: the first section will look at the events of September 1791 and the death of Francis Kotzwara and Susannah Hill's trial. The second section will look at the curious publication that arose from it in some detail and consider how its author uses the story of Hill and Kotzwara to discuss the nature of sexual deviance, prostitution, and the purpose of sexual relations. It is a curious and at times ambiguous document. It could be a political satire, produced during a well-documented period of national soul-searching about gender roles or a thinly disguised advertisement for sex aids.[14] It might also be seen as a form of erotica, a romanticization of prostitution, and possibly a discussion piece on the nature of punishment and its purpose. Section three will develop one aspect of the pamphlet's content: an observation concerning the effects of hanging on the human body and the implications this had for public execution in the light of eighteenth-century concerns about the gallows spectacle, something which is highlighted by recent research into the criminal corpse.[15] It would seem that autoerotic asphyxiation was known about in the 1790s and is not a more 'modern' phenomenon.[16] Arguably Kotzwara was not the first but simply the most publicized victim of this particular form of thrill seeking. At least two previous deaths in the 1700s can be ascribed to misadventures with autoerotic asphyxiation and the Marquis de Sade's *Justine* (1791) includes a very graphic description of the act.

This unusual case has surfaced before but was previously confined largely to the pages of medical journals or the work of forensic scientists. Indeed 'Kotzwarism' has become shorthand for autoerotic asphyxiation in some circles.[17] William Ober used the case in a brief article in which he discusses examples of 'erotic hanging' in art and literature.[18] However, Ober merely utilizes the pamphlet as a source of information for the Kotzwara case; he does not interrogate its nature or purpose. Nor is this the first time that this pamphlet has come to the attention of historians. In his 1988 study of Enlightenment erotica, Peter Wagner discussed *Modern Propensities* alongside other examples of medical and paramedical literature, which included sex guides, tracts condemning masturbation, and peculiar practices such as flagellation and sadomasochism.[19] He concluded that the pamphlet had been written by 'an eccentric quack named Martin Vanbutchell' who was 'engaged in the promotion of suffocation and strangulation for sexual pleasure', and rather dismissed the article as a less than subtle advertisement for various aids for improving sexual performance.[20] Julia Peakman also mentioned the Kotzwara case briefly but suggested the author of *Modern Propensities* 'considered the episode comedic'.[21] In this chapter, I will analyze the case and the pamphlet from a new perspective: one that considers the history of crime alongside that of sexuality, an area that has largely been ignored but is potentially a rich source of research for historians in both disciplines.

The Life of Susannah Hill and the Death of Francis Kotzwara

The pamphlet presents a heavily stylized account of Susannah's path towards prostitution and her appearance at the Old Bailey.[22] Susannah Hill followed a pathway that would have resonated with many readers in the late eighteenth century who were familiar with representations of prostitution in print culture. According to this source, Susannah was raised in Frome, in Somerset by 'honest' and 'industrious' parents, and educated for a life in domestic service.[23] This role she played until, aged 19, she fell in love with a 'reputable' farmer's son and imagined a future where she could leave behind the 'drudgery of servitude' for a life of married bliss. However, Susannah fell pregnant and found herself out of a position with little chance of gainful employment as a 'respectable' servant.

This then was an oft-told story of a naive and unworldly country girl undone by a young man more intent on fulfilling his lusts than his obligations. Susannah's illegitimate child died within a few weeks of its birth, while (after about a year), with Susannah pregnant once more, her young man found work in London and decamped there, promising to return soon but never doing so. Having miscarried her second child, with money running out, her lover showing no signs of returning to Frome, Susannah pawned what few possessions she had and set off for the capital to find him. She was eventually reunited with her beau only to find him living with an older woman of ill repute (dubbed a 'jezebel') and seemingly reluctant to provide for her. Her fate was secured: Susannah, without money, friends or any prospects, was forced to become what so many young migrant women became in eighteenth-century London, one of thousands of the 'girls of the town' for whom: 'Every day is . . . a day of misery, a pitiful repetition of the same illegal contracts, yet without which they must literally starve'.[24] Thus, by the late summer of 1791, Susannah was almost living out the plot of Hogarth's *Harlot's Progress*.

Hogarth's harlot (Moll Hackabout) has been described as 'both criminal and victim, commodity and trophy, beautiful and diseased' who summed up 'the pleasures, fears, and sentiments' of contemporary Londoners.[25] Since Hogarth's six print series had been published in 1730 and was the first of several successful publications for the artist, it is likely that Moll's story was a very familiar one by the late 1700s. Joseph Addison and Richard Steele (of *The Spectator*) had already successfully sentimentalized the fall of young women into prostitution while the Reformation of Manners campaigners strove to drive them from the streets;[26] the efforts of each side of the debate helped to create a contemporary discourse that saw the 'whore' as both victim and social menace.[27] Hogarth used Moll to critique eighteenth-century society and to pour scorn on the 'respectable' figures that exploited her for pleasure and profit, or to satisfy their own perverted sense of morality, as well as showing the inevitability of Moll's fall from innocence. Similarly the author of *Modern Propensities* used Susannah's story for a variety of purposes, such as her resort to the use of pawnbrokers ('swelling the stock of the Three Blue Balls'), and descent into poverty ('compleatly [sic] shut out from the all the comforts of society'), and then prostitution. In the course of this slide into the debauched world of London prostitution Susannah, we are told, passed up the opportunity of redemption by ignoring the attention of a 'certain pale-faced Quaker' (whom she probably approached for money, as he is described as a 'Lombard Street discounter').[28]

Into this world came a little known musician and composer named Francis Kotzwara (or more properly František Kočvara). Kotzwara had been born in Prague in 1730 and was in his early sixties when he visited Susannah.[29] Francis worked at the King's Theatre in London (at Haymarket, now known as Her Majesty's Theatre), featured in a command performance of the Messiah before the king and queen, and wrote a number of sonatas including one that celebrated the battle of Prague in 1757, when Austrian troops held off the might of Frederick of Great.[30] Apparently he had fought 'several duels, being a good fencer' and once paid his landlord in kind, by executing his portrait when he was short of funds.[31] More pertinently, Kotzwara had a 'penchant for wine and women' as well as some rather peculiar sexual preferences.[32] The *Public Advertiser* described him as a man who 'had fallen a sacrifice to irregular passions'.[33] At her trial, Hill's victim was described by the prosecuting counsel as 'grossly immoral'.[34]

The Death of Francis Kotzwara

The exact details of what happened that day can only have been known by the two protagonists but the pamphlet's author was able to draw upon a printed record of the Old Bailey trial; an account that has survived and that has been consulted here.[35] Naturally we should treat both accounts with some caution because they represent a constructed narrative of events rather than necessarily reflecting factual accuracy.[36] The pamphlet's account of the death is indicative of other forms of contemporary crime narratives, such as the Old Bailey Proceedings and 'Last Confessions', in that it imagines events that the author did not himself witness that have been presented in a form that would be familiar to the reader. However, the presented 'facts' do demonstrate some consistency between the newspaper reports of the pretrial hearing before a London magistrate and a surviving record of what was said at the Old Bailey.[37] Between one and two o'clock in the afternoon of September 2, 1791 Kotzwara supposedly visited Susannah at 5 Vine Street, near the Strand, an area he may well have been familiar with since he lodged at 35 Berwick Street, in nearby Soho. Susannah's address suggests that she was a relatively poor and unspectacular prostitute who was living, rather like Hogarth's *Moll*, a hand-to-mouth existence.[38]

After eating a meal and presumably establishing a fee for Susannah's services, the pair retired to a back room where 'several acts of indecency passed between them' before the composer made a rather strange request.[39] He asked Susannah to cut off his penis or possibly his testicles (the author of the pamphlet simply refers to his 'means of generation' while the trial record states that 'he desired to have *it* severed [my emphasis] for which service he offered her a Guinea').[40] Not surprisingly Susannah refused and so Francis requested instead that she hang him for five minutes saying, and this was Susannah's own recollection in court of the conversation, that it 'would do everything he wished for and would raise his letch or lust'.[41] After sending her out to buy some cord he tied it himself, with her help, to the parlour door. She then helped him put the rope around his own neck so that he was suspended, but quite low down as this illustration (Figure 5.1) suggests:

MODERN PROPENSITIES.

Figure 5.1 Illustration from *Modern propensities; or, an essay on the art of strangling*. Anon.

As William Ober points out, there are several reasons why we should treat this representation with caution. He sees the bottle that Kotzwara is holding as a visual metaphor for masturbation and not unreasonably suggests that the couple were unlikely have remained fully clothed by this stage of proceedings. Nor are the smiles particularly convincing.[42] Nevertheless the image does indicate that the rope was tied – as the trial report states – to the handle of the door and not to a higher place. After five minutes Susannah cut him down and he fell on his face, seemingly unconscious. Susannah panicked and rushed out of her house shouting, 'I have hanged a man! and I am afraid he is dead'. A nearby publican went to fetch help and eventually a surgeon arrived who 'attempted to bleed him'.[43] Francis was beyond medicine however and Susannah was quickly arrested for his murder.

At the inquest Susannah deposed that Francis had 'shewed [her] many scars on his body, which he said, had, at his desire, been inflicted by females'.[44] She went on to protest that 'if the gentleman had a mind to hang himself, it was no business of hers'.[45] A witness claimed to be able to produce others who would testify that Francis had been seen in Charing Cross, 'offering any woman two guineas to cut off his ears'.[46] Despite the evidence that seemed to make it particularly clear that Susannah could not have hanged Francis without his acquiescence, the coroner's jury returned a verdict of murder.[47] Susannah was indicted for 'feloniously willfully and with malice aforethought' making an assault that led to the composer's death and was sent to Newgate Gaol to await trial at the Old Bailey.[48]

The Trial of Susannah Hill

That most famous of all eighteenth-century barristers, William Garrow, acted for the crown. Instead of starting by outlining the guilt of the accused, Garrow set about a deliberate process designed to obscure the facts of the case from the court and the wider public. He lamented that there were 'men who, to gratify the most unwarrantable species of lust, resorted to methods at which reason and morality revolted'.[49] Garrow told the court that Susannah's complicity in the 'grossly immoral' act that had led to Kotzwara's death meant that at the very least she was guilty of aiding and abetting a suicide. Her attitude towards the dead man was careless in the extreme and her behaviour entirely consistent, he added, with 'her abandoned way of life'.[50] In his view she could not but be aware of the consequences of suspending the musician by his neck, regardless of his instructions or desire for her to do so. According to the surviving account of the trial, Garrow stated that he wanted Susannah punished to protect society and ensure that such 'miserable and detestable practices would in the end be eradicated'.[51]

Garrow's opening address makes it clear that he thought this a prurient case that needed to be dealt with swiftly and with as little fuss as possible. He insisted that the trial record be destroyed and no account be published for fear of corrupting the morals of the public. *The Times* reported that 'it was the particular request of the Court, that the notes taken by the short-hand writers might be torn', while *Lloyd's Evening Post* stated they would refrain from setting out the details of the case on grounds of decency, adding that there had already been rather too much publicity.[52] Garrow's approach is consistent with the Old Bailey's attitude towards sodomy trials throughout the eighteenth century. As Peakman has noted:

By the end of the eighteenth century the crime [of buggery] had become so disgraceful in public perception that the [Old Bailey] court decided to suppress reporting the crime publicly, possibly thinking that the more the subject was aired, the more men might be likely to try it.[53]

Garrow may well have been trying to apply the same rationale to this instance of autoerotic asphyxiation; by hushing it up he presumably believed he would prevent future tragedies but also repress the knowledge that hypoxia was a potential path to sexual gratification (something Ober is at pains to refute,[54] as will be discussed later in this chapter).

After an hour where just a handful of witnesses (including a Bow Street officer and one of Hill's neighbour) gave evidence and there were reported to have been a couple of long discussions between the judge, Garrow, and the Recorder of London (who in 1790 was Sir William Rose), Justice Gould stopped the trial and directed the jury to acquit the prisoner. The evidence, even by eighteenth-century standards, was flimsy at best. The nature of the crime, and the scandalous circumstances of the death of a foreign musician, and the need to draw a veil over the whole sorry affair may well have convinced him that any further investigation into Hill's guilt or innocence was unnecessary.

The strange case of Francis Kotzwara was not the first of its kind, nor the first to be hushed up by the London courts. As several of the metropolis' papers noted in their reporting of Kotzwara's death and the subsequent inquest, a similar incident had occurred during the magistracy of Sir John Fielding at Bow Street, between 1754 and 1780. On this occasion a prostitute had been charged with hanging a 'depraved African'.[55] The woman was distracted when her pimp quarreled with someone outside and she forgot her client, who died. She was tried at the Old Bailey court, acquitted of murder, and the papers 'torn' (i.e., destroyed) by the court.

Lloyd's Evening Post reported, again in the aftermath of the Kotzwarra inquest, that:

> Peter Motteux, the well-known translator of Don Quixote into English, lost his life in the same manner, and from the same cause, as the man who was hanged in Vine-street. Mr. Motteux had taken two women of the town into a tavern in St. James's, who, by his desire, hanged him, and were to have cut him down in five minutes. Just at this period, a trumpet was heard in the street, and some procession went along: the curiosity of the girls was excited; and when they returned to relieve the suspended gallant, he was quite dead.[56]

The trial of those accused of Motteux's murder was reported in the Proceedings of 1718 but, apart from a remark by Motteux's servant that he saw bruising on his master's head and 'a Circle about his neck' (suggestive of autoerotic asphyxiation), this case was reported differently.

The author of *Modern Propensities* clearly believed Motteux had fallen victim to the same dangerous sexual practice as Kotzwara, as he mentioned him in his text, describing him as an 'eminent and strangulous [sic] hero'.[57] In October 1791 the *Bon Ton Magazine* used the Kotzwara case to highlight the practice, this time for the amusement of its readership. It describes the antics of 'Sir Barnaby Bowstring' who was enjoying the 'physical excitements of strangulation' when he heard 'a woman vociferate the death of Kotzwarra! [sic] and fearful lest he should follow the example of the debilitated fiddler, he starts from the hands of his fair adjuster'.[58] The *Bon Ton Magazine* for April 1793 also suggested that a man from Bristol had attempted to try out the technique (but no outcome is given).[59]

Modern Propensities and Contemporary Sex Literature

As a result the case was hushed up, for reasons of its immoral nature. Indeed, if the system had worked properly and the court's instructions had been carried out to the letter I doubt we would ever have heard of it.[60] However, as the reporting of both the Kennedy and Gordon cases show, the authorities of the day found keeping the public unaware of what happened behind closed doors considerably difficult. At least one individual had an eye on a potentially lucrative market for this sorry tale and obtained a copy of the trial record that allowed the creation of a 43-page pamphlet entitled *Modern Propensities: or, An Essay on the Art of Strangling.*

The pamphlet is a commentary on the state of society, and on what constitutes appropriate, and inappropriate, forms of sexual activity.[61] The anonymous author begins his discussion with a flamboyant attempt at scene setting ('At a period when the kingdoms of the earth are shook upon their settled foundations'[62]), something in keeping with Peakman's analysis of forms of erotica in this period.[63] The French Revolution was in quite recent memory, the execution of the Bourbons had recently taken place and the world of politics had been turned on its head yet, as he puts it, 'the world of animal existence is still the same'.[64] While he admits that the enlightened world of the eighteenth century offered a range of new and interesting pleasures and delights, the most 'extatic' [sic] pleasure is still derived from 'the conjunctive means by which [the human] species is perpetuated'.[65] So while the pamphleteer addresses a number of issues in his publication, he makes it quite clear that his primary focus is on sex. The work was published and sold in several locations but notably in Paternoster Row, near St Paul's cathedral. That street was notorious throughout the period for its associations with the trade in printed pornography.[66] This sort of pseudo-medical text was typical of the time and the careful way in which the author addresses what is a potentially controversial topic suggests that he was aware of recent prosecutions of printers for the publishing of erotic material.[67] While the detail in this pamphlet is pretty restrained by modern standards, the fact that it discusses sex (indeed 'deviant' sex) means that it could have been purchased by those who were reading it for purposes other than simple enlightenment.[68] The fact that the pamphlet was reproduced in three parts in consecutive editions of the *Bon Ton Magazine* (described as 'one of the first monthly pornographic journals in England'[69] and 'the most important of [the] predecessors of *Playboy*'[70]) also suggests the publishers believed the content would arouse their readership.

The author of *Modern Propensities* is quite demonstrative about the purpose of sex, which was reproduction.[71] By the later 1700s, it appears that reproductive sex meant a fairly conventional rendering of the missionary position in which male orgasm was the desired outcome. So, for example, we could point to an increasing discourse that outlined the negative effects or consequences of masturbation, particularly after the publication of Samuel Tissot's *Onanism* in 1758, and other works by authors such as Venette and the anonymous author of *Aristotle's Masterpiece*, as well as the later work on 'Generation' by Dr Graham.[72] All provided their readership with 'a possible source of knowledge about sex', and both McClaren and Hitchcock have noted that it is possible that their readers used the information contained in reverse – i.e., to indulge in activities that were unlikely to result in conception. Thus, Hitchcock suggests that 'by denigrating perhaps the single most common sexual practice, this literature valorizes a crude, phallocentric emphasis on penetration, over all else'.[73] This was linked to a very understandable emphasis on the importance of fertility and procreation, especially amongst the upper classes. Children were essential to ensuring the longevity of the family name, to securing inherited funds and positions. The Georgian elite may often have been portrayed as pleas-seeking libertines but they all needed heirs to survive them.

Therefore we find the author discussing possible 'quack' cures for impotence such as Dr Graham's so-called Celestial bed or Martin Vanbutchell's elastic garters.[74] Graham was fascinated by the new science of electricity, which he claimed to have studied in Philadelphia. His Celestial bed was 'twelve feet long by nine wide' and supported by 'pillars of brilliant glass', all beautifully decorated. It could be tilted so that a man might 'follow his lady down-hill' (to aid conception) and was built upon a system of electromagnets (to stimulate both parties). Dr Graham made all sorts of spurious 'scientific' claims for his invention in a 1783 article.[75] He also used this piece to condemn prostitution and propose a tax on men who remained unmarried. Whether Graham's moralizing was a product of his form moral convictions or a reflection of his desire to promote his products is open to question but he was not shy of putting himself in the limelight. Graham opened two shows in London in the 1780s—the Temple of Health at the Adelphi and a second, the Temple of Prolific Hymen on Pall Mall. Here he entertained large audiences with his demonstrations of the Celestial bed and pioneered the use of musical therapy.[76] Graham was a consummate self-publicist although ultimately his business sense seems to have let him down; the Celestial bed never made him any money despite (or perhaps because of) it costing the princely sum of two guineas to attend his performances.[77] By 1782 Graham was almost bankrupt and he died a lunatic in 1794. Nevertheless, many readers of *Modern Propensities* would have been familiar with his exploits and those of other 'quacks', like Chevalier Bartholomew Ruspini (who arrived in London in the 1750s). Ruspini had become famous for treating the Prince of Wales in the 1780s and so secured the position of surgeon-dentist to the future George IV.[78] *Modern Propensities* references Graham's 'bliss-giving machine' and notes that the 'ELECTRIC QUALITIES' are 'within the recollection of thousands'.[79] Quacks such as Graham were well-versed in the use of newsprint to promote their own products and cures and to denigrate those of rivals. So-called advertising professors (such as the unfortunate Dr Rock who was lampooned by Hogarth in *A Harlot's Progress*) colluded with newspapers – sharing the profits of sales of medicines and inserting spurious articles (or 'puffs') on the efficacy of this or that cure, which were little more than publicity for new products.[80] Newspapers were full of advertisements for pills and 'nostrums' to cure all sorts of diseases and address all kinds of maladies and weaknesses as well as plugs for lectures and pamphlets that discussed and described all manner of medical topics. *Modern Propensities* emulates these works – such as *Aristotle's Masterpiece*.[81] It also echoes (albeit in a more carefully constructed manner) the execution broadsides of the eighteenth century and the narratives of crime produced by the Ordinary of Newgate and the publishers of the Old Bailey Proceedings.[82]

Modern Propensities is a more detailed discussion piece. It takes the reader on a journey through a variety of strange and peculiar pastimes and seeks to entertain rather than lecture on the subject of sex. Perhaps, as Peakman has identified, in other works it shows the ways in which the links between science and erotica and new discoveries and 'enlightenment' ideas were being incorporated into writing about sex.[83] I will return to the topic of sex and aids to sexual performance (in particular Vanbutchell and the use of strangulation) shortly but before that I would like to address another way in which we might interpret this curious document.

The Sex (or Gender) Panic of the 1790s

The anonymous author's style of writing echoes contemporary satires on the nobility, such as Charles Pigott's *The Jockey Club* (and its follow up, *The Female Jockey Club*) that were published in the 1790s.[84]

Various notable persons are mentioned by name (such as the Duchess of Devonshire[85] and Lady Aylesbury)[86] or alluded to (such as the unnamed 'General S___')[87] in the manner that Pigott used to expose the scandals of the day, and so this would have been a sensational and familiar read for many of those that purchased it. In *The Jockey Club*, Pigott set out to shame the nobility (and in particular the person of the Prince of Wales) by portraying them as immoral and corrupt. Thus these attacks by Pigott are redolent of those made by 'Junius' on some of George III's ministers. The anonymous letter writer drew attention to questions of the Duke of Grafton's 'private sexual morality', in particular publicly criticizing him for taking his mistress to the opera in 1768.[88] As Donna Andrew has observed, in the last years of the 1760s England witnessed a

> continuing and growing trend of newspaper and magazine reportage of the salacious and anti-social sexual activities of the well-born and infamous. Beginning with the publication of Junius' criticism of Grafton for political immorality, which his private immorality mirrored, through the affair of the Duke of Cumberland and Lady Grosvenor, which implicated figures among the very highest rungs of privilege and social hierarchy, the press soon realized the advantages and interest to be gained from this sort of reporting.[89]

There are strong echoes of this in Pigott's writing. For example he described the 'ageing Duchess of Bedford' as someone who 'dispensed her patronage to young men in return for sexual favours'.[90] Nick Rogers has identified Pigott as a radical with the intent to 'discredit the aristocracy's right to rule and to trumpet the downfall of what he saw as an undeniably decadent order'. Rogers points to an increasing contemporary interest in the publication of cases of 'criminal conversation' (divorce) and the trade in 'aristocratic erotica' across the eighteenth century.[91] It was not unusual for political satire and sexual misbehaviour to be interconnected in texts from the seventeenth century, as Toulalan has noted.[92] Moreover, if one agrees with Foucault's notion of sexuality as essentially 'bourgeois', then it is easy to read Pigott *et al* as a commentary on the worst excesses of the ruling class and therefore the illegitimacy of their power.[93] In the context of the 1790s and the publication of this pamphlet, I think we need to be careful, however, of seeing the author of *Modern Propensities* as a dangerous radical.

The late 1780s and 1790s certainly represent a period of heated political debate following events across the Channel – events that the author referred to at the start of his pamphlet. In addition, London witnessed a series of attacks on women by the so-called Monster. A number of women, including 'respectable' women, were subjected to physical and verbal abuse by a strange individual who often inveigled them into his immediate proximity with the ruse of inviting them to smell his nosegay. As they came close he made sexually suggestive comments and stabbed them in the face or the backside. Some, as a result of the layers of clothing that fashionable women wore, did not realize they had been attacked until they got home. A moral panic then ensued before an artificial flower-maker named Rhynwick Williams was put on trial at the Old Bailey on a charge of wounding in July 1790. The jury found him guilty, but the judge (Justice Buller) deferred sentence because of concerns he had about the nature of the indictment. In the end he went to gaol for six years.[94] The 'Monster Panic' can be viewed as a conservative backlash aimed at restoring the patriarchal status quo at a time when all sorts of 'rights' were seemingly up for discussion.[95]

Similarly *Modern Propensities* should be read in the context of the 'gender panic' that gripped Britain in the aftermath of the Revolution in France (and the loss of the American colonies). As noted previously, Binhammer has described this turbulent period as one that was synonymous with political and social challenges to the established status quo.[96] The pamphlet's author notes the 'severity of morals at this period'.[97] During the 'sex' or 'gender' panic, notions of femininity were widely discussed and disputed and attempts were made to redraw gender boundaries that had been mutable or blurred from the 1770s onwards. In the inherent deviancy exposed by *Modern Propensities*, in its discussion of Kotzwara and Hill's fall ('the result of deviations from the regular paths of prudence'),[98] we can discern a moralizing tone that links this publication very clearly to other calls for a return to 'normality', such as those by Hannah More, and a reestablishment of more conventional ideals of masculinity and femininity.[99] Arguably it was getting harder to be different in the 1790s (as the celebrated Chevalier D'Eon discovered on his second visit to England after 1785) and Kotzwara's peculiar 'perversion' may have manifested itself as a suitable example of how dangerous such subversion could be. It probably helped the anonymous author's case that the musician was, like D'Eon, a foreign curiosity and not a red-blooded Englishman. The so-called sex panic manifested itself in all sorts of condemnatory publications, and *Modern Propensities* is indicative of this 'fear over the basic degeneracy of the morals of the age',[100] something that is clear in Garrow's expression of his disgust of the case. Given the attached concern about the increasing numbers of prostitutes in London, the desire of the court to hush up this sordid episode is certainly suggestive of other examples of the 'sex panic' of the 1790s. Therefore, by drawing on some of the rhetoric of contemporary satires on politics, the state of society, and perhaps reflecting an educated interest in contemporary debates on a host of issues, the author may have partly been riding the political zeitgeist in the hope of selling more copies.

As Binhammer argues: 'Sex panic literature frequently used the trope of the French Revolution in order to conflate – both literally and metaphorically – female sexuality and the nation'.[101] *Modern Propensities* utilizes the Revolution in a similar way, suggesting that the world has been turned upside down ('convulsed and inverted'[102]), and so attempts to reinforce the conventional view that the purpose of sex was reproduction. So, for *Modern Propensities*, Susannah's 'fall' might have been precipitated by a man but it was her desire (or the reciprocation of Kotzwara's at least) that led her to the precipice. She was, like Hogarth's Moll, both victim and polluter of morals. Her fate (and that of so many London prostitutes) was, in the words of the pamphlet's author, 'dreadful monuments of the effects of unlawful desires'.[103] Her corruption was completed by her decision to leave the relative sanctuary of Frome for the dangers of the metropolis. In short, then, she brought it upon herself, and her appearance in court, and associations with such a deviant sexual practice, was entirely consistent with contemporary views about the immorality of women in a period of history where sexuality and the proper conduct of women in particular were bound up with notions of the state of society more generally. Moreover, as the prosecution of individual immorality through the courts (notably of course the church courts which had effectively disappeared by the late 1700s), 'ever more energy was expended on the inculcation of sexual mores through education, literature, and social norms', as Faramerz Dabhoiwala has written. 'For women in particular', Dabhoiwala notes, 'especially those in middling and polite society, the result may well have been a tightening of moral control, rather than the reverse'.[104]

While it is likely that selling numerous copies of the pamphlet was uppermost in the author's (and his publisher's) mind, I would suggest that he had other aims in view. This brings us to the third area of interest stimulated by this curious document and its underlying narrative: the area concerned with sexual performance and the best means of overcoming impotence.

Autoerotic Asphyxiation and Contemporary Concerns About the Execution of Felons

Having detailed several instances where those suffering from various manifestations of sexual impotence turned to internal stimulants, (such as the aforementioned 'General S____' who swallowed a 'double portion of liquid love potion'), with spectacularly disastrous consequences, the pamphlet's author suggests that there are other 'equally efficacious' external 'expedients', which are much safer.[105] He introduces the topic in a typically euphemistic manner that echoes the ways in which contemporary erotica deployed what Karen Harvey has described as 'cloaks of metaphor and suspended denouements'.[106] This is what the author has to say:

> When, by too frequent use and overstraining of the vitals, nature becomes sluggish, and the corporeal fluids begin to linger in their respective revolutions; the mind, however active, is of itself incapable of communicating that sympathetic energy and tone, which, at a former period, it accelerated even by a single glance of thought.[107]

What he is alluding to is that impotence is a symptom of the ageing process. What follows is a discussion of attempts at remedying this problem, leading to an observation about the effects of strangulation on the human body. As a part of this exposition, the author mentions flagellation (both as a method of scourging and a form of sexual stimulation) before going into a lengthy examination of the effects of hanging on executed prisoners. His analysis is focused on the Ordinary of Newgate, the prison chaplain who listened to, wrote up, and profited from the last confessions of those condemned to be executed at Tyburn and, later, outside the debtor's door at the London prison. One particular Ordinary (dubbed 'Parson Manacle') took a great interest in the hanged and the contents of their pockets – the implication being he was more interested in their worldly goods than their immortal souls. However, by trying to make sure he got hold of any valuables that had remained on them at the time of their execution, he inadvertently made a curious discovery that concerned the physical conditions of their lower bodies. What the Ordinary noted was that 'at least four-fifths of his periodical flocks were scarcely suspended between heaven and earth, or in other words, launched into eternity, than they evinced certain emotions and commotions'. In short, he observed that hanging sometimes produced erections and orgasms – via the same autoerotic asphyxiation that Kotzwara craved from Susannah – or as the pamphlet's author delicately put it: 'all flesh must die to live again'. While life appeared to have left the corpses of the hanged men, in 'those centrical and critical parts the symptoms of life and vigour were expressly evident'.[108] The parson appears not only to have helped himself to the trimmings from the pockets of executed male criminals but also to have enjoyed the sexual benefits of a gaol full of terrified women. By offering them the chance to become pregnant (and so delay if not avoid altogether, the hangman's noose by 'pleading the belly'), he both pimped out the female prisoners to others for a fee and had sexual relations with them himself. On one occasion, however, he seems to have contracted a sexually transmitted disease that rendered him impotent. And so, given his knowledge of the benefits of hanging he then began to experiment with autoerotic asphyxiation himself.

In purporting to help a distressed female prisoner ('Mrs Birdlime') who was afraid of her own execution, he acquired a rope and involved her in the process of helping him partially strangle himself. Her duty was to cut the rope 'the moment she saw any appearance of actual danger' even though he was at all times able to put his legs down and save himself.[109] This echoes the Kotzwara case where the image from *Modern Propensities* (see Figure 5.1) shows Francis with his legs touching the floor. In a report of a death from hanging in June of 1791, it was noted that a farmer was 'was found hanging by the neck, not suspended from the ground, but on his knees'.[110] According to modern forensic science asphyxiation 'caused by hanging is by far the most common form of accidental auto-erotic fatality' and actual suicide is not intended even if the risk is part of the thrill. So Parson Manacle and Kotzwara's arrangement of the rope within touching distance of the ground is typical of more recent reported incidents of asphyxia or sexually related hypoxia.[111] According to our narrator, the woman, although shocked by his suggestion, acquiesced to his demands and was apparently reassured that hanging was actually quite painless. The Ordinary also found the experiment to his satisfaction, achieving the results he had hoped for in overcoming his impotence. After several further successful dalliances, he finally left himself suspended too long and was found dead in a cell by a gaoler; the affair was hushed up and his death attributed to 'gaol fever' (typhus). Sadly no contemporary record of 'Parson Manacle' appears to have survived, but while the story may be apocryphal it is still valuable as a source for understanding contemporary attitudes towards hanging.[112]

What the author of the pamphlet concludes from this is that hanging, or the process of shutting off the blood supply, can be an effective remedy for erectile dysfunction. He then goes on to advertise the benefits of Vanbutchell's elastic garters (also known as 'spring bands'),[113] which he says have benefitted several members of the aristocracy. The science of strangulation, he argued, was still in its infancy and anyone reading his pamphlet was advised that while in the future it may be possible to deploy a means of autoerotic asphyxiation that is safe, for the meantime readers are urged to stick to more reliable remedies such as Dr Vanbutchell's own patent 'and astonishing Nostrum', the Balsam of Life, which not only appeared to be able to restore the physical but had the added bonus of being able to 'preserve wives from corruption, and produce children of the true athletic stamina'.[114] While the 'balsam of life' might be viewed as another quack cure for all ills, it would seem that Vanbutchell was ahead of his time in applying the science of auto-asphyxiation to prolonged or sustained penile erections, at least for commercial purposes; indeed an advertisement in the London press recommended the use of Vanbutchell's 'spring-band garters' at the upcoming masquerade to be held at Ranelagh Gardens, promising to make the wearers 'superlatively happy!'[115]

Other Concerns About the Public Execution
of Criminals

The revelation regarding the effects of hanging on the male body can also be factored into contemporary debates surrounding the efficacy of hanging as a punishment and of the wider effects of public execution on the crowd.[116] In the later eighteenth century there was a growing disquiet about the public execution of criminals, for reasons of taste and decency as well as the efficacy of hanging as a deterrent for crime.[117] As was noted in the introduction to this volume, for the most part comment was directed at the behaviour of the execution crowd who were the intended audience for this demonstration of state power over the body of the condemned.[118] Hanging was intended as a deterrent; while there had been notable improvements in policing agencies (such as the creation of the Bow Street 'runners' and the reform of the night watch in Westminster and the City of London),[119] there was no universal method of catching criminals or preventing crime – prosecutions relied upon the efforts of the victims and entrepreneurial thief-takers some of whom were shamelessly corrupt and traded on the availability of government rewards that sent men and women to Tyburn regardless of their guilt or innocence.[120] All the state had to fall back on was the public spectacle of a steady stream of malefactors dancing the so-called Tyburn jig in the hope that this prevented others from following their example.

Contemporary commentators condemned the practice. Execution was inefficient, it set a bad example of state cruelty, and it was argued that the crowds that gathered were becoming inured to the scene or were brutalized by it. Reports of executions were sometimes peppered with accounts of pickpockets preying on the watching crowds and of the consumption of alcohol and the avoidance of work. The carnivalesque atmosphere was roundly condemned. One commentator writing to the papers around the time of Susannah's case reflected one widely held view that hanging was an inappropriate and outmoded form of execution for an enlightened civilized society: 'Hanging is a slow and awkward contrivance, and the sufferer is often seen to struggle with death for some moments after his launch into the air' he wrote, and others echoed this viewpoint within parliament and society.[121] It also came to be seen as archaic and representative of an early modern past that was out of step with 'enlightened' and 'modern' England. The cruelty of the hanging ritual had become 'disturbing and negative' in the eyes of several reformers.[122] Public execution also presented a risk to public safety and offended public morals. As Laqueur noted prostitution and sex were often associated with execution crowds: 'Ribald sexuality, male potency and death – intimately bound together in the carnivalesque – are also ubiquitously associated in the imagery of eighteenth-century executions'.[123] All of these arguments were to become central tenets in the attempts of early nineteenth-century reformers to restrict or abolish the practice of hanging and of public execution. I wonder in all this discussion about the effects upon the crowd: how many people witnessed an involuntary bulge in the breeches or saw the consequence of hangings immediately afterwards? Dr Iwan Bloch, the early sexologist and 'discoverer' of de Sade, certainly believed there were clear connections to be drawn between the execution spectacle and sexual arousal. In discussing public execution in England, Bloch noted that there was

> a secret passion which draws countless people to the horrible spectacle of a public execution; and it is an excitation with definitely marked erotic undertones that takes possession of them during the performance itself. This is the terrifying theme of the Marquis de Sade's novels that are not the products of an idle fantasy but really mirror actual happenings.[124]

Bloch suggested that Kotzwara was influenced by what he had seen because, like so many other 'execution habitués', including the essayist Boswell and George Selwyn (the politician that had intervened to help save the Kennedy brothers and who had travelled to Paris to see the regicide Damiens executed), he had regularly attended executions at Tyburn.[125] Of course others might have learned a very different lesson, as Julie Peakman suggests: she argues that knowledge of what happened to the human body at executions might have deterred people from attempting auto-asphyxiation. 'Seeing the victims evacuating their bodily fluids and writhing and jerking could not', she writes, 'have been a pleasant sight'.[126] Not pleasant at all, at least not for the majority, but revealing nonetheless. It is some evidence at least that those viewing the execution of felons were aware of the physical transformations that their bodies underwent.

Recent research reveals that the dissection of criminals condemned under the 1752 Murder Act were witnessed by large numbers of ghoulish onlookers.[127] Crowds gathered as the corpses of criminals were carried into the anatomization room; many more saw them as they were cut down after death. Bodies were supposed to be suspended for an hour after execution to ensure that death had occurred (although it is likely that this rule was frequently ignored).[128] Therefore, it is unlikely that the Ordinary was the only person to notice the effects of hanging on the male body. So, as the anonymous creator of *Modern Propensities* suggested, if hanging held such unexpected pleasures was it perhaps losing its fear amongst the populace? This is of course very unlikely, but given that the 'bloody code' actually spared many more from the noose than it killed there does seem to be a recognition amongst some leading contemporaries that the punishment of hanging had lost its power to *control* the

populace. The side effects of hanging had been known for some considerable time as one contemporary poem noted:

> In our town the other day
> They hanged a man to make him pay
> For having raped a little girl.
> As life departed from the churl
> The townsfolk saw, with great dismay
> His organ rise in boldest way
> A sign to all who stood around
> That pleasure e'en in death is found.[129]

William Ober, a forensic scientist, is skeptical that hanging would rou-
tinely produce the results that 'Parson Manacle' or Kotzwara and others
desired. While he accepts that it is possible, and does happen, 'there is no
physiologic mechanism for producing [such] an effect of the genitalia'.[130]
Ober explains the presence of semen in the undergarments of hanged
criminals as merely reflecting the 'passive emptying of the bladder, rec-
tum, and seminal vesicles when the cervical cord and autonomic nervous
system are disrupted and the usual controls abolished'. It is possible then
that what the Ordinary and onlookers at executions were witnessing was
in fact priapism ('which is pathological') rather than erections (which are
physiological).[131] However, whether an eighteenth-century audience was
able to discern the difference is a moot point; to the uneducated observer
it would still appear that the hanged man had enjoyed a brief moment of
ecstasy before his life was finally extinguished on the gallows.

In 1783 the 'traditional procession of the condemned to Tyburn' was
abandoned and a scaffold was erected outside Newgate to encompass
the 'new drop' method of hanging.[132] This had been used once before to
execute Earl Ferrers in 1760 but became the usual way of dispatching
felons from the 1780s. The drop was supposedly introduced to make the
management of execution easier for the sheriffs but also because it was
suggested that this was in some way more scientific and humane. Gatrell
pours scorn on this supposition, arguing that hanging remained a very
inexact and cruel punishment right through to the end of the 1800s.[133]
However, the proud sheriffs commissioned an image of their new device
that shows a raised platform beneath a fixed gallows (see Figure 5.2).

On a signal the hangman would remove a pin, causing the platform to
fall away and the bodies of the convicts to fall through, snapping their
necks.[134] At this point the lower halves of those executed may have disappeared from public view. I say 'may' here because it is quite hard to
be absolutely sure of what an execution looked like or how much was
visible to the observer. We know that the structure outside Newgate was
raised up eight feet from the ground, which made the 'condemned more

Figure 5.2 'The Platform and Gallows at Newgate Prison, Old Bailey, City of London', (1783). Anon.

Source: Heritage Image Partnership Ltd/Alamy Stock Photo

readily visible to everyone in the street', but the bottom of the platform was draped in black cloth (to give the proceedings a funeral aspect perhaps).[135] In Rowlandson's 1806 engraving (see Figure 5.3), we can see the whole body of the condemned after they are dispatched by the hangman. But was this image, (see Figure 5.4) imbued as it was with artistic licence, deliberately intended perhaps to echo Hogarth's mid-century engraving of the carnivalesque execution at Tyburn?

Fisher Nuttall's print (see Figure 5.5), created three years after Rowlandson, shows the platform with the height exaggerated (it looks as if it is at least twice the height of contemporary reports) but make it appear that, as the bodies dropped, they became slightly more obscured from those watching.

There are several well-known records of witnesses to hangings, including Dickens and Thackeray, but as was discussed in the introduction, much of what was written or said is either euphemism or concentrates on the crowd and the moments leading up to the execution itself. Thackeray describes all the events leading up to Courvoisier's hanging (in 1840) but averts his eyes at the point at which the hood is drawn over the condemned man's head.[136] Similarly, while there is quite a full description of the crowd within *The Groans of the Gallows, or the Past and*

Figure 5.3 Thomas Rowlandson, 'An Execution Outside Newgate Prison', (c.1806)
Source: Heritage Image Partnership Ltd/Alamy Stock Photo

Figure 5.4 William Hogarth, 'The Idle 'Prentice Executed at Tyburn': *Industry and Idleness*, plate 11. September 30, 1747. Harris Brisbane Dick Fund, 1932

Source: www.metmuseum.org/art/collection/search/399844

VIEW OF AN EXECUTION BEFORE THE DEBTORS DOOR OF NEWGATE.

Figure 5.5 Fisher Nuttall, 'View of an Execution Before the Debtor's Door of Newgate', (1809)

Source: © Museum of London

Present Life of William Calcraft The Living Hangman of Newgate (London, 1846), there is no actual commentary on the hanging process. W. H. Maxwell also offers more than one recollection of hangings in Ireland in the late eighteenth and early nineteenth centuries but again we get no description of the death itself. Understandably, perhaps, he seems reluctant to share the event graphically.[137] As one author has noted, 'canons of decorum and middle-class squeamishness dictated that the ugly reality of protracted death by strangulation should be glossed over, usually by some variant of "launched into eternity" '.[138]

Clearly we cannot say for certain that contemporaries introduced the 'new drop' in order to protect the public from seeing the involuntarily effects of hanging on the human body, but this may have formed a part of their rationale for so doing. It may have influenced later discussions to remove executions from public view entirely after 1868. Execution by hanging was a very physical, painful, and unpleasant process as one pamphlet from 1837 felt obliged to demonstrate: 'Horrid convulsions agitate the body, in its ineffectual attempts to inspire', the *Penny Satirist* explained, 'the countenance becomes distorted with each agonising gasp: the eyes protrude from their sockets, and are suffused with blood, the tongue is forced into the mouth, and blood bursts from the ears'.[139] These visible signs of cruelty were used by abolitionists throughout the late eighteenth and early decades of the nineteenth century in their campaign against the 'bloody code' and it may well be the case that other, normally unspoken effects of hanging were noted as well.

It seems reasonable to suppose that the advocates of the abolition of the public execution (if not hanging as a method of execution itself) would have used this argument in private debates but perhaps not publicly, for reasons of taste and decency. Hanging continued as a punishment in England but its use was increasingly restricted. The number of people that could view public executions (and the effect on the condemned felon) was effectively constrained both by moving gallows within the close proximity of a gaol and by introducing the 'drop', and then (from the late 1860s) taking it behind prison walls. As Steve Poole argues, this may not have been much of a factor outside of London where the gallows procession and crude form of execution persisted into the 1800s.[140] To what degree an almost unspoken discussion of the physical effects of hanging had on this change is hard to measure but perhaps warrants consideration. In doing so, it reminds us that Foucault's fascinating explanation for the retreat from public displays of state violence does not allow room for a more nuanced and cultural alternative; in rejecting 'humanity' he has also perhaps underestimated the extent to which 'good taste' was offended by the gallows spectacle.[141] After all, John Beattie noted that the process of prosecution and punishment was not driven by a 'simple and single set of motives and concerns' and this can be seen in changes across policing, prosecution, and punishment in the late eighteenth and early nineteenth centuries.[142] By looking at both what *is* and what *is not* described, at public executions we have a much better chance of fully understanding the multiple casual factors behind changes to the process of hanging offenders.[143]

It has been shown that autoerotic asphyxiation was by no means unknown in eighteenth-century London but at least some people wished for it to be less well known, William Garrow amongst them. This strange sexual practice went against the contemporary understanding of what represented appropriate forms of sexual behaviour which, by the 1790s, were pretty much restricted to methods designed for procreation—anything else was deemed perverse and perhaps even, a bit *foreign*, especially in the context of the 1790s 'panic' about gender and sex. Of course we should be mindful that the printing (and survival) of a contemporary pamphlet is not indicative in any way of its reach or influence but we might presume that its author believed it worth writing and distributing. Thus this curious pamphlet may well be an elaborate advertisement but at the same time if offers an interesting insight into late eighteenth-century society and its print culture. It draws on classical themes, politics, and popular satire; it echoes contemporary forms of erotica and social commentary and it clearly disregards the injunction against the publication of the details of certain criminal trials.[144] Perhaps by accident if not by design it calls into question the state's use of hanging as a method of punishment, in public at least.

In 1791, the Marquis de Sade published *Justine*, which he had written during his confinement in the Bastille in 1787. In one scene, the character of Roland practices autoerotic asphyxiation, putting his life in Therese's hands. He mounted a stool, put a rope around his neck, and then she removed the stool on his signal. The result was 'symptoms of pleasure [that] ornament his countenance and at practically the same instant jets of semen spring nigh to the vault. When 'tis all shot out . . . I rush to cut him down, he falls, unconscious, but thanks to my ministrations he quickly recovers his senses'.[145]

Conclusions

Was Kotzwara familiar with *Justine*? It seems unlikely given the timing but it is just possible that he obtained a copy since it was quite possible he spoke and read French. It is more likely, however, that Francis arrived at his discovery of the benefits of hypoxia via attendance at executions, by word of mouth or by happenstance. Kotzwara's case is sometimes cited as the first example of autoerotic asphyxiation to be clearly identified. As such, this curious episode perhaps represents the beginnings of a history of sadomasochism in this country— something that was clearly occurring long before Sade's first novella was widely known. Peter Motteux, the 'depraved African', and Kotzwarra were experimenting with forms of deviant sexuality in a society determined to establish a one-size-fits-all model of sexual conduct. Garrow's attempt to put the genie back in the bottle failed and the resulting literature derived from the trial shows us that our Georgian ancestors were every bit as sexually adventurous as any society before or since. More importantly, the publication of *Modern Propensities* reveals a sophisticated author quite adept at exploiting contemporary attitudes towards sexuality and fears about sexual freedoms and practices for base commercialism. While this might not surprise us, it does contribute to a growing understanding of the rich multiplicity of conduct literature, paramedical tracts, erotica, and satire in Georgian England and suggests a knowing audience that was cognizant with this vibrant cornucopia of writing. Furthermore, *Modern Propensities*, and the case from which it takes it central narrative, adds nuance to debates surrounding the public execution of criminals. I am not suggesting for a minute that the new drop and the eventual removal of the gallows spectacle were entirely occasioned by a squeamishness resulting from the sight of erections in those being dispatched 'into eternity' but instead that by looking at the ritual of execution more closely we might better understand that those campaigning for its abolition (or its removal behind prison walls) had multiple reasons for doing so. Thus, while this otherwise insignificant case of the accidental death of a Bohemian musician might appear to have little to offer on the surface, a detailed analysis of the Hill/Kotzwara case allows useful insight into a period when ideas about sex and ideas about the body of the criminal were experiencing considerable scrutiny. Moreover, I think we can also draw some conclusions about why the authorities chose to draw a veil over the death of Francis Kotzwara even if that meant releasing his killer. One can argue of course that no homicide was proven, but there can be no doubt as to Susannah Hill's responsibility since by her own admission she 'hanged a man'. She was guilty, by most definitions, at least, of manslaughter, and under eighteenth-century law could have punished by imprisonment (branding, as we have noted, was abolished by the early 1790s). That she was not, and her trial was not only abandoned but also entirely struck from the record, is testimony once more to the power of the Hanoverian system to pick and choose which individuals to make examples of. It served no one to hang or imprison a lowly London prostitute for the killing of a minor foreign musician. Much better, then, that the whole affair was quietly hushed up and forgotten. Unfortunately for William Garrow and his colleagues, someone had not read the memo and the story leaked out into the public domain, albeit in a limited way. We have no idea of the reach of *Modern Propensities* or at what effect it had. Nor of course do we know what became of Susannah Hill, but she most probably continued to ply her trade in London until poverty or disease got the better of her. Her case is a final reminder that discretion, circumstance, and connections – much more than legal arguments and evidence-based decision-making – determined who was prosecuted and ultimately left to hang in eighteenth-century England.

Notes

1. Anon, *Modern Propensities: Or an Assay on the Art of Strangling etc. Illustrated with Several Anecdotes, with Memoirs of Susannah Hill and a Summary of Her Trial at the Old Bailey, on Friday, September 16, 1791, on the Charge of Hanging Francis Kotzwara at Her Lodgings in Vine Street, on September 2* (London, 1791).
2. Devereaux, 'Recasting the Theatre of Execution'; Laqueur, 'Crowds, Carnival, and the State'; Smith, 'Civilized People Don't Want to See That Kind of Thing'; Wilf, 'Imagining Justice'.
3. Julie Peakman, *Mighty Lewd Books: The Development of Pornography in Eighteenth-Century England* (Basingstoke, Palgrave Macmillan, 2003); Sarah Toulalan, *Imagining Sex: Pornography and Bodies in Seventeenth-Century England* (Oxford, Oxford University Press, 2007), p. 65.
4. Tim Hitchcock, 'Redefining Sex in Eighteenth-Century England', *History Workshop Journal*, Vol. 41 (Spring 1996), p. 188.

5. Peakman, *Mighty Lewd Books*; Toulalan, *Imagining Sex*; Karen Harvey, *Reading Sex in the Eighteenth Century: Bodies and Gender in English Erotic Culture* (Cambridge, Cambridge University Press, 2004).

6. Roy Porter, 'Sexual Advice Before 1800', in R. Porter and M. Teich (eds.), *Sexual Knowledge, Sexual Science: The History of Attitudes to Sexuality* (Cambridge, Cambridge University Press, 1994), p. 138.

7. Tim Hitchcock, *English Sexualities, 1700–1800* (Basingstoke, Palgrave Macmillan, 1997), pp. 50–51; Paul-Gabriel Boucé, 'Some Sexual Beliefs and Myths in Eighteenth-Century Britain' (pp. 30–31) and Robert A. Erickson, 'The Books of Generation: Some Observations on the Style of the British Midwife Books, 1671–1764' (pp. 74–94), both in Paul-Gabriel Boucé (ed.), *Sexuality in Eighteenth-Century Britain* (Manchester, Manchester University Press, 1982).

8. Julie Peakman, 'Sexual Perversion in History: An Introduction', in Julie Peakman (ed.), *Sexual Perversions, 1670–1890* (Basingstoke, Palgrave Macmillan, 2009), pp. 3–4.

9. Toulalan, *Imagining Sex*, p. 77.

10. Binhammer, 'The Sex Panic', p. 411.

11. Nicholas Rogers, 'Pigott's Private Eye: Radicalism and Sexual Satire in Eighteenth-Century England', *Journal of the Canadian Historical Association*, Vol. 4 (1993), p. 251.

12. Toulalan, *Imagining Sex*, p. 55.

13. Kim M. Phillips and Barry Reay (eds.), *Sexualities in History: A Reader* (London, Routledge, 2002), p. 35.

14. Binhammer, 'The Sex Panic'.

15. Elizabeth T. Hurren, 'The Dangerous Dead: Dissecting the Criminal Corpse', *Lancet*, Vol. 382, No. 9889 (2013), pp. 302–3.

16. In February 1994 Stephen Milligan MP was found dead in his home, the cause attributed to autoerotic asphyxiation. Michael Hutchence was believed to have died in similar circumstances in 1997 despite the verdict of suicide given by the coroner. More recently the actor David Carradine died from accidental asphyxiation in Thailand and there was evidence that this was another incident of sexual practice gone wrong.

17. Stephen G. Michaud and Roy Hazelwood, *The Evil That Men Do: FBI Profiler Roy Hazelwood's Journey into the Minds of Sexual Predators* (Basingstoke, Palgrave Macmillan, 2010), p. 67.

18. William B. Ober, 'The Sticky End of Frantisek Koczkwara, Composer of the "Battle of Prague"', *American Journal of Forensic Medicine and Pathology*, Vol. 5, No. 2 (1984), p. 147.

19. Peter Wagner, *Eros Revived: Erotica of the Enlightenment in England & America* (London, Paladin Books, 1988).

20. Ibid., pp. 24–26.

21. Julie Peakman, *A Cultural History of Sexuality, Volume 4: Sexuality in the Enlightenment* (London, Bloomsbury, 2011, 2014), p. 18.

22. An advert for *Modern Propensities* appeared in the London press within days of the trial, on the 17 September 1791, *Morning Post and Daily Advertiser*, 17 September 1791.

23. Anon, *Modern Propensities*.

24. Ibid., p. 38.

25. Ronald Paulson, *Hogarth's Harlot: Sacred Parody in Enlightenment England* (Baltimore, MA, John Hopkins University Press, 2003), p. 27.

26. Faramerz Dabhoiwala, 'Sex and Societies for Moral Reform, 1688–1800', *Journal of British Studies*, Vol. 46, No. 2 (April 2007), pp. 290–319.

27. Laura J. Rosenthal, *Infamous Commerce: Prostitution in Eighteenth-Century British Literature and Culture* (Ithaca, NY, Cornell University Press, 2015).

28. Anon, *Modern Propensities*, pp. 34–39.

29. Although at least one newspaper incorrectly records his age as between 40 and 50, *London Chronicle*, 3 September 1791.

30. *Morning Post and Daily Advertiser*, 17 September 1791.

31. Ibid.

32. Wagner, *Eros Revived*, pp. 24–26.

33. *Public Advertiser*, 6 September 1791.

34. Anon, *The Trial of Susannah Hill for the Willful Murder of Francis Kotzwara, September the 2nd 1791 at Justice Hall in the Old Bailey* (Boston Medical Library, 1791).

35. Ibid.

36. Natalie Zemon Davis, *Pardon Tales and Their Tellers in Sixteenth-Century France* (Stanford, Stanford University Press, 1988).

37. Anon, *The Trial of Susannah Hill*.

38. *Harris' List of Covent Garden Ladies* was published on an annual basis between 1757 and 1795 and offered its readers a guide to London's prostitutes. It gave details of their looks, personality, prosperity to alcoholism, comments on their sexual abilities and specialism (often heavily coded), and the price one could expect to pay. Susannah does not feature in any edition I have so far been able to consult. Hallie Rubenhold, *The Covent Garden Ladies: The Extraordinary Story of Harris' List* (London, Random House, 2012).

39. Anon, *Modern Propensities*, p. 12.

40. Ibid., p. 7.

41. Ibid., p. 13.

42. Ober, 'The Sticky End of Frantisek Koczkwara', p. 146.

43. Anon, *Modern Propensities*, p. 44.

44. *London Chronicle*, 1 September 1791.

45. *Morning Chronicle*, 5 September 1791.

46. *Whitehall Evening Post*, 1–3 September 1791.

47. *The Times*, 6 September 1791.

48. MJ/SP/1791/05 OB/SP/286; Anon, *The Trial of Susannah Hill*, p. 2.

49. Anon, *Modern Propensities*, p. 41.

50. Ibid.

51. Anon, *The Trial of Susannah Hill*, p. 10.

52. *The Times*, 16 September 1791; *Lloyd's Evening Post*, 16 September 1791.

53. Peakman, 'Sexual Perversion in History', p. 14.

54. Ober, 'The Sticky End of Frantisek Koczkwara', p. 148.

55. *The Times*, 17 September 1791.

56. *Lloyds Evening Post*, 5 September 1791.

57. Anon, *Modern Propensities*, p. 28.

58. *Bon Ton Magazine*, 8 October 1791.

59. *Bon Ton Magazine* (London), April 1793.

60. The trial was not recorded in the Old Bailey Proceedings either on account of the nature of the case and the threat to public morality, or because Susannah was acquitted and there was policy of not publishing details of trials that ended thus. However, it is possible that this was treated as an 'ignoramus' (as 'no true bill') because the judge stopped the trial and *directed* the jury to acquit. This seems unlikely because the newspapers are quite clear in stating that the bill of indictment against Hill was 'found' by the Grand Jury

(*Evening Mail*, 12 September 1791) and *The Times* (17 September 1791) noted that 'the Jury returned a verdict of Not Guilty' after 'having engaged the court nearly an hour'.

61. Katherine Crawford, 'Erotica: Representing Sex in the Eighteenth Century', in Peakman (ed.), *Cultural History of Sexuality*, p. 204.
62. Anon, *Modern Propensities*, p. 5.
63. Peakman, *Mighty Lewd Books*, p. 4.
64. Anon, *Modern Propensities*, p. 5.
65. Ibid.
66. Harvey, *Reading Sex in the Eighteenth Century*, p. 41; Peakman, *Mighty Lewd Books*, p. 23.
67. Peakman, *Mighty Lewd Books*, pp. 42–44.
68. Julie Peakman, *The Pleasure's All Mine: A History of Perverse Sex* (London, Reaktion Books, 2013), p. 53.
69. Binhammer, 'The Sex Panic', p. 409.
70. Peter Wagner, 'The Pornographer in the Courtroom', in Boucé (ed.), *Sexuality in Eighteenth-Century Britain*, p. 132.
71. Roy Porter, ' "The Secrets of Generation Displayed": *Aristotle's Master-Piece* in Eighteenth-Century England', in Robert P. Maccubbin (ed.), *'Tis Nature's Fault: Unauthorized Sexuality During the Enlightenment* (Cambridge, Cambridge University Press, 1987), p. 5.
72. Peakman, *The Pleasure's All Mine*, p. 60; Anon, *Aristotle's Master-Piece: Or the Secrets of Generation Displayed in the Parts Thereof* (London, 1684); Nicholas Venette, *Mysteries of Conjugal Love* (London, 1703); James Graham MD, *A Lecture on the Generation, Increase, and Improvement of the Human Species* (London, 1783).
73. Hitchcock, 'Redefining Sex', pp. 193–94.
74. Anon, *Modern Propensities*, pp. 7, 29.
75. Graham, *A Lecture on the Generation*.
76. Lydia Syson, *Doctor of Love: James Graham and His Celestial Bed* (London, Alma Books, 2008).
77. Adrian Teal, 'Quacks and Hacks: Georgian Medicine and the Power of Advertising', *The Lancet*, Vol. 383, No. 9915 (2014), p. 2.
78. Ibid.
79. Anon, *Modern Propensities*, p. 8.
80. Teal, 'Quacks and Hacks', p. 4.
81. This title went under several names but this is the one most commonly referred to by historians of sexuality. I have consulted Anon., *Aristotle's Book of Problems with Other Astronomers, Astrologers and Physicians, Concerning the State of Man's Body* (London, c.1715). This was actually a birthing manual aimed at healthy reproduction rather than a treatise concerning sex.
82. Rawlings, *Drunks, Whores and Idle Apprentices*; Shoemaker, 'The Old Bailey Proceedings and the Representation of Crime'; Richard M. Ward, *Print Culture, Crime and Justice in 18th-Century London* (London, Bloomsbury, 2014).
83. Peakman, *Mighty Lewd Books*, p. 89.
84. Anna Clark, *Scandal: The Sexual Politics of the British Constitution* (Princeton, NJ, Princeton University Press, 2004), pp. 117–19; other publications – such as *Town and Country Magazine, Oxford Magazine, Bingley's Journal* – played 'significant role in making the adultery of the famous not only widely known but a topic of discussion among the hoi polloi'. Donna Andrew, *Aristocratic Vice: The Attack on Duelling, Suicide, Adultery, and*

Gambling in Eighteenth-Century England (New Haven and London, Yale University Press, 2013), p. 139.

85. Anon, *Modern Propensities*, p. 9.
86. Ibid., p. 29.
87. Ibid., pp. 10–11.
88. Andrew, *The Attack*, p. 137.
89. Ibid., p. 146.
90. Rogers, 'Pigott's Private Eye', p. 259.
91. Ibid., p. 251.
92. Toulalan, *Imagining Sex*, p. 55.
93. Phillips and Reay (eds.), *Sexualities in History*, p. 35.
94. This turned on a technicality – was it a misdemeanor or a felony? Most probably it did not much matter which it was in legal terms, the authorities needed a scapegoat and regardless of whether Williams was indeed the 'Monster' society required that someone was punished for the outrages.
95. Mary Wollstonecraft's *Vindication of the Rights of Women* appeared in 1792, following Tom Paine's *Rights of Man* in the previous year. See also Katherine Binhammer, 'Thinking Gender with Sexuality in 1790s' Feminist Thought', *Feminist Studies*, Vol. 28, No. 3 (2002), pp. 667–90.
96. Binhammer, 'The Sex Panic', p. 411.
97. Anon, *Modern Propensities*, p. 36.
98. Ibid.
99. Dror Wahrman, 'Percy's Prologue: From Gender Play to Gender Panic in Eighteenth-Century England', *Past & Present*, Vol. 159 (1998), p. 121; Clark, *Scandal*, pp. 123–24.
100. Binhammer, 'The Sex Panic', p. 411.
101. Ibid., p. 416.
102. Anon, *Modern Propensities*, p. 5.
103. Ibid., p. 37.
104. Dabhoiwala, 'Sex and Societies for Moral Reform', p. 319.
105. Ibid., p. 12.
106. Harvey, *Reading Sex in the Eighteenth Century*, p. 1.
107. Anon, *Modern Propensities*, p. 13.
108. Ibid., p. 18.
109. Ibid., p. 23.
110. *Whitehall Evening Post*, 7 June 1791.
111. Michaud and Hazelwood, *The Evil That Men Do*, p. 70.
112. Given that the anonymous pamphleteer was writing in the 1790s, a number of candidates for the historical 'Parson Manacle' are possible. Thomas Purney resigned from the position from ill health in 1725 and died in 1727. He was often satirized. James Guthrie was dismissed in 1746 because he was deemed unfit, physically, to continue as Ordinary. John Wood also resigned due to ill health in 1774. None were declared to have died in office or of typhus however, which supports a thesis that 'manacle' was an amalgam of a number of clerics, fitting contemporary narratives of venality in public office.
113. *Morning Herald*, 5 June 1788.
114. Anon, *Modern Propensities*, p. 28.
115. *Morning Herald*, 5 June 1788.
116. Gatrell, *The Hanging Tree*.
117. See for example: Devereaux, 'England's "Bloody Code" in Crisis and Transition', pp. 71–113; Richard R. Follett, *Evangelicalism, Penal Theory and the Politics of Criminal Law Reform in England, 1808–30* (Basingstoke,

Palgrave Macmillan, 2001); Gatrell, *Hanging Tree*; Phil, Handler, 'Forgery and the End of the "Bloody Code" in Early Nineteenth-Century England', *The Historical Journal*, Vol. 48, No. 3 (2005); Randall McGowen, 'The Image of Justice and Reform of the Criminal Law in Early Nineteenth-Century England', *Buffalo Law Review*, Vol. 32, No. 1 (1983); Potter, *Hanging in Judgment*.

118. Foucault, *Discipline and Punish*.

119. Beattie, *The First English Detectives*; Gray, *Crime, Prosecution and Social Relations*; Andrew T. Harris, *Policing the City: Crime and Legal Authority in London, 1780–1840* (Columbus, Ohio State University Press, 2004).

120. Howson, *Thief-Taker General*; Paley, 'Thief-Takers in London in the Age of the McDaniel Gang, c. 1745–1754'.

121. *Diary or Woodfall's Register*, 20 January 1790.

122. McGowen, 'The Body and Punishment', p. 655.

123. Indeed not only were prostitutes in evidence mingling with the crowds (along with other 'criminal' elements) but 'advertisements for new editions of Onamia, Dr. Drakes and Several Physicians Opinions of Hermaphrodites, or for patent medicine to cure clap or impotency fill the back of even the Ordinary of Newgate's most pious accounts'. Laqueur, 'Crowds, Carnival, and the State', pp. 347–48.

124. Iwan Bloch, *The Sexual Extremities of the World* (New York, Book Awards, 1964), p. 152.

125. Ibid., p. 165.

126. Peakman, *The Pleasure's All Mine*, p. 383.

127. Ward, *A Global History of Execution*; Hurren, *Dissecting the Criminal Corpse*; King, *Punishing the Criminal Corpse*.

128. Given that crowds would sometime seek to liberate bodies of loved ones before they could be taken by the surgeons for dissection, some of those hanged were cut down much sooner. In 1745 Abraham Dealtry was taken down 'after 10 minutes and put in a coffin'; in 1740 William Duell was only hanged for 22 minutes before he was driven to Surgeon's hall in London. Hurren, *Dissecting the Criminal Corpse*, pp. 39–40; See also Peter Linebaugh, 'The Tyburn Riot and the Criminal Law', in Hay (ed.), *Albion's Fatal Tree*, pp. 65–117.

129. Quoted in Roger Byard, 'Autoerotic death—characteristic features and diagnostic difficulties', *Journal of Clinical Forensic Medicine*, No. 1 (1994), p. 72.

130. Ober, 'The Sticky End of Frantisek Koczkwara', p. 148.

131. Ibid.

132. Devereaux, 'The City and the Sessions Paper', pp. 470–71.

133. Gatrell, *Hanging Tree*, pp. 46, 53–54.

134. 'The New Drop at Newgate', *Gentleman's Magazine* (1783) in Gatrell, *Hanging Tree*, p. 53.

135. Devereaux, 'Recasting the Theatre of Execution', p. 156.

136. William M. Thackeray, *Going to See a Man Hanged* (London, 1840).

137. W. H. Maxwell, 'Last Scenes of the Condemned: By an Eye-Witness', *Bentley's Miscellany* (London), 1849.

138. John Tulloch, 'The Privatising of Pain', *Journalism Studies*, Vol. 7, No. 3 (2006), p. 439.

139. Anon, *Penny Satirist 1:7* (3 June 1837), in Yetter (ed.), *Public Execution in England*.

140. Poole, 'For the Benefit of Example', p. 73.

141. Foucault, *Discipline and Punish*, p. 92.

142. Beattie, *Crime and the Courts*, p. 621.

143. Foucault, *Discipline and Punish*, p. 92.

144. There had long been a restriction on the publishers of the Old Bailey Sessions Papers not to share potentially corrupting details of trials that involved rape or sodomy. After 1787 the City authorities (who authorized publication) seem to have insisted that the Sessions Papers omitted cases that might offer readers (i.e., those with criminal intent) useful advice on how to avoid conviction. This, Simon Devereaux suggests, represents a break from a Wilkite insistence in the 1770s that the Sessions Papers served to demonstrate that 'the administration of justice was evenhanded'. In 1790 acquittals were excluded entirely from the Sessions Papers for two years. They were reinstated in 1793; both decisions were motivated by a need to save (and then make) money from selling the Sessions Papers. Readers apparently wanted to know about those cases where defendants had been found not guilty. Devereaux, 'The City and the Sessions Paper', pp. 492–93.

145. Marquis De Sade, *Justine or the Misfortunes of Virtue* (1791, 1797).

6   Conclusions

This study set out to consider what factors influenced discretionary decision-making in the last decades of the eighteenth century. This is a subject that has received plenty of attention from the mid-1970s onwards following the publication of Douglas Hay's seminal essay 'Property, Authority and the Criminal Law'.[1] Without revisiting that debate it is necessary, however, to note that Hay was looking at the operation of the criminal justice system outside of London and only in regards to property crime. Those that came after Hay, either to critique or dismiss his thesis (Langbein),[2] or to revise it (King),[3] similarly concentrated on property offending. Peter King argued that there was a clear rationale behind the decisions that sent some offenders to the gallows while sparing others, and historians of crime now largely accept that age, gender, social status, and previous convictions all played a part in influencing decision-making. It is also widely agreed that decision-making rested with a broader societal grouping than Hay's original work had allowed. The fate of a thief did not rest wholly in the hands of a judge who was, quite evidently, a member of a privileged elite. Instead, discretion extended to include the jurors that sat in judgement (who were wealthy and 'middling' but not fundamentally of the elite). Moreover, plenty of discretion was enjoyed and exercised by the victims of crime (who were often property owning, but rarely aristocratic) who decided whether to pursue a prosecution in the first place. John Langbein might have been over-egging the pudding by insisting that the 'bloody code' existed to protect the property of the humblest in the land just as much as it did that of the richest,[4] but the laws concerning property theft were, up to a point, equitable.

We cannot deny, however, that discretion played a huge part in deciding who was hanged and who was not. That the 'victims' of gallows were, as Peter Linebaugh has discussed,[5] overwhelmingly young, male, and working class, suggests that it was this demographic that most concerned Hanoverian society and those applying its laws. So we can probably be fairly clear, then, that in a system where evidence (as we understand it today at least) was less important than the 'character' of the person supplying it, it is likely that decisions as regards guilt or innocence were often subjective. Put another way, if the person in the dock looked like the sort of individual one expected to commit a crime and those giving evidence against him or her were deemed credible by the jury (because perhaps they recognized them as social equals or as subordinates for whom they had some level of trust), then a conviction was highly likely to follow. If, however, the accused or their defence counsel (if they had one) could create some element of doubt in the minds of the jurors (something Charlotte Walker was adept at for many years),[6] then a conviction might be avoided. Ultimately, once a prosecution had been brought and an indictment approved by the grand jury, most discretionary power rested with the jury who could convict, acquit, or bring in a partial verdict (effectively restricting the judge's ability to hand down a death sentence).[7] Thereafter, discretion passed to the judge in sessions, who could order a felon to be hanged, transported, or to suffer a lesser punishment. Following the completion of a trial, the judge at a county assizes had the power to reprieve or respite an execution. In London, this power rested with the king and his ministers in council.[8]

It was the post-trial pardoning process that dominated two of the four case studies considered by this volume. In the case of Matthew and Patrick Kennedy, it was shown that while the council might have wished to make an exception and allow them both to live, Lord Mansfield was clear that an example had to be made and one of them had to hang. That his authority was overridden is demonstrative of the power of elite connections working behind the scenes to save them. Once this strategy was put at risk by the intervention of similarly vocal (if not as powerful) forces intent on exposing corruption in high office, Mansfield used his position at King's Bench to ensure that Mrs Bigby's appeal of murder failed. The wider network of privilege was able to bring its financial muscle to bear on the case, first by delaying the proceedings (which would have increased the widow's costs) and then second by offering her a compensatory bribe to drop the legal effort to hang her husband's murderers.

Yet while elite connections ultimately proved successful in the Kennedy case, they were far less useful to Thomas Gordon, despite the fact that his father's network included the brother of the reigning monarch and one of the most important 'political' women of the age. Francis Gordon, we should remember, was able to engage the support of the Dukes and Duchesses of Gloucester and Gordon. This enabled him to get a sit-down audience with George III who, reportedly at least, was most willing to help secure young Thomas a conditional pardon. 'Old man' Gordon also deployed the Duchess of Gordon to help. She was very close to the Prime Minister, William Pitt, and therefore ideally placed to persuade him to act to save Thomas' life. There are several smaller factors that could explain why these efforts failed (such as the fact that Maria, Duchess of Gloucester, was not welcome at court, and that the Duke of Gordon was sick in the weeks leading up to Thomas' execution), but it seems likely that it was politics that meant that Thomas Gordon hanged while the Kennedy brothers escaped the noose and sailed for a new life in the Americas.

In both cases the defendants had been convicted of killing an officer of the law: a watchman – John Bigby – in 1769 and a parish constable – George Linnell – in 1788. Both represented an assault on authority and so might be expected to have resulted in a conviction and punishment, yet only Gordon was hanged. There was evidential doubt in both cases: two or more persons beat John Bigby to death in a brutal assault and it was argued that the Kennedys were not present. The jury chose not to believe this, however, and a conviction followed. We do not have the detailed case notes for the Gordon case and so have been forced to reconstruct it from the pardoning files, but to most observers it would appear that this was an example of justifiable homicide. Thomas fired at the 'mob' of people that were besieging the home of his elderly parents. He feared for his and their life and the destruction of their property. A better defence case might have seen him acquitted of murder and found guilty instead of manslaughter, a quite common outcome in the 1700s, as the introduction to this study has shown.

Which means I believe that we need to look beyond the evidence (such as it is) for the murders and those guilty of them. We also need to look beyond the elite connections that both parties were able to assemble. Instead it is reasonable to argue that these cases were ultimately decided by the political circumstances that pertained at the time. In 1770 (when the Kennedy brothers went on trial) the government was in a position of relative strength, despite the attacks of the opposition radicals. While political opponents like the anonymous 'Junius' and the former Wilkite Horne Tooke were throwing verbal and printed brickbats at George III's ministry, it was more than able to resist. In Mansfield it had a sharp and competent legal operator and the domestic and international situation was largely calm. Wind forward to 1788/9 however and a very different political climate presented itself. George III was recovering from his first major outbreak of 'madness' and political moves to replace him with his son as Regent were underway. On the continent all manner of revolutionary rhetoric was threatening the rule of law and the very fabric of monarchy. Quite simply, had Thomas Gordon shot and killed George Linnell a decade earlier he may not have paid for it with his life. In the summer of 1789, no English Prime Minister could allow a 'cop killer' (to use a modern expression) to escape justice; it would have sent out entirely the wrong message, regardless of Thomas' youth and previous good character.

Circumstances also played a key role in the other cases described here and impacted their protagonists in different ways. Arguably the most unusual case was that of Susannah Hill, who found herself in the Old Bailey dock for a homicide she certainly had not intended. Francis Kotzwara's was a death by misadventure, his own misadventure in seeking a peculiar form of sexual gratification. There was plenty of doubt as to how culpable Susannah was, but not enough to stop the prosecution reaching the Old Bailey courtroom. Once there the trial was closed down fairly quickly but not, I would argue, because the 'evidence' was insufficient on its own to obtain a conviction. Indeed a conviction for manslaughter was probable, given Susannah's social status as a 'common prostitute' and since she admitted tying the rope around his neck. There was no doubt that she had killed the Czech composer, the only doubt lay in whether she had intended to. The case was thrown out not for legal reasons but to preserve public decency. Susannah got away with homicide because the 'powers that be' deemed it to be expedient. Moreover the tragedy occurred at a time when 'deviant' sexuality was under threat more broadly. The 1790s witnessed attempts to put a lid on all sorts of forms of revolutionary or alternative culture and the 'sex panic' of the 1790s was a reflection of this. In this atmosphere of sexual conservatism it seems likely that the author of 'Modern Propensities' was tapping into a wider debate (perhaps in the hope of selling copies and promoting his own aids to sexual reproduction). The prevailing atmosphere also necessitated an embargo on trials that were either scandalous (as Hill's was) or demonstrated that defendants might 'get away with it'.[9]

If Susannah Hill was an indirect beneficiary of turbulent times (when Thomas Gordon had suffered from them), then Henry Stroud was a clear victim of circumstances. There was little or nothing in the published court records, or indeed in any other records of the case, to clearly point to Stroud as the person most responsible for Daniel Clarke's murder in April 1771. The pattern drawer had been pursued through the streets and gardens of Spitalfields for several hours before he ended up in a pond at Weaver's Fields. Battered, bruised, and bleeding from several wounds he finally succumbed to his injuries and died in the late afternoon. In the immediate aftermath, the silk weaving community of East London closed ranks and acted to prevent anyone being held accountable. Eventually three persons were arrested and put on trial for Clarke's murder, despite the reality that dozens of people, if not hundreds, had played their part in his death. Without the evidence to prosecute most or even many of those responsible, the authorities – notably Justice Wilmot, a man desperate to maintain a sense of his fragile authority – opted to go for a mixture of the 'usual' or 'most obvious' suspects. Clarke was responsible for the conviction and execution of two men and connected – as an informer – to the death of others. The three defendants on trial for killing him were all connected in some way to the 'cutters' that had recently hanged for the disturbances that taken place in the area. Robert Campbell was still at large and wanted in connection with the attacks on Daniel Clarke's looms, Antis Horsford's husband had been hanged on Clarke's evidence, and Henry Stroud was married to the daughter of William Eastman, another weaver who met his end on the gallows. On the basis of the testimony presented at the Old Bailey, only Campbell really had a case to answer and that was pretty tenuous at best. Unfortunately for him his face fitted the sort of person the authorities believed could have been responsible. Antis Horsford was effectively cleared since nothing against her would stick and perhaps there was no appetite to hang her. Stroud emerged as the least likely of the trio and may even have tried to rescue Clarke from the mob. He should have been cleared as well but he was victim to a very local conspiracy hatched by neighbours who had a grudge against him. This should not come as a surprise, as historians of witchcraft persecutions have established; a system that relies on witness testimony and that is unsupported by forensic science and underpinned by venality and corruption is likely to create multiple miscarriages of justice.[10] Moreover the desire of the authorities to reestablish order in Spitalfields required a quick trial and the execution of the guilty. As Shoemaker has observed, 'participants in the largest riots were treated less leniently by the government; the threat posed by any significant riot that involved violent attacks on individuals, widespread destruction of property, or opposition to government policies had to be answered firmly'.[11] There was no attempt to save Henry Stroud or Robert Campbell, despite both of them protesting their innocence. The papers did acknowledge that the courts might have got the judgement on Stroud wrong but by then he had already been hanged. His execution – alongside Campbell's – took place close to the scene of the crime and was accompanied by a show of military strength by the state. Justice Wilmot and his fellow magistrates wanted no repeat of the chaotic scenes that had accompanied Eastman's execution a year or so earlier. The power of the public execution was in its ability to deter others from crime and demonstrate the authority of the state. This was much harder to control several miles from Newgate Gaol or even at Tyburn's 'triple tree'. While the execution procession and crude roadside gallows hanging may have persisted in rural and provincial England into the 1800s it was brought to a controlled and more reliable position outside Newgate Gaol in the capital. The experience of hanging riotous 'cutters' may well have informed the decision to hang offenders outside the debtor's door on Newgate Street.

So what are we to make of these four cases and what they can tell us about judicial decision-making in the late eighteenth century? I believe there are several conclusions we can draw. First, evidence was much less important to the judicial process in the last quarter of the 1700s than it became by the end of the next century, and certainly by today's standards. Character and social status were much more important in determining guilt and punishment than anything resembling crude forensics. This is equally applicable to homicide, an area of the law that is much less well studied than it should be, and to property crime (where most of the previous analysis of the use of discretion has focused attention). Second, and perhaps self-evidently given the first point, homicide convictions were determined by other factors, most of which were only loosely connected to the actions that caused the death of the victim. These factors or circumstances could be localized (as with the Clarke murder) or global (as was the case with the killing of Constable Linnell). It is very hard then to make useful theoretical modules of homicide convictions beyond some kind of analysis of their typology (as was carried out in the introductory chapter). Third, while punishment outcomes in property cases were open to discretionary leniency the same leniency was not supposed to be applicable in homicide cases. Under the terms of the 1752 Murder Act executions were supposed to take place within days of conviction and 'all convicted murderers were [supposed to be] either dissected or gibbeted'.[12] I have added 'supposed to be' to King's statement because clearly in some instances they were not. Both Thomas Gordon and the Kennedy brothers should have been hanged and then dissected within days of conviction. Gordon was respited for the best part of a year while the Twelve Judges considered the legality of his conviction. Thereafter, once the Northampton assizes judge directed that he should die several weeks were allowed for his father to try and save his life, if not his liberty. This failed but Gordon was not dissected; instead his body was returned to his father for burial. Matthew and Patrick Kennedy not only escaped execution, they were also helped to make a new life in the American colonies, an opportunity denied to many other convict transportees. So discretion in punishment, something historians are familiar with in property crime cases, must now be extended to homicides prosecuted under the Murder Act.

These cases may be unusual but others may yet emerge which give weight to an argument that discretion was more widespread than perhaps we have acknowledged. I think a further conclusion must be that the pardoning process needs more study to better understand how it operated across the period from the Glorious Revolution to the late 1800s. Clearly contemporaries, while they may not have understood how the various machinations of the process worked, had a very good knowledge that it did. The idea that all of these discussions taking place behind closed doors engendered a mystical sense of the ruling elite's paternalism is strained by some of the examples shown here. The Gordon case was widely discussed in London and regional papers, the fate of the Kennedy brothers was equally present in the public domain, as was the campaign by 'persons of quality' and 'some courtesans' to save them. Francis Kotzwara's fate was quickly and quietly hushed up, or at least it should have been, while dark rumours circulated that Henry Stroud was a scapegoat for others. Londoners and those reading the London papers (or the provincial ones that largely took their copy from them) were arguably better informed about crime in the second half of the eighteenth century than any generation before them. Newspapers, pamphlets, execution broadsides, the Sessions Papers (the Old Bailey Proceedings), and the Ordinary of Newgate's 'last dying confessions' all offered a rich source of news about crime and criminality. Of course much of this was carefully orchestrated to present the view of law and order that the government and City authorities wanted, but this was not an uneducated or naive audience, as Shoemaker correctly observes. It 'is likely', he argues 'that at least some Londoners read the Proceedings skeptically, as a deliberate intervention, on the side of the authorities and the property-owning classes, in the century-long debate over how to respond to the apparently rising tide of criminality in London'.[13] Readers were well informed and could see for themselves the state of crime in the capital, much more so, I would suggest, than modern contemporary consumers of crime news. That the government and others strove desperately to control the news agenda should be a reminder that alternative viewpoints existed.

What this also tells us is that crime, justice, and punishment were intimately interwoven with, and inseparable from, politics and political scheming. The period in which all four of these case studies occurred was one riven by an increasingly acrimonious debate about the abuse of executive power and the existence of a secretive group of ministers (in other words an inner cabinet) that was 'assumed to be using government patronage to overcome parliamentary resistance to its numerous nefarious activities, manipulating and coercing the ostensible ministers, and thus gradually asserting autocratic power without responsibility'.[14] Simon Devereaux highlighted that the special situation pertaining to pardoning and execution in London was closely linked to the concerns of government. Given that decisions about who would hang and who would be spared were taken at the end of an Old Bailey Sessions with the 'Recorder's Report', this gave considerable power to those in elevated positions of power. I think Devereaux is correct in concluding that the

> scale of execution at the Old Bailey may therefore have been far more precisely reflective of governmental – and perhaps, by extension, parliamentary and press – concerns and perceptions of crime and the criminal law than was that of individual counties outside the metropolis.[15]

However, I believe this also requires some adjustment. That decision-making was reflective of wider concerns about crime and justice is undeniable, indeed that is a situation that continues to this day. As Martin Wiener noted, the principles of law 'never operate in a world of their own; principles, rules, and procedures arise and are applied within specific political, social, and cultural contexts'.[16] Various factors affected an individual's experience of the law. Wiener refers to race, gender, and class as factors that might have caused some defendants in murder trials to be treated differently, at different times. Similarly this volume showcases four separate and entirely different cases of homicide, all of which were affected by prevailing political, social, and cultural trends, events, or mores.

What this small selection of cases suggests however is that decision-making was influenced by other factors, not necessarily those affecting the nation or society as a whole, but derived from more personal motives. This also has implications for how contemporaries viewed the hanging ritual and those condemned to die by it. We are aware that a vigorous debate unfolded across the eighteenth and early nineteenth century focused on the merits of public execution.[17] Those, like Lord Ellenborough, who believed that 'the task of justice was to shock' insisted on retaining a powerful weapon in the fight to prevent crime. Supporters of hanging argued, as McGowen has eloquently expressed it, that 'justice possessed dignity, firmness and authority. This power was to be celebrated; it was both necessary and good'.[18] But what if people – 'the people' indeed – saw it to be neither necessary nor good? What if it was seen as arbitrary and venal: did that not undermine the entire rule of law? Moreover, if, as the case of Susannah Hill and her unfortunate client suggests, the public were increasingly aware that public hanging had the potential to reveal physical reactions that society would prefer to remain hidden, to what extent might this have been factored into debates about the appropriateness of public executions? Was this part of the 'uneasiness caused by the spectacle' that criminal law reformers demanding abolition referred to?[19]

The micro-history or case study approach that has been taken here can do much to help us understand the past and the context in which events occurred. However, I am very conscious that for each of these cases it has been necessary to draw on different sorts of (albeit related) source material. For the Kennedy case the trial record was useful but much of the detail from the pardoning process that followed it does not exist outside the newspaper account and some private papers. For Henry Stroud the Old Bailey Proceedings are key because aside from the correspondence between Justice Wilmot and the ministry no state papers exist because there was no appeal for a pardon (because the state and the Murder Act made it impossible for an appeal to be formulated, let alone heard). By contrast the Gordon example has no real trial record at all (merely the judge's report of it) but it does have a lot of material from the key protagonists (from Francis Gordon to William Pitt, and the Dukes and Duchesses of Gloucester and Gordon). It was also played out in the pages of the press. As we know, there is no record of Susannah Hill's trial in the Old Bailey Proceedings, and minimal newspaper coverage, but two alternative printed sources have allowed us to reconstruct events in 1791. Can all these various sources be marshalled to be useful comparative tools? Or must we only explore comparative histories using identical forms of source material? Sadly our ancestors rather failed us in keeping precise and easily dissectible records of the events they experienced and most, if not all, are handed down to us with a degree of political, moral, or religious bias. I have tried to pick my way through the various sources available here to create my own interpretation of what happened in each of these four mini-histories and what we might glean from them. I also recognize that this selection of homicide cases might be seen as untypical. Moreover critics may regard individual tales of murder and manslaughter as atypical of crime in general, given how rare, relative to other offences, they were. This is partly why historians of crime have avoided homicide as a subject area and concentrated instead on the huge numbers of property offenders who were sentenced to hang or be transported in the last decades of the eighteenth century. Yet surely murder and public attitudes to it have much to tell us about the justice system of the day, of contemporary concerns, and public interaction with criminality? Martin Wiener certainly believes we can learn a lot from the representation of homicide in popular culture.[20]

My approach is open to criticism and to other interpretations of the information I have used. However, I am not worried of accusations that I am guilty of speculating; if we do not speculate, then we cannot hypothesize and that will lead to some very dry and unimaginative history. In all of these lives lost (and saved) there are lessons to learn about the way the criminal justice system operated in the past and, perhaps, how it continues to operate today.

Notes

1. Hay, 'Property, Authority, and the Criminal Law'.
2. Langbein, 'Albion's Fatal Flaws'.
3. King, *Crime, Justice and Discretion*.
4. Langbein, 'Albion's Fatal Flaws'.
5. Linebaugh, *The London Hanged*.
6. Clayton, 'The Life and Crimes of Charlotte Walker'.
7. Beattie, *Crime and the Courts*, pp. 420–21; Lemmings, *Law and Government in England*, p. 68.
8. Beattie, *Policing and Punishment in London*; Devereaux, 'The City and the Sessions Paper'; Devereaux, 'The Bloodiest Code'.
9. Shoemaker, 'The Old Bailey Proceedings and the Representation of Crime'.
10. See, for example, Robin Briggs, *Witches & Neighbours: The Social and Cultural Context of European Witchcraft* (London, Fontana Press, 1996).
11. Shoemaker, 'The London "Mob" ', p. 299.
12. King, *Punishing the Criminal Corpse*, p. 6.
13. Shoemaker, 'The Old Bailey Proceedings and the Representation of Crime', p. 580.
14. Jay, *Most Humble Servants*, p. 35.
15. Devereaux, "England's "Bloody Code" in Crisis and Transition', p. 80.
16. Wiener, 'Murder and the British Historian', p. 2.
17. Gatrell, *Hanging Tree*; Handler, 'Forgery and the End of the "Bloody Code" in Early Nineteenth-Century England'; McGowen, 'The Body and Punishment'; Potter, *Hanging in Judgment*; J. A. Sharpe, 'Civility, Civilizing Processes and the End of Public Punishment in England', in Peter Burke, Brian

Harrison, and Paul Slack (eds.), *Civil Histories: Essays Presented to Sir Keith Thomas* (Oxford, Oxford University Press, 2001).

18. McGowen, 'A Powerful Sympathy', pp. 315–16.
19. McGowen, 'Civilizing Punishment', p. 262.
20. Martin Wiener, 'Alice Arden to Bill Sykes: Changing Nightmares of Intimate Violence in England, 1558–1869', *Journal of British Studies* (April 2001), pp. 184–212.

Bibliography

Archival Resources

London Metropolitan Archives.
OB/SP/1771/001-028.
National Archives.
HO47/8/51-56.
KB1/26.
PCMO2/166.
State papers (Gale MC 4300007429-2/58).
TS 11/169.
T 1/484/256-259.

Online Resources

Dictionary of National Biography [www.oxforddnb.com].
Digital Panopticon [www.digitalpanopticon.org].
History of Parliament Online [www.historyofparliamentonline.org].
London Lives [www.londonloives.org].
Old Bailey Online [www.oldbaileyonline.org].
Survey of London [www.britishhistory.ac.uk].

Newspapers

Bath Chronicle.
Bingley's Journal.
Bon Ton Magazine.
Diary or Woodfall's Register.
Dublin Mercury.
English Chronicle or Universal Evening Post.
Gazetteer and New Daily Advertiser.
General Evening Post.
Independent Chronicle.
Lloyd's Evening Post.
London Chronicle.
London Evening Post.
London Gazette.

Middlesex Journal or Chronicle of Liberty.
Morning Chronicle.
Morning Herald.
Morning Post and Daily Advertiser.
Morning Star.
The New London Magazine.
North Briton.
Northampton Mercury.
Oracle Bell's New World.
Public Advertiser.
St James' Chronicle or the British Evening Post.
The Times.
Westminster Journal.
Whisperer.
Whitehall Evening Post.
World.

Printed Works Before 1900

Anon. *Aristotle's Book of Problems with Other Astronomers, Astrologers and Physicians, Concerning the State of Man's Body* (London, c.1715).

Anon. *Aristotle's Master-Piece: Or the Secrets of Generation Displayed in the Parts Thereof* (London, 1684).

Anon. *Genuine Copies of All the Letters Which Passed Between the Right Honourable the Lord Chancellor and the Sheriffs of London and Middlesex and Between the Sheriffs and the Secretary of State Relative to the Execution of Doyle and Valine* (London, R. Davis, 1770).

Anon. *Hanging Not Punishment Enough* (London, 1701).

Anon. *Letter from a Spitalfields Weaver, to a Noble Duke* (London, 1765).

Anon. *Modern Propensities: Or an Assay on the Art of Strangling etc. Illustrated with Several Anecdotes, with Memoirs of Susannah Hill and a Summary of Her Trial at the Old Bailey, on Friday, September 16, 1791, on the Charge of Hanging Francis Kotzwara at Her Lodgings in Vine Street, on September 2* (London, 1791).

Anon. *The Trial of Susannah Hill for the Willful Murder of Francis Kotzwara, September the 2nd 1791 at Justice Hall in the Old Bailey* (Boston Medical Library, 1791).

Barnewall, R. V. *Reports of Cases Argued and Determined in the Court of King's Bench* (London, 1818).

Barry, Edward (Rev.). *A Supplement to the Present Practice of a Justice of the Peace; and Complete Library of Parish Law* (London, 1792).

Blackstone, William. *Commentaries on the Laws of England*, Vol. 4 (Oxford, 1765).

Blackstone, William. *Reports of Cases Determined in the Several Courts of Westminster-Hall, from 1746 to 1779*, Vol. 2 (London, 1828).

Burn, Richard. *Justice of the Peace and Parish Officer*, Vol. 2 (London, 1785).

Burrow, Sir James. *Reports of Cases Argued and Adjudged in the Court of King's Bench During the Time Lord Mansfield etc.* (London, 1790).

Butler, James Davie. 'British Convicts Shipped to American Colonies', *The American Historical Review*, Vol. 2, No. 1 (October 1896).

The Cambridge Magazine: Or, Universal Repository of Arts, Sciences, and the Belles Letters (London, Thomas Evans, 1769).

Campbell, R. *The London Tradesman, Being a Compendious View of All the Trades, Professions, Arts, Both Liberal and Mechanic, Now Practiced in the Cities of London and Westminster* (London, T. Gardner, 1747).

Dickinson, William. *A Practical Exposition of the Law: Relative to the Office and Duties of a Justice of the Peace*, Vol. 1 (London, 1813).

Graham MD, James. *A Lecture on the Generation, Increase, and Improvement of the Human Species* (London, 1783).

Holyoake, George J. *Public Lessons of the Hangman* (London, 1864).

Hyde East, Edward. *Esq of the Inner Temple, a Treatise of the Pleas of the Crown*, Vol. 1 (London, 1803).

Jesse, J. H. *George Selwyn and His Contemporaries, with Memoirs and Notes* (London, 1843).

Kelly's Directory (1894).

Kendall, E. A. *An Argument for Construing Largely the Right of an Appellees of Murder to Insist on His Wager of Battle and Also for Abrogating Writs of Appeal* (London, 1818).

Knapp, Andrew. *The New Newgate Calendar . . . To Which Is Added a Correct Account of the Various Modes of Punishment of Criminals in Different Parts of the World*, Vol. 3 (London, 1826).

Leach, T. *Cases in Crown Law, Determined by the Twelve Judges; By the Court of King's Bench; and by Commissioners of Oyer and Terminer, and General Gaol Delivery* (London, 1792).

A List of the Society for the Encouragement of Arts, Manufactures and Commerce (London, 18 August 1766).

Long, Edward. *A History of Jamaica, or, General Survey of the Antient and Modern State of That Island; with Reflections on Its Situation, Settlements, Inhabitants*, Vol. 2 (London, 1774).

Mandeville, Bernard. *Fable of the Bees: Or, Private Vices, Public Benefits* (London, 1714).

The Manuscripts of J. B. Fortescue Esq, Preserved at Dropmore, Vol. I, Royal Manuscripts Commission Thirteenth Report, Appendix, Part II (1892).

Maxwell, W. H. 'Last Scenes of the Condemned: By an Eye-Witness', *Bentley's Miscellany* (London), 1849.

Millingen, John Gideon. *The History of Duelling: Including, Narratives of the Most Remarkable Personal Encounters That Have Taken Place from the Earliest Period to the Present Time*, Vol. 2 (London, 1841).

Newman, Alan. *Criminal Executions in England with Remarks on the Penal Code, Prison Discipline and Abuses, and Other Subjects Connected with the Punishment and Prevention of Crime* (Paternoster Row, London, B. Steill, 1830).

Sade, Marquis De. *Justine or the Misfortunes of Virtue* (1791, 1797).

Shaw, Joseph. *Parish Law or a Guide to Justices of the Peace, Ministers, Church-Wardens, Overseers of the Poor, Constables, Surveyors of the Highways, Vestry-Clerks, and All Others Concerned in Parish Business*, 3rd ed. (London, 1736).

Stephen, Leslie. 'Chatham, Francis, and Junius', *The English Historical Review*, Vol. 3, No. 10 (April 1888).

Stephen, Sir James Fitzjames. *A History of the Criminal Law of England*, Vol. II (London, Macmillan & Co., 1883).

Thackeray, William M. *Going to See a Man Hanged* (London, 1840).

Venette, Nicholas. *Mysteries of Conjugal Love* (London, 1703).

Printed Works Post 1900

Andrew, Donna T. *Aristocratic Vice: The Attack on Duelling, Suicide, Adultery, and Gambling in Eighteenth-Century England* (New Haven and London, Yale University Press, 2013).

Andrew, Donna T. 'The Code of Honour and Its Critics: The Opposition to Dueling in England, 1700–1850', *Social History*, Vol. 5 (1980).

Archer, John E. ' "Men Behaving Badly"? Masculinity and the Uses of Violence, 1850–1900', in Shani D'Cruze (ed.), *Everyday Violence in Britain, 1850–1950* (Harlow, Longman, 2000).

Archer, John E. 'Mysterious and Suspicious Deaths: Missing Homicides in North-West England (185–1900)', *Crime, History & Societies*, Vol. 12, No. 1 (2008).

Aspinall, A. (ed.). *The Later Correspondence of George III, Volume 1: December 1783 to January 1793* (Cambridge, Cambridge University Press, 1962).

Ayling, Stanley. *George the Third* (New York, Alfred A. Knoff, 1972).

Baird, Rosemary. *Mistress of the House, Great Ladies and Grand Houses* (London, Weidenfeld & Nicolson, 2003).

Banner, Stuart. *The Death Penalty: An American History* (Cambridge, MA, Harvard University Press, 2003).

Beattie, John. *Crime and the Courts in England, 1660–1800* (Princeton, NJ, Princeton University Press, 1986).

Beattie, John. *The First English Detectives: The Bow Street Runners and the Policing of London, 1750–1840* (Oxford, Oxford University Press, 2014).

Beattie, John. *Policing and Punishment in London, 1660–1750: Urban Crime and the Limits of Terror* (Oxford, Oxford University Press, 2001).

Beattie, John. "The Royal Pardon and Criminal Procedure in Early Modern England', *Historical Papers/Communications Historiques*, Vol. 22, No. 1 (1987).

Bellany, Alastair. 'The Murder of John Lambe: Crowd Violence, Court Scandal and Popular Politics in Early Seventeenth-Century England', *Past & Present*, No. 200 (August 2008).

Bentley QC, D. R. (ed.). *Select Cases from the Twelve Judges' Notebooks* (London, John Rees, 1997).

Binhammer, Katherine. 'The Sex Panic of the 1790s', *Journal of the History of Sexuality*, Vol. 6, No. 3 (1996).

Binhammer, Katherine. 'Thinking Gender with Sexuality in 1790s' Feminist Thought', *Feminist Studies*, Vol. 28, No. 3 (2002).

Bird, W. 'Liberties of Press and Speech: "Evidence Does Not Exist to Contradict the . . . Blackstonian Sense" in Late 18th Century England?' *Oxford Journal of Legal Studies*, Vol. 36, No. 1 (2016).

Black, Jeremy. *George III: America's Last King* (New Haven & London, Yale University Press, 2006).

Bloch, Iwan. *The Sexual Extremities of the World* (New York, Book Awards, 1964).

Boucé, Paul-Gabriel. (ed.), *Sexuality in Eighteenth-Century Britain* (Manchester, Manchester University Press, 1982).

Bowyer, T. H. 'Junius, Philip Francis and Parliamentary Reform', *Albion: A Quarterly Journal Concerned with British Studies*, Vol. 21, No. 3 (Autumn, 1995).

Brooke, John. *King George III* (London, Constable, 1972).

Brookman, Fiona. *Understanding Homicide* (London, Sage, 2005).

Brumwell, Stephen and Speck, W. A. *Cassell's Companion to Eighteenth Century Britain* (London, Orion, 2001).

Campbell, Ruth. 'Sentence of Death by Burning for Women', *Journal of Legal History*, Vol. 5 (1984).

Clark, Anna. *Scandal: The Sexual Politics of the British Constitution* (Princeton, NJ, Princeton University Press, 2004).

Clayton, Mary. 'The Life and Crimes of Charlotte Walker, Prostitute and Pickpocket', *The London Journal*, Vol. 33, No. 1 (2008).

Cockburn, J. S. 'Patterns of Violence in English Society: Homicide in Kent 1560–1985', *Past and Present*, Vol. 103 (1991).

Conquergood, Dwight. 'Lethal Theatre: Performance, Punishment, and the Death Penalty', *Theatre Journal*, Vol. 54, No. 3 (October 2002).

Cox, David J. *A Certain Share of Low Cunning: A History of the Bow Street Runners, 1792–1839* (London, Routledge, 2012).

Crawford, Katherine. 'Erotica: Representing Sex in the Eighteenth Century', in Julie Peakman (ed.), *Cultural History of Sexuality. Volume 4: Sexuality in the Enlightenment* (London, Bloomsbury, 2011, 2014).

Cross, Arthur Lyon. 'Judges in the British Cabinet and the Struggle Which Led to Their Exclusion After 1806', *Michigan Law Review*, Vol. 20. No.1 (November 1921).

Dabhoiwala, Faramerz. 'Sex and Societies for Moral Reform, 1688–1800', *Journal of British Studies*, Vol. 46, No. 2 (April 2007).

Davis, Natalie Zemon. *Pardon Tales and Their Tellers in Sixteenth-Century France* (Stanford, Stanford University Press, 1988).

Devereaux, Simon. 'The Abolition of the Burning of Women in England Reconsidered', *Crime, History & Societies*, Vol. 9, No. 2 (2005).

Devereaux, Simon. 'The Bloodiest Code: Counting Executions and Pardons at the Old Bailey, 1730–1837', *Law, Crime and History*, No. 1 (2016).

Devereaux, Simon. 'The City and the Sessions Paper: "Public Justice" in London, 1770–1800', *Journal of British Studies*, Vol. 35, No. 4 (October 1996).

Devereaux, Simon. 'The Criminal Branch of the Home Office 1782–1830', in G. Smith, S. May, and S. Devereaux (eds.), *Criminal Justice in the Old World and the New: Essays in Honour of J.M. Beattie* (Toronto, Toronto Centre of Criminology, 1998).

Devereaux, Simon. 'England's "Bloody Code" in Crisis and Transition: Executions at the Old Bailey, 1760–1837', *Journal of the Canadian Historical Association*, Vol. 24, No. 2 (2013).

Devereaux, Simon. 'Recasting the Theatre of Execution: The Abolition of the Tyburn Ritual', *Past and Present*, Vol. 202 (2009).

Dodsworth, Francis. *Masculinity as Governance: Police, Public Service and the Embodiment of Authority, c. 1700–1850* (Basingstoke, Palgrave Macmillan, 2007).

Durston, Gregory. *Crime and Justice in Early Modern England: 1500–1750* (Chichester, Barry Rose Limited, 2004).

Dyndor, Zoe. 'The Gibbet in the Landscape: Locating the Criminal Corpse in Mid-Eighteenth-Century England', in R. Ward (ed.), *A Global History of Execution and the Criminal Corpse* (Basingstoke, Palgrave Macmillan, 2015).

Ehrman, J. *William Pitt: The Years of Acclaim* (London, Constable, 1969).

Ekirch, A. Roger. *Bound for America: The Transportation of British Convicts to the Colonies, 1718–1775* (Oxford, Clarendon Press, 1987).

Emmerichs, M. Beth. 'Getting Away with Murder: Homicide and the Coroners in Nineteenth-Century London', *Social Science History*, Vol. 25 (2001).

Emsley, Clive. *Hard Men: The English and Violence Since 1750* (London, Hambledon Continuum, 2005).

Follett, Richard R. *Evangelicalism, Penal Theory and the Politics of Criminal Law Reform in England, 1808–30* (Basingstoke, Palgrave Macmillan, 2001).

Foucault, Michel. *Discipline and Punish: The Birth of the Prison* (Harmondsworth, Penguin, 1977).

Gatrell, V. A. C. *The Hanging Tree: Execution and the English People, 1770–1868* (Oxford, Oxford University Press, 1994).

George, M. Dorothy. *London Life in the Eighteenth Century* (Harmondsworth, Penguin, 1925, 1966).

Ginzburg, Carlo. *Threads and Traces: True False Fictive* (Berkeley, CA, University of California Press, 2012).

Gould, Jack. 'The Culworth Gang', *Northamptonshire Past & Present*, Vol. 53 (2000).

Gray, Drew D. *Crime, Policing and Punishment in England, 1660–1914* (London, Bloomsbury, 2016).

Gray, Drew D. *Crime, Prosecution and Social Relations: The Summary Courts of the City If London in the Late Eighteenth Century* (Basingstoke, Palgrave Macmillan, 2009).

Gray, Drew D. 'Making Law in Mid-Eighteenth-Century England: Legal Statutes and Their Application in the Justicing Notebook of Phillip Ward of Stoke Doyle', *The Journal of Legal History*, Vol. 34, No. 2 (2013).

Gray, Drew D. and King, Peter. 'The Killing of Constable Linnell: The Impact of Xenophobia and of Elite Connections on Eighteenth-Century Justice', *Family & Community History*, Vol. 16, No. 1 (2013).

Handler, Phil. 'Forgery and the End of the "Bloody Code" in Early Nineteenth-Century England', *The Historical Journal*, Vol. 48, No. 3 (2005).

Harris, Andrew T. *Policing the City: Crime and Legal Authority in London, 1780–1840* (Columbus, Ohio State University Press, 2004).

Harvey, Karen. *Reading Sex in the Eighteenth Century: Bodies and Gender in English Erotic Culture* (Cambridge, Cambridge University Press, 2004).

Hatley, V. A. (ed.). *Northamptonshire Militia Lists, 1777*, Vol. 25 (Northampton, Northamptonshire Record Society Publications, 1973).

Hay, Douglas. 'Property, Authority and the Criminal Law', in D. Hay (ed.), *Albion's Fatal Tree: Crime and Society in Eighteenth-Century England* (Harmondsworth, Penguin, 1975).

Hay, Douglas. 'Writing About the Death Penalty', *Legal History*, Vol. 6 (2006).

Hertz, Gerald B. 'The English Silk Industry in the Eighteenth Century', *The English Historical Review*, Vol. 24, No. 96 (October 1909).

Hibbert, Christopher. *George III: A Personal History* (Houndmills, Penguin, 1998).

Hitchcock, Tim. *English Sexualities, 1700–1800* (Basingstoke, Palgrave Macmillan, 1997).

Hitchcock, Tim. 'Redefining Sex in Eighteenth-Century England', *History Workshop Journal*, Vol. 41 (Spring 1996).

Hitchcock, Tim and Shoemaker, Robert. *London Lives: Poverty, Crime and the Making of a Modern City, 1690–1800* (Cambridge, Cambridge University Press, 2015).

Hitchcock, Tim and Shoemaker, Robert. *Tales from the Hanging Court* (London, Hodder Arnold, 2006).

Howson, Gerald. *Thief-Taker General: The Rise and Fall of Jonathan Wild* (London, Hutchinson, 1970).

Hurren, Elizabeth T. 'The Dangerous Dead: Dissecting the Criminal Corpse', *Lancet*, Vol. 382 (2013).

Hurren, Elizabeth T. *Dissecting the Criminal Corpse: Staging Post-Execution Punishment in Early Modern England* (Basingstoke, Palgrave Macmillan, 2016).

Hyde, Ralph. *The A to Z of Georgian London*, London Topographical Society Publication No. 126 (London, London Topographical Society, 1982).

Ignatieff, Michael. *A Just Measure of Pain: The Penitentiary in the Industrial Revolution, 1750–1850* (Basingstoke, Macmillan Press, 1978).

Jarrett, Derek. *England in the Age of Hogarth* (New Haven and London, Yale University Press, 1974).

Jay, Stewart. *Most Humble Servants: The Advisory Role of Early Judges* (New Haven and London, Yale University Press, 1997).

Kent, Joan R. *The English Village Constable 1580–1642: A Social and Administrative Study* (Oxford, Oxford University Press, 1986).

Kilday, Anne-Marie and Nash, David (eds.). *Law, Crime & Deviance Since 1700: Micro-Studies in the History of Crime* (London, Bloomsbury, 2017).

King, Peter. *Crime, Justice and Discretion in England, 1740–1820* (Oxford, Oxford University Press, 2000).

King, Peter. *Crime and Law in England, 1750–1840: Remaking Justice from the Margins* (Cambridge, Cambridge University Press, 2006).

King, Peter. 'Decision-Makers and Decision-Making in the English Criminal Law, 1750–1800', *Historical Journal*, Vol. 27, No. 1 (1984).

King, Peter. 'Gender, Crime and Justice in Late Eighteenth and Early Nineteenth-Century England', in M. Arnot and U. Usborne (eds.), *Gender and Crime in Modern Europe* (London, UCL Press, 1999).

King, Peter. 'The Impact of Urbanization on Murder Rates and on the Geography of Homicide in England and Wales, 1780–1850', *The Historical Journal*, Vol. 53, No. 3 (2010).

King, Peter. 'Newspaper Reporting and Attitudes to Crime and Justice in Late-Eighteenth and Early-Nineteenth-Century London', *Continuity and Change*, Vol. 22, No. 1 (2007).

King, Peter. 'Newspaper Reporting, Prosecution Practice and Perceptions of Urban Crime: The Colchester Crime Wave of 1765', *Continuity and Change*, Vol. 2, No. 3 (1987).

King, Peter. 'Punishing Assault: The Transformation of Attitudes in the English Courts', *Journal of Interdisciplinary History*, Vol. 27, No. 1 (Summer 1996).

King, Peter. *Punishing the Criminal Corpse, 1770–1840: Aggravated Forms of the Death Penalty in England* (Basingstoke, Palgrave Macmillan, 2017).

King, Peter. 'The Summary Courts and Social Relations in Eighteenth-Century England', *Past & Present*, Vol. 183, No. 1 (2004).

King, Peter and Ward, Richard. 'Rethinking the Bloody Code in Eighteenth-Century Britain: Capital Punishment at the Centre and on the Periphery', *Past and Present*, Vol. 228 (2015).

Landau, Norma 'The Trading Justice's Trade', in Norma Landau (ed.), *Law, Crime and English Society, 1660–1830* (Cambridge, Cambridge University Press, 2002).

Langbein, John H. 'Albion's Fatal Flaws', *Past and Present*, Vol. 98 (February 1983).

Langbein, John H. *The Origins of the Adversary Criminal Trial* (Oxford, Oxford University Press, 2003).

Laqueur, Thomas W. 'Crowds, Carnival, and the State in English Executions, 1604–1868', in A. L. Beier et al. (eds.), *The First Modern Society* (Cambridge, Cambridge University Press, 1989).

Lemmings, David. *Law and Government in England During the Long Eighteenth Century: From Consent to Command* (Basingstoke, Palgrave Macmillan, 2011).

Lemmings, David. 'Negotiating Justice in the New Public Sphere', in David Lemmings (ed.), *Crime, Courts and the Press in Early Eighteenth-Century Britain 1750–1850* (Farnham, Ashgate, 2012).

Linebaugh, Peter. *The London Hanged: Crime and Civil Society in the Eighteenth Century* (Harmondsworth, Penguin, 1991).

Macalpine, Ida and Hunter, Richard. *George III and the Mad Business* (New York, NY, Pantheon Books, 1970).

McGowen Randall. 'The Body and Punishment in Eighteenth-Century England', *Journal of Modern History*, Vol. 59 (1987).

McGowen, Randall. 'Civilizing Punishment: The End of the Public Execution in England', *Journal of British Studies*, Vol. 33, No. 3 (July 1994).

McGowen, Randall. 'Forgery and the Twelve Judges in Eighteenth-Century England', *Law and History Review*, Vol. 29, No. 1 (February 2011).

McGowen, Randall. 'A Powerful Sympathy: Terror, the Prison, and Humanitarian Reform in Early Nineteenth-Century England', *Journal of British Studies*, Vol. 25, No. 3 (July 1989).

McKenzie Andrea. *Tyburn's Martyrs: Execution in England, 1675–1775* (London, Hambledon Continuum, 2007).

Michaud, Stephen G. and Hazelwood, Roy. *The Evil That Men Do: FBI Profiler Roy Hazelwood's Journey into the Minds of Sexual Predators* (Basingstoke, Palgrave Macmillan, 2010).

Morgan, Gwenda and Rushton, Peter. *Eighteenth-Century Transportation: The Formation of the Criminal Atlantic* (Basingstoke, Palgrave Macmillan, 2004).

Morgan, Gwenda and Rushton, Peter. 'The Magistrate, the Community and the Maintenance of an Orderly Society in Eighteenth-Century England', *Historical Research*, Vol. 76, No. 191 (2003).

Moss, Richard and Illingworth, Iris. *Pattishall a Parish Patchwork* (Northampton, Millcop Publishing, 2000).

Neeson, J. M. *Commoners: Common Right, Enclosure and Social Change in England, 1700–1820* (Cambridge, Cambridge University Press, 1993).

Ober, William B. 'The Sticky End of Frantisek Koczkwara, Composer of the "Battle of Prague"', *American Journal of Forensic Medicine and Pathology*, Vol. 5, No. 2 (1984).

Paley, Ruth. 'Thief-Takers in London in the Age of the McDaniel Gang, c.1745–1754', in D. Hay and F. Synder (eds.), *Policing and Prosecution in Britain, 1750–1850* (Oxford, Oxford University Press, 1989).

Palk, Deirdre. *Gender, Crime and Judicial Discretion, 1780–1830* (Woodbridge, Boydell & Brewer, 2006).

Palk, Deirdre (ed.). *Prisoners' Letters to the Bank of England, 1781–1827* (Loughborough, London Record Society, 2007).

Paulson, Ronald. *Hogarth's Harlot: Sacred Parody in Enlightenment England* (Baltimore, MA, Johns Hopkins University Press, 2003).

Peakman, Julie. *A Cultural History of Sexuality, Volume 4: Sexuality in the Enlightenment* (London, Bloomsbury, 2011, 2014).

Peakman, Julie. *Mighty Lewd Books: The Development of Pornography in Eighteenth-Century England* (Basingstoke, Palgrave Macmillan, 2003).

Peakman, Julie. *The Pleasure's All Mine: A History of Perverse Sex* (London, Reaktion Books, 2013).

Peakman, Julie (ed.). *Sexual Perversions, 1670–1890* (Basingstoke, Palgrave Macmillan, 2009).

Phillips, Kim M. and Reay, Barry (eds.). *Sexualities in History: A Reader* (London, Routledge, 2002).

Poole, Steve. ' "For the Benefit of Example" ': Crime Scene Executions in England, 1720–1830', in Richard Ward (ed.), *A Global History of Execution and the Criminal Corpse* (Basingstoke, Palgrave Macmillan, 2015).

Porter, Roy. ' "The Secrets of Generation Displayed": Aristotle's Master-Piece in Eighteenth-Century England', in Robert P. Maccubbin (ed.), *'Tis Nature's Fault: Unauthorized Sexuality During the Enlightenment* (Cambridge, Cambridge University Press, 1987).

Porter, Roy. 'Sexual Advice Before 1800', in R. Porter and M. Teich (eds.), *Sexual Knowledge, Sexual Science: The History of Attitudes to Sexuality* (Cambridge, Cambridge University Press, 1994).

Potter, Harry. *Hanging in Judgment: Religion and the Death Penalty in England from the Bloody Code to Abolition* (Norwich, SCM Press, 1993).

Rabin, Dana. 'Drunkenness and Responsibility for Crime in the Eighteenth Century', *Journal of British Studies*, Vol. 44. No. 3 (July 2005).

Rawlings, Phillip. *Drunks, Whores and Idle Apprentices. Criminal Biographies of the Eighteenth Century: Criminal Biographies of the 18th Century* (London, Routledge, 1992).

Reynolds, Elaine. *Before the Bobbies: The Night Watch and Police Reform in Metropolitan London, 1720–1830* (Redwood City, Stanford University Press, 1998).

Rice, Geoffrey W. *The Life of the Fourth Earl of Rochford (1717–1781) Eighteenth-Century Anglo-Dutch Courtier, Diplomat, and Statesman. Book 2* (Lewiston, Queenstown, Lampter, Edwin Mellen Press, 2010).

Riddell, W. R. 'Appeal of Death and Its Abolition', *Michigan Law Review*, Vol. 24, No. 8 (June 1926).

Rodger, N. A. M. *The Insatiable Earl: A Life of John Montagu, Fourth Earl of Sandwich, 1718–1792* (London, Norton, 1993).

Rogers, Nicholas. 'Pigott's Private Eye: Radicalism and Sexual Satire in Eighteenth-Century England', *Journal of the Canadian Historical Association*, Vol. 4 (1993).

Rosenthal, Laura J. *Infamous Commerce: Prostitution in Eighteenth-Century British Literature and Culture* (Ithaca, NY, Cornell University Press, 2015).

Rubenhold, Hallie. *The Covent Garden Ladies: The Extraordinary Story of Harris' List* (London, Random House, 2012).

Rudé, George. *Wilkes and Liberty: A Social Study of 1763 to 1774* (Oxford, Oxford University Press, 1962).

Sabin, A. K. *The Silk Weavers of Spitalfields and Bethnal Green, with a Catalogue and Illustrations of Spitalfields Silks* (London, Board of Education, 1931).

Schwartz, L. D. *London in the Age of Industrialisation: Entrepreneurs, Labour Force and Living Conditions, 1700–1850* (Cambridge, Cambridge University Press, 1992).

Sharpe, J. A. 'Civility, Civilizing Processes and the End of Public Punishment in England', in Peter Burke, Brian Harrison, and Paul Slack (eds.), *Civil Histories: Essays Presented to Sir Keith Thomas* (Oxford, Oxford University Press, 2001).

Sharpe, J. A. 'Debate: The History of Violence in England; Some Observations', *Past and Present*, Vol. 108 (1985).

Shoemaker, Robert B. *The London Mob: Violence and Disorder in Eighteenth-Century England* (London, Hambledon Continuum, 2004).

Shoemaker, Robert B. 'The Old Bailey Proceedings and the Representation of Crime and Criminal Justice in Eighteenth-Century London', *Journal of British Studies*, Vol. 47, No. 3 (2008).

Shoemaker, Robert B. 'The Taming of the Duel: Masculinity, Honour and Ritual Violence in London, 1660–1800', *Historical Journal*, Vol. 45, No. 3 (2002).

Shore, Heather. *London's Criminal Underworlds, c.1720-c.1930: A Social and Cultural History* (Basingstoke, Palgrave Macmillan, 2015).

Shorrocks, D. M. M. 'Transportation of Felons from Sandwich to Virginia, 1721–1773', *The Virginia Magazine of History and Biography*, Vol. 68, No. 3 (July 1960).

Simpson, Antony. 'Dandelions on the Field of Honour: Dueling, the Middle Classes, and the Law in Nineteenth-Century England', *Criminal Justice History*, Vol. 9 (1998).

Smith, Greg T. 'Civilized People Don't Want to See That Kind of Thing: The Decline of Public Punishment in London, 1760–1840', in Carolyn Strange (ed.), *Qualities of Mercy: Justice, Punishment and Discretion* (Vancouver, 1996).

Snell, K. D. M. *Parish and Belonging: Community, Identity and Welfare in England and Wales 1700–1950* (Cambridge, Cambridge University Press, 2006).

Spierenburg, Pieter. *A History of Murder: Personal Violence in Europe from the Middle Ages to the Present* (Cambridge, Cambridge University Press, 2008).

Steedman, Carolyn. 'Lord Mansfield's Women', *Past & Present*, No. 176 (August 2006).

Stone, Lawrence. 'Interpersonal Violence in English Society, 1300–1980', *Past and Present*, Vol. 101 (1983).

Syson, Lydia. *Doctor of Love: James Graham and His Celestial Bed* (London, Alma Books, 2008).

Taylor, Howard. 'Rationing Crime: The Political Economy of Criminal Statistics Since the 1850s', *Economic History Review*, Vol. 51 (1998).

Teal, Adrian. 'Quacks and Hacks: Georgian Medicine and the Power of Advertising', *The Lancet*, Vol. 383, No. 9915 (2014).

Thompson, E. P. *Whigs & Hunters: The Origin of the Black Act* (Harmondsworth, Penguin, 1975, 1990).

Toulalan, Sarah. *Imagining Sex: Pornography and Bodies in Seventeenth-Century England* (Oxford, Oxford University Press, 2007).

Tulloch, John. 'The Privatising of Pain', *Journalism Studies*, Vol. 7, No. 3 (2006).

Vaver, Anthony. *Bound with an Iron Chain: The Untold Story of How the British Transported 50,000 Convicts to Colonial America* (Westborough, MA, Pickpocket Publishing, 2011).

Wagner, Peter. *Eros Revived: Erotica of the Enlightenment in England & America* (London, Paladin Books, 1988).

Wahrman, Dror. 'Percy's Prologue: From Gender Play to Gender Panic in Eighteenth-Century England', *Past & Present*, Vol. 159 (1998).

Walliss, Jon. *The Bloody Code in England and Wales, 1760–1830* (Basingstoke, Palgrave Macmillan, 2018).

Ward, Richard (ed.). *A Global History of Execution and the Criminal Corpse* (Basingstoke, Palgrave Macmillan, 2015).

Ward, Richard. *Print Culture, Crime and Justice in 18th-Century London* (London, Bloomsbury, 2014).

Watson, J. Steven. *The Reign of George III, 1760–1815* (Oxford, Clarendon Press, 1960).

White, Jerry. *London in the Eighteenth Century: A Great and Monstrous Thing* (London, The Bodley Head, 2012).

Wiener, Martin. 'Alice Arden to Bill Sykes: Changing Nightmares of Intimate Violence in England, 1558–1869', *Journal of British Studies* (April 2001), pp. 184–212.

Wiener, Martin. *Men of Blood: Violence, Manliness, and Criminal Justice in Victorian England* (Cambridge, Cambridge University Press, 2004).

Wiener, Martin. 'Murder and the British Historian', Presidential Address of the North American Conference on British Studies, 2003, *Albion: A Quarterly Journal Concerned with British Studies*, Vol. 36, No. 1 (Spring 2004).

Wilf, Stephen. 'Imagining Justice: Aesthetics and Public Executions in Late Eighteenth-Century England', *Yale Journal of the Humanities*, Vol. 5, No. 1 (1993).

Wood, John Carter. *Violence and Crime in Nineteenth-Century England: The Shadow of Our Refinement* (London, Routledge, 2004).

Yetter, Leigh (ed.). *Public Execution in England, 1573–1868. Volume 5: Public Execution in England, 1777–1868* (London, Pickering & Chatto, 2010).

Unpublished Thesis

Kilburn, Matthew C. 'Royalty and Public in Britain: 1714–1789', Thesis submitted for the degree of Doctor of Philosophy (Oxford University, 1997).

Index